UNDERSTAND YOUR LEGAL SYSTEM

LAW IN REAL LIFE

Common Legal Questions Americans Ask - Answered

NGOZI E. BOLIN, ESQ.

Cover by Jim Olen.

Legal Disclaimer

Important Notice to Readers

THIS BOOK IS PROVIDED FOR INFORMATIONAL AND EDUCATIONAL PURPOSES ONLY AND IS NOT INTENDED TO CONSTITUTE LEGAL ADVICE.

No Attorney-Client Relationship

The information contained in this book does not create an attorney-client relationship between the author, publisher, and any reader or user of this material. Reading this book, accessing its content, or using any information contained herein does not establish any professional relationship or create any duties or obligations on the part of the author or publisher to any reader.

Not a Substitute for Professional Legal Counsel

The content of this book is general in nature and may not apply to your specific situation. Legal matters are highly fact-specific and jurisdiction-dependent. Laws, regulations, court decisions, and legal interpretations change frequently and vary significantly between jurisdictions. Nothing in this book should be used as a substitute for competent legal advice from a licensed attorney in your jurisdiction who is familiar with the specific facts of your case.

YOU SHOULD ALWAYS CONSULT WITH A QUALIFIED ATTORNEY BEFORE MAKING ANY LEGAL DECISIONS OR TAKING ANY ACTION BASED ON INFORMATION CONTAINED IN THIS BOOK.

Accuracy and Currency of Information

While every effort has been made to ensure the accuracy of the information contained in this book at the time of publication, the author and publisher make no representations or warranties regarding the completeness, accuracy, reliability, or currency of the information provided. Laws and legal precedents change constantly, and what may have been accurate at the time of writing may no longer be current or applicable.

The information in this book reflects the law as understood by the author as of the publication date. Legal developments occurring after the publication date are not reflected in this material.

Jurisdictional Limitations

Laws vary significantly among different countries, states, provinces, and localities. The information in this book may be based primarily on the laws of specific jurisdictions and may not be applicable in your location. Local laws should always be consulted, and local legal counsel should be retained for matters involving specific jurisdictions.

Limitation of Liability

TO THE FULLEST EXTENT PERMITTED BY LAW, THE AUTHOR, PUBLISHER, EDITORS, CONTRIBUTORS, AND DISTRIBUTORS OF THIS BOOK DISCLAIM ALL LIABILITY FOR ANY LOSS, DAMAGE, OR INJURY ARISING FROM THE USE OF OR RELIANCE ON THE INFORMATION CONTAINED HEREIN, WHETHER SUCH LIABILITY ARISES IN CONTRACT, TORT, STRICT LIABILITY, OR OTHERWISE.

This limitation applies to all damages or injuries, including but not limited to:

- Direct, indirect, incidental, and consequential damages
- Lost profits or business opportunities
- Legal fees and costs

- Punitive or exemplary damages
- Any other economic or non-economic losses

No Warranties

THIS BOOK IS PROVIDED "AS IS" WITHOUT WARRANTY OF ANY KIND, EXPRESS OR IMPLIED, INCLUDING BUT NOT LIMITED TO WARRANTIES OF MERCHANTABILITY, FITNESS FOR A PARTICULAR PURPOSE, OR NON-INFRINGEMENT.

Individual Circumstances

Every legal situation is unique. The examples, case studies, and scenarios presented in this book are for illustrative purposes only and may not reflect the full complexity of actual legal situations. The outcomes described may not be achievable in your circumstances, and past results do not guarantee future outcomes.

Updates and Revisions

The author and publisher are under no obligation to update or revise the content of this book to reflect changes in the law or legal practice. Readers are encouraged to verify all information with current legal sources and qualified legal professionals.

Third-Party Content and References

Any references to third-party materials, websites, organizations, or publications are provided for informational purposes only and do not constitute an endorsement of such materials or entities. The author and publisher are not responsible for the content, accuracy, or availability of third-party materials.

Compliance with Professional Rules

Readers who are legal professionals should ensure that their use of any information in this book complies with applicable professional conduct rules, ethical requirements, and licensing obligations in their jurisdiction.

Intellectual Property Notice

This book is protected by copyright and other intellectual property laws. The information provided is for personal, educational, and non-commercial use only. Any commercial use, reproduction, or distribution requires express written permission from the copyright holder.

Severability

If any portion of this disclaimer is held to be invalid or unenforceable, the remaining portions shall remain in full force and effect.

BY READING AND USING THIS BOOK, YOU ACKNOWLEDGE THAT YOU HAVE READ, UNDERSTOOD, AND AGREE TO BE BOUND BY THE TERMS OF THIS DISCLAIMER.

IF YOU DO NOT AGREE WITH THESE TERMS, DO NOT USE THIS BOOK.

Contents

Introduction

Most Americans do not learn the law in classrooms or courtrooms. They learn it in moments of urgency: late at night, on a phone screen, typing a question into a search bar. What does "indicted" mean? Can my landlord evict me? What happens if I get arrested? Do I need a prenup? These are not academic curiosities. They are real problems, tied to jobs, families, freedom, money, and identity.

This book begins where people actually encounter the law: not in statutes or in case reporters, but in search results.

Every year, millions of legal questions are typed into Google and other search engines by people trying to understand their rights, their risks, and their options. The patterns are revealing. Americans most often search for basic legal definitions, criminal process terms, employment rights, family law issues, housing disputes, immigration status, and questions about money, accidents, and contracts. These searches tell a simple story: the law is everywhere in daily life, yet rarely explained in plain language.

The questions people ask online reflect genuine anxiety and confusion. They want to know if they can be fired for missing work due to illness. They wonder whether a verbal agreement is legally binding. They search frantically to understand what happens after a DUI arrest or how long they have to respond to a lawsuit. These are not hypothetical scenarios. They are urgent, personal crises that demand immediate answers, often at times when professional help is unavailable or unaffordable.

Yet the information people find online is often incomplete, outdated, or written in dense legal terminology that obscures more than it clarifies. Legal advice websites may be accurate but impenetrable. Social media threads offer conflicting opinions from strangers. Government websites, while authoritative, are frequently written for lawyers rather than ordinary citizens. The result is a frustrating paradox: legal information is more accessible than ever before, but genuine understanding remains elusive.

Law in Real Life is written for people who are not lawyers but who live under the law every day.

This book does not assume prior legal knowledge. It avoids unnecessary jargon, explains legal concepts in clear terms, and focuses on how the law operates in practice, not just in theory. When legal terms are unavoidable, they are defined carefully and illustrated with examples drawn from common experiences. When rules vary by state, that reality is made explicit, and readers are guided toward resources for finding their specific state's laws. The goal is not to turn readers into attorneys, but to give them enough understanding to recognize issues, ask better questions, and avoid preventable mistakes.

The approach here is deliberately practical. Rather than offering exhaustive legal analysis, this book prioritizes the information people actually need when facing real situations. It answers the questions that keep people awake at night: What are my options? What are the deadlines? What could go wrong if I do nothing? What should I say or not say? When is this serious enough to hire a lawyer?

Just as important, this book is organized around how legal problems actually arise. Most people do not experience the law in neat categories. A car accident can lead to insurance disputes, medical bills, employment problems, and lawsuits. A divorce can trigger housing issues, financial strain, and child custody disputes. An arrest can affect immigration status, employment, and future opportunities. The chapters in this book reflect that interconnected reality, showing how one legal issue often cascades into others and how understanding these connections can help people navigate complex situations more effectively.

Each chapter is built around real scenarios and common questions. The explanations are grounded in how legal processes actually unfold: what happens first, what comes next, what documents matter, what decisions need to be made, and what mistakes are most common. Where possible, the book provides concrete guidance, such as what to bring to a legal appointment, what questions to ask a lawyer, or what records to keep for future reference.

This is also a book about limits. Laws change constantly through new legislation, court decisions, and regulatory updates. Facts matter enormously in legal disputes, and small details can determine outcomes. Results depend on jurisdiction, timing, individual circumstances, the quality of evidence, and countless other variables. Nothing here replaces professional legal advice from a licensed attorney who can review your specific situation, apply the current law in your state, and advocate on your behalf.

Instead, this book serves as a bridge between confusion and clarity: a starting point for understanding what is happening, what questions to ask, and when it is time to seek help from a qualified lawyer. It is designed to help readers recognize when a situation has legal implications, understand the basic framework of how the law addresses that situation, and make informed decisions about next steps. Sometimes that means taking immediate action. Sometimes it means gathering information before making a move. And sometimes it means recognizing that professional help is not optional but necessary.

Ultimately, legal knowledge is a form of personal protection. People who understand the basics of the law are better equipped to protect their rights, their families, and their futures. They are less likely to panic when legal problems arise, less likely to be misled by inaccurate information or bad advice, and more likely to make informed decisions under pressure. They can spot warning signs earlier, preserve important evidence, meet critical deadlines, and avoid actions that might harm their position

Legal literacy also changes the balance of power in interactions where one party understands the law and the other does not. Landlords, employers, creditors, and government agencies all operate within legal frameworks, and they often rely on the assumption that ordinary people do not understand their rights. When people know the basic rules, they can push back against unlawful demands, negotiate from a position of knowledge, and recognize when they are being treated unfairly.

Moreover, understanding the law reduces fear and helplessness. Legal problems are frightening precisely because they feel incomprehensible and beyond control. When people understand what is happening and why, they regain a sense of agency. They can participate meaningfully in their own legal matters rather than feeling like passive subjects of an inscrutable system.

The law should not feel like a foreign language spoken only by professionals. It governs everyday life, and it belongs to everyone. It determines whether you can be evicted, whether you owe a debt, whether you have recourse when harmed, whether your marriage can be dissolved, whether you can keep your children, whether you can enter or remain in the country, whether you will face criminal punishment, and countless other matters that shape the course of a human life.

Despite its profound impact, the law is rarely taught outside of professional training. Most Americans complete their education without ever learning basic legal concepts, their constitutional rights, how courts work, or how to find legal help. This absence leaves people vulnerable and dependent on others to explain systems that directly affect them.

This book is an invitation to understand it. Not completely, because that would require years of study, but sufficiently. Enough to navigate common legal situations with confidence. Enough to recognize when something is wrong. Enough to ask the right questions. Enough to protect yourself and the people you care about. Enough to feel less afraid and more prepared when the law enters your life, as it inevitably will.

PART I: Understanding the Basic Legal System

1

How the American Legal System Actually Works

For many people, the American legal system feels confusing, intimidating, or deliberately opaque. Courtrooms seem formal and mysterious, legal language feels impenetrable, and outcomes often appear unpredictable. Yet at its core, the system follows a structure that, once understood, makes most legal problems far less frightening.

This chapter explains the foundations of the U.S. legal system in plain language: what kinds of cases exist, who makes and enforces the laws, who decides disputes, and why the rules can change dramatically from one state to another. Understanding these basics empowers you to recognize when you have a legal problem, know where to look for answers, and make informed decisions about whether you need professional help.

Civil Law vs. Criminal Law

One of the most important distinctions in American law is between criminal law and civil law. Many people assume all legal cases involve crimes. Most do not. Understanding the difference affects everything from what rights you have to what outcomes are possible.

Criminal Law: When the Government Prosecutes

Criminal law deals with behavior that the government has decided is harmful to society as a whole. These cases are brought by the state or federal government, not by private individuals. If you are charged with a crime, the case name will look something like *State of California v. Smith* or *United States v. Johnson*. That wording matters: it means the government is accusing someone of breaking the law.

The theory behind criminal law is that certain actions are so harmful they threaten the community, not just individuals. Murder, theft, assault, fraud, and drug offenses are all crimes because society has an interest in preventing and punishing them. Even if a specific person is harmed (a victim), the case belongs to the government, and the government decides whether to prosecute.

Criminal cases can result in serious penalties. You could face jail or prison time, probation, fines paid to the government, community service, mandatory treatment programs, or a permanent criminal record that affects employment, housing, education opportunities, professional licensing, and other aspects of life. A felony conviction (the most serious category of crime) can result in the loss of certain rights, including the right to vote in some states, the right to own firearms, and eligibility for some government benefits.

Because the consequences are so severe, criminal defendants are given strong constitutional protections. These include:

The right to remain silent, protected by the Fifth Amendment. You cannot be forced to testify against yourself or answer questions from police or prosecutors.

The right to an attorney, guaranteed by the Sixth Amendment. If you cannot afford a lawyer, one will be appointed for you at no cost.

The presumption of innocence. You are assumed innocent until proven guilty. The burden of proof rests entirely on the government.

The requirement of proof beyond a reasonable doubt. This is the highest standard of proof in American law. The government must prove its case so thoroughly that no reasonable person would have serious doubts about your guilt.

Protection against double jeopardy. You cannot be tried twice for the same crime after being acquitted.

The right to a speedy and public trial. You cannot be held indefinitely without being charged and tried.

These protections exist because the power imbalance between an individual and the government is so enormous. When the full weight of the state is directed at prosecuting you, constitutional safeguards help level the playing field.

Not all crimes are equal. They are typically divided into categories based on severity:

Felonies are the most serious crimes, punishable by more than one year in prison. Examples include murder, rape, armed robbery, and major drug trafficking.

Misdemeanors are less serious crimes, typically punishable by up to one year in jail, fines, or both. Examples include petty theft, simple assault, vandalism, and first-time DUI in some states.

Infractions (or violations) are minor offenses that typically result only in fines, not jail time. Traffic tickets are the most common example.

The category matters enormously. A felony conviction has lifelong consequences that extend far beyond any sentence you serve. Misdemeanors are less damaging but still create a criminal record. Understanding what you are charged with is the first step in understanding what you are facing.

Civil Law: When Private Parties Dispute

Civil law, by contrast, governs disputes between private parties: individuals, businesses, or organizations. Civil cases include divorces, landlord-tenant disputes, employment claims, personal injury lawsuits, contract disputes, probate matters (dealing with estates after someone dies), property boundary disagreements, debt collection, and intellectual property disputes.

In these cases, one party (the plaintiff) claims that another party (the defendant) caused harm or violated a legal duty. The plaintiff is seeking some kind of remedy or relief from the court, not asking the government to punish someone. Civil law exists to resolve disagreements, compensate victims, and enforce private agreements and responsibilities.

Civil cases do not result in jail time. Instead, outcomes usually involve:

- **Money damages** paid from one party to another to compensate for harm
- **Injunctions**, which are court orders requiring someone to do something or stop doing something
- **Declaratory judgments**, where the court clarifies legal rights or relationships
- **Specific performance**, where someone is ordered to fulfill a contract they agreed to
- **Property transfers or divisions**, such as in divorce or estate cases

The burden of proof is also lower in civil cases. The standard is typically **"a preponderance of the evidence,"** which means the claim just needs to be more likely true than not. This is often thought of as 51% or more likely, or "more probable than not." This lower standard exists because the consequences are less severe (no loss of liberty) and because requiring absolute certainty would make it nearly impossible to resolve private disputes.

Unlike criminal cases, you do not have an automatic right to a free lawyer in civil matters. If you cannot afford an attorney, you may represent yourself (called appearing "pro se"), seek help from legal aid organizations that serve low-income people, or try to find a lawyer willing to work on contingency (taking a percentage of any money you win rather than charging upfront).

Civil lawsuits follow a predictable process. The plaintiff files a complaint describing the harm and what they want. The defendant files an answer responding to the allegations. Both sides exchange information through "discovery," a process that can include written questions, document requests, and depositions (sworn testimony taken before trial). Many cases settle during this phase. If no settlement is reached, the case goes to trial, where a judge or jury decides the outcome. The losing party may appeal if they believe legal errors were made.

When One Event Triggers Both Criminal and Civil Cases

It's important to understand that a single event can trigger both types of cases. For example:

A car accident caused by drunk driving may lead to criminal charges brought by the state (for driving under the influence) and a separate civil lawsuit brought by the injured person (seeking money for medical bills and other damages).

An assault may result in criminal prosecution by the district attorney and a civil lawsuit by the victim for medical expenses, lost wages, and pain and suffering.

Fraud in a business transaction might lead to criminal charges for theft or embezzlement and a civil lawsuit by the defrauded party to recover money.

These cases are completely separate and proceed independently, even though they arise from the same facts. They can even reach different results. Someone might be found "not guilty" in criminal court (because the government could not prove guilt beyond a reasonable doubt) but still be held liable in civil court (because the plaintiff proved their case by a preponderance of the evidence). This happened in several famous cases where criminal acquittals were followed by civil liability verdicts.

Understanding whether your problem is criminal or civil changes everything about how you should respond. If you are contacted by police or charged with a crime, you need a criminal defense attorney immediately and should exercise your right to remain silent until you have one. If you are being sued or considering suing someone else, you are dealing with a civil matter, and the urgency and process are different.

Federal Law vs. State Law

Another major source of confusion is the division of power between federal law and state law. Understanding this split is essential because it determines which rules apply to your situation and which courts can hear your case.

How Federal and State Power Is Divided

The United States operates under a **federal system**, meaning power is shared between a national government (in Washington, D.C.) and 50 individual state governments. This design was deliberate. The founders wanted a national government strong enough to function effectively but also wanted to preserve state independence and prevent too much power from concentrating in one place.

The U.S. Constitution gives the federal government authority over certain specific areas. These include:

- **Interstate commerce** (business that crosses state lines)
- **Immigration and naturalization** (who can enter or become a citizen)
- **National defense and foreign policy** (military and treaties)
- **Federal taxes** (income tax, corporate tax, estate tax)
- **Patents and copyrights** (protecting intellectual property nationally)
- **Bankruptcy** (providing uniform debt relief processes)
- **Disputes between states** (resolving conflicts between state governments)
- **Civil rights** (enforcing constitutional protections)
- **Currency and banking regulation** (controlling money supply and financial institutions)

The Constitution reserves most other legal matters to the states. This is sometimes called "police power," the general authority to regulate for health, safety, and welfare.

State Law Controls Most Daily Life

As a result, **most laws that affect daily life are state laws, not federal ones**. The following areas are primarily or exclusively governed by state law:

- **Marriage and divorce**, including age requirements, waiting periods, grounds for divorce, and property division
- **Child custody and support**, with each state setting its own standards for the best interests of children
- **Property ownership and real estate**, including how property is bought, sold, titled, and taxed
- **Most criminal offenses**, such as theft, assault, murder, rape, and burglary (the vast majority of crimes are prosecuted under state law)
- **Traffic laws**, including speed limits, DUI standards, and licensing

requirements

- **Employment rules**, such as minimum wage (though federal law sets a floor), overtime, workers' compensation, and workplace safety
- **Landlord-tenant regulations**, including eviction procedures, security deposit rules, and habitability standards
- **Personal injury law** (tort law), covering car accidents, medical malpractice, product liability, and slip-and-fall cases
- **Contract law**, governing agreements between private parties
- **Probate**, which determines how estates are handled after death
- **Professional licensing**, regulating doctors, lawyers, contractors, and other professions
- **Education requirements**, with states controlling public school curricula and standards
- **Consumer protection laws**, regulating businesses and protecting buyers

Each state writes its own rules on these topics. The variations can be enormous. California's employment laws look nothing like Texas employment laws. Florida's landlord-tenant law differs dramatically from New York's. Some states recognize common-law marriage; others do not. Some states allow capital punishment; others have abolished it. Gun laws, marijuana laws, tax rates, and countless other rules vary widely.

Federal Law's Important Role

Federal law still plays an important role in many areas:

Federal crimes, including tax evasion, wire fraud, mail fraud, drug trafficking across state lines, counterfeiting, terrorism, kidnapping that crosses state lines, bank robbery, and immigration violations

Civil rights violations, such as discrimination based on race, color, religion, sex, or national origin

Employment discrimination under laws like Title VII of the Civil Rights Act, the Americans with Disabilities Act, and the Age Discrimination in Employment Act

Social Security and Medicare disputes

Bankruptcy proceedings, which follow federal law exclusively

Securities fraud and financial crimes involving stocks, bonds, and investment fraud

Environmental law, with federal agencies like the EPA setting and enforcing national standards

Federal constitutional questions, such as First Amendment free speech issues or Fourth Amendment search and seizure questions

When Federal and State Law Overlap

Sometimes federal and state law overlap or address the same topic. When they directly conflict, federal law generally takes priority under the "supremacy clause" of the Constitution, but only within the areas where the federal government is allowed to act. This balance is the reason something can be legal under state law but illegal under federal law, or vice versa.

For example, several states have legalized marijuana for medical or recreational use under state law. However, marijuana remains illegal under federal law as a Schedule I controlled substance. This creates a conflict where state-legal businesses could theoretically face federal prosecution, though federal enforcement priorities have changed over time. Similarly, some cities have higher minimum wages than federal law requires. Federal law sets a floor, but states and cities can be more generous.

Understanding which level of government controls an issue helps you find the right laws and the right courts. If your problem involves immigration, federal taxes, or patent law, you are in federal territory. If it involves divorce, a landlord dispute, or a DUI, you are almost certainly dealing with state law. Some issues (like employment discrimination) might be governed by both federal and state law, giving you options for where to file claims.

Courts, Judges, Juries, and Lawyers

The legal system functions through courts, each with defined roles and responsibilities. Understanding who does what helps demystify the process and clarifies what to expect if you are involved in a legal case.

The Court System: State and Federal

There are both state court systems and a separate federal court system, and each is organized in levels or tiers. These are truly separate systems with their own judges, rules, and procedures. Most cases are filed in state courts because most legal issues involve state law.

Trial courts are where cases begin. They are sometimes called "courts of first instance." This is where evidence is presented, witnesses testify, and initial decisions are made. Trial courts handle fact-finding: determining what actually happened in a dispute. Witnesses appear in person, documents are introduced as evidence, and testimony is given under oath. In the federal system, these are called District Courts. In state systems, they might be called Circuit Courts, Superior Courts, County Courts, or District Courts, depending on the state.

Within state systems, trial courts are often divided by the type or size of case. Small claims courts handle disputes involving small amounts of money (typically $5,000 to $10,000, depending on the state). Family courts handle divorces, custody, and support issues. Probate courts deal with estates and wills. Traffic courts handle traffic violations. Criminal courts may be separated into different divisions for misdemeanors versus felonies. Understanding which specific court handles your type of case is important because filing in the wrong court can delay or derail your case.

Appeals courts (also called appellate courts) review decisions made by trial courts. They do not re-examine the facts or hear new evidence. Instead, they review whether the law was applied correctly and whether proper procedures were followed. Appeals are based on written briefs (legal arguments) and sometimes oral arguments where lawyers answer judges' questions. If appellate judges find legal errors that affected the outcome, they can reverse or modify trial court decisions or send the case back to the trial court for further proceedings. In the federal system, these are called Courts of Appeals or Circuit Courts (there are 13 federal circuits dividing the country geographically). States have their own appellate courts with various names, and some states have intermediate appellate courts plus a highest court.

At the top are **supreme courts**, which are the highest courts in their respective systems. The **U.S. Supreme Court** is the highest court in the nation for federal law and constitutional questions. It hears only a tiny fraction of cases that request review (about 1-2% of petitions). When the Supreme Court decides a case, its interpretation of federal law or the Constitution is final and binding on all lower courts throughout the country. Each state also has its own highest court, usually called the State Supreme Court (though some states use different names: New York's highest court is the Court of Appeals, while Texas has separate supreme courts for civil and criminal matters). State supreme courts have the final word on interpreting their own state's laws and constitution.

Jurisdiction: Which Court Has Authority

Not every court can hear every case. Courts must have **jurisdiction**, the legal authority to decide a particular case. Jurisdiction depends on several factors:

Subject matter jurisdiction: Does the court have authority over this type of case? Federal courts have limited jurisdiction and can only hear certain types of cases (federal question cases involving federal law or the Constitution, and diversity cases where parties are from different states and the amount in controversy exceeds $75,000). State courts have general jurisdiction and can hear almost any type of case.

Personal jurisdiction: Does the court have authority over the defendant? Generally, you can be sued in the state where you live or where you do business. You can also be sued where the events giving rise to the lawsuit occurred.

Territorial jurisdiction: Courts only have power within their geographic boundaries.

Understanding jurisdiction is crucial because filing in the wrong court wastes time and money. If you sue someone in a court that lacks jurisdiction, your case will be dismissed, and you will have to start over elsewhere.

What Judges Do

Judges oversee cases and perform several critical functions. They are not simply referees; they are active participants who ensure the legal process works correctly.

Judges:

- **Rule on legal questions and objections**, such as whether evidence is admissible or whether certain legal arguments are valid
- **Interpret statutes and constitutional provisions**, deciding what laws mean when their language is unclear or disputed
- **Ensure proper procedures are followed**, making sure both sides get fair treatment and constitutional rights are respected
- **Manage the courtroom**, maintaining order and decorum

- **Issue rulings and orders**, such as granting or denying motions, issuing search warrants, setting bail, or ordering injunctions
- **Sentence convicted defendants** in criminal cases (within limits set by law)
- **Decide cases in bench trials**, where the judge determines both the facts and the law without a jury

Judges may be selected through different methods depending on the system. Federal judges are appointed by the President and confirmed by the Senate, and they serve for life (unless they resign or are removed). State judges may be appointed by governors, elected by voters, or selected through merit-based systems, and they typically serve fixed terms. The method of selection can influence judicial independence and decision-making.

Good judges are impartial, knowledgeable about the law, patient with people unfamiliar with legal procedures, and committed to fairness. They should not favor one side over the other based on personal feelings or outside pressure.

The Role of Juries

Juries are groups of ordinary citizens selected from the community to evaluate evidence and decide factual questions in certain cases. Jury service is both a right and a civic duty. The jury system reflects the fundamental belief that community judgment plays an important role in justice and acts as a check on government power.

In **criminal trials**, juries decide whether the defendant is guilty or not guilty. They must follow the judge's instructions on the law but have complete authority over factual questions: Did the defendant commit the acts charged? Has the government proven its case beyond a reasonable doubt? Criminal juries must typically reach a unanimous verdict, though some states allow non-unanimous verdicts for certain crimes.

In **civil cases**, juries determine whether someone is liable (legally responsible) and, if so, how much money in damages should be awarded. The jury evaluates evidence, weighs witness credibility, and applies the relevant legal standards to the facts. Civil juries do not always need to be unanimous; many states allow verdicts if a supermajority agrees (such as 9 out of 12 jurors).

Juries are typically made up of 6 to 12 people, depending on the type of case and jurisdiction. Potential jurors are questioned during a process called voir dire, where lawyers and the judge ask questions to identify bias or conflicts of interest. Lawyers can strike potential jurors "for cause" (if bias is shown) or through "peremptory challenges" (a limited number of strikes for any reason, except race or gender discrimination).

Not all cases involve juries. Many are decided by judges alone, particularly in matters like family law, probate, and small claims. Parties sometimes waive their right to a jury trial, choosing instead to have a judge decide the case (a bench trial). Civil litigants may prefer bench trials when they believe a judge will better understand complex technical or legal issues. Criminal defendants sometimes choose bench trials when they fear jury prejudice or believe a judge will be more sympathetic.

The right to a jury trial is constitutionally protected in criminal cases (Sixth Amendment) and in federal civil cases where the amount in controversy exceeds $20 (Seventh Amendment). State constitutions provide similar protections for state cases.

How Lawyers Fit In

Lawyers act as advocates and advisors within the legal system. They are professionals trained in legal analysis, research, writing, and courtroom practice. Lawyers do much more than argue cases. They:

- **Explain complex legal concepts** in plain language
- **Research applicable laws and precedents** to build strong arguments
- **Prepare legal documents**, including contracts, wills, complaints, motions, and briefs
- **Negotiate settlements** and agreements on behalf of clients
- **Advise clients on strategy and risk**, helping them understand options and consequences
- **Represent clients in court**, presenting evidence and making arguments
- **Protect clients' rights** and ensure fair treatment

The type of lawyer depends on the case:

Prosecutors (also called district attorneys, state's attorneys, or U.S. attorneys) represent the government in criminal cases. They have enormous power: they decide what charges to bring, whether to offer plea bargains, and whether to dismiss cases. Prosecutors work for the state or federal government, not for crime victims.

Defense attorneys represent people accused of crimes. They may be privately retained (hired by the defendant or their family) or court-appointed public defenders (government lawyers assigned to represent people who cannot afford private counsel).

Plaintiff's attorneys represent people or entities bringing civil lawsuits. They may work on contingency (taking a percentage of any money recovered) or charge hourly fees.

Defense attorneys in civil cases represent defendants being sued. They are typically paid by the hour or by insurance companies.

Transactional attorneys help with business deals, contracts, real estate purchases, and other non-litigation matters.

Family law attorneys handle divorces, custody disputes, and related matters.

Estate planning attorneys draft wills, trusts, and powers of attorney.

While lawyers are central to the system and provide essential expertise, not all legal matters require one. Small claims court (for disputes involving smaller amounts of money), certain administrative hearings, traffic court, and some basic legal filings are often designed to be accessible to non-lawyers representing themselves. Many courts provide forms and instructions for common filings like restraining orders, name changes, or simple divorces.

However, for serious matters, having a lawyer is usually critical. Criminal charges (especially felonies), lawsuits involving substantial money, child custody battles, complex business disputes, and situations that could significantly affect your rights or future all warrant professional legal help. An experienced lawyer knows procedures, deadlines, legal arguments, and strategic options that non-lawyers would miss. Mistakes in legal proceedings can be permanent and irreversible.

Finding and affording a lawyer can be challenging. Legal aid organizations provide free services to low-income people for certain types of cases. Bar associations often have referral services. Some lawyers offer free initial consultations. Contingency fee arrangements (where the lawyer gets paid only if you win) are common in personal injury cases. Understanding when professional help is essential and when it is optional is a key theme throughout this book.

Why Laws Differ So Much by State

One of the most frustrating aspects of American law for ordinary people is that the "right answer" to a legal question often depends on where you live. Something that is perfectly legal in one state may be illegal in a neighboring state. Rights, deadlines, procedures, and penalties can vary dramatically. Understanding why this happens helps you navigate the system more effectively.

The Structure Creates Variation

This variation exists because states are independent legal authorities within the federal system. Each state has:

- **Its own constitution** (separate from the U.S. Constitution), which establishes the structure of state government and protects additional rights
- **Its own legislature** that passes laws (called statutes)
- **Its own court system** that interprets those laws and creates precedent through judicial decisions
- **Its own regulatory agencies** that enforce laws and create detailed rules (called regulations or administrative law)

States pass their own criminal codes, family laws, property rules, consumer protection laws, and business regulations based on local values, political preferences, history, geography, and economic priorities.

Examples of State-by-State Differences

Over time, states have made different choices that reflect their unique populations and priorities. Here are just a few examples:

Criminal law: Some states have the death penalty; others have abolished it. Marijuana possession is legal for recreational use in some states, decriminalized in others, and a serious crime in still others. DUI penalties, mandatory minimum sentences, three-strikes laws, and expungement opportunities all vary.

Family law: Some states recognize common-law marriage (where a couple is legally married without a formal ceremony if certain conditions are met); most do not. Divorce grounds, property division rules, alimony guidelines, and child support calculations differ. Some states prioritize joint custody; others have different presumptions.

Property law: Community property states (Arizona, California, Idaho, Louisiana, Nevada, New Mexico, Texas, Washington, Wisconsin, and Alaska by agreement) treat most property acquired during marriage as jointly owned. Separate property states follow different rules. Homestead exemptions (protection of your home from creditors) range from unlimited protection to very limited protection depending on the state.

Employment law: Minimum wage varies, with some states and cities setting rates well above the federal minimum. Some states are "at-will employment" states (you can be fired for almost any reason), while others provide greater worker protections. Rules about breaks, overtime, final paycheck timing, and non-compete agreements differ significantly.

Consumer protection: Some states have strong lemon laws for defective cars; others have weaker protections. Interest rate caps on loans, debt collection rules, and small claims court limits vary. Some states prohibit certain contract terms that other states allow.

Landlord-tenant law: Security deposit limits, required disclosures, eviction procedures, notice requirements, and tenant rights vary enormously. What constitutes adequate heat or habitability in Maine differs from Florida.

Traffic and licensing: Speed limits, right-turn-on-red rules, cell phone use while driving, graduated licensing for young drivers, and requirements for obtaining a driver's license all differ. Some states require vehicle safety inspections; others do not.

Gun laws: Background check requirements, waiting periods, concealed carry permits, open carry laws, and restrictions on certain weapons vary dramatically. What is legal in one state may be a felony in another.

Taxes: Seven states have no income tax. Sales tax rates range from zero to over 10% when local taxes are included. Property tax rates vary widely. Estate and inheritance taxes exist in some states but not others.

These differences are not accidents or mistakes. They are deliberate features of the system, reflecting the principle that states can serve as "laboratories of democracy," experimenting with different approaches to policy problems.

If one state's approach works well, other states may adopt it. If it fails, the damage is limited to that state.

What This Means for You

For individuals, this reality means that **legal information must always be read with location in mind**. A rule you find in a book, online article, or even from a friend's experience may be completely accurate in one state and totally wrong in another. Someone giving you advice based on their own legal experience in a different state may be steering you wrong, even with the best intentions.

When researching legal questions, always verify:

- **Which state's law applies** to your situation
- **Whether federal law also applies** and potentially preempts state law
- **Whether local city or county ordinances** add additional requirements

This variation also matters if:

You **move from one state to another**. Laws you relied on may no longer apply. Contracts, licenses, legal documents, and rights you had may need to be updated or re-established.

Your **legal issue involves people or property in multiple states**. Choice of law rules (which state's law applies) can be complex.

You are **considering where to file a lawsuit or other legal action**. Sometimes the choice of location (venue) can significantly affect the outcome. Forum shopping (choosing the most favorable location) is a legitimate strategy within legal and ethical limits.

Understanding which level of government (federal or state) controls an issue and which specific state's law applies is often the first and most important step in solving a legal problem. Getting this wrong can waste significant time, money, and effort.

Why This Structure Matters

The American legal system can seem overwhelming because it is layered, decentralized, and genuinely complex. Multiple levels of government, different types of courts, varying procedures, and 50 different state systems all operating simultaneously create real challenges for anyone trying to understand their rights and responsibilities.

But once you understand its basic architecture (the distinction between criminal versus civil matters, the division between federal versus state authority, the roles of courts versus lawyers, and how juries fit in), you can orient yourself much more quickly when problems arise.

Every legal issue, no matter how complicated it first appears, begins with the same fundamental questions:

Is this a criminal or civil matter? Are you facing potential jail time and prosecution by the government, or is this a dispute with another private party? The answer determines your rights, the burden of proof, and what outcomes are possible.

Is it governed by state law or federal law? Which set of rules applies, and which might take priority if there's a conflict? This determines where you look for answers and which courts have jurisdiction.

Which court has authority? Where would this case be filed, and which court system would handle it? Understanding jurisdiction helps you avoid wasting time in the wrong forum.

Who is responsible for proving what? What's the burden of proof, and which party has to meet it? This affects both strategy and likely outcomes.

Do I need a lawyer? How serious are the consequences? How complex is the process? Can I afford to make mistakes? This determines whether self-help is realistic or professional assistance is necessary.

Answering those questions does not require a law degree or years of legal training. It requires a framework for thinking about legal problems systematically. It requires knowing which questions to ask first.

This chapter provides that framework. It gives you the foundational concepts you need to make sense of almost any legal situation you might encounter. With this foundation, you can:

- Recognize when something is a legal problem requiring action
- Understand where to look for applicable laws and rules
- Evaluate information you find online or hear from others

- Make informed decisions about when to seek professional help
- Understand what is happening if you become involved in a legal case
- Protect your rights and avoid common mistakes

The rest of this book builds directly on these fundamentals, applying these concepts to the specific legal issues Americans search for most often online: the problems that arise in real life, often unexpectedly, when it matters most and when you need clear, practical guidance. Each chapter will return to these core concepts, showing how they apply in specific contexts like employment disputes, landlord-tenant problems, debt collection, family law, small business issues, and encounters with law enforcement.

Understanding the structure of the legal system is the first step toward navigating it successfully. Legal problems are less frightening when you understand how the system works, what your options are, and what to expect. This knowledge doesn't replace professional legal advice when it's needed, but it helps you recognize when you need that advice, ask the right questions, and make better decisions about protecting yourself and your rights.

2

Legal Words People Search For

When people search for legal help online, they often are not asking about complex strategies or rare doctrines. They are trying to understand a single word they just heard on the news, from a police officer, in a court document, or from a lawyer. These words carry serious consequences, yet they are rarely explained clearly.

This chapter breaks down some of the most commonly searched legal terms in America: what they actually mean, what they do not mean, and why misunderstanding them can lead to costly mistakes.

Indictment

The word indictment often sounds like a declaration of guilt. It is not.

An indictment is a formal accusation that a person has committed a crime. It usually comes from a grand jury, a group of citizens who review evidence presented by prosecutors and decide whether there is enough reason to charge someone. Importantly, an indictment is not a verdict. It does not mean the person is guilty.

In many jurisdictions, prosecutors are not required to prove the case beyond a reasonable doubt at this stage. They only need to show that there is probable cause to believe a crime occurred and that the accused may have committed it. Defense attorneys are often not present during grand jury proceedings, and the accused usually does not testify.

An indictment simply moves a case forward into the criminal justice process. Guilt or innocence is determined later (often months or years later) through plea negotiations, trials, or dismissals.

What happens after an indictment? Once a person is indicted, they will typically be arraigned, which means they appear before a judge to hear the charges and enter a plea. The case then proceeds through the pretrial phase, where both sides exchange evidence, file motions, and prepare their strategies. Most cases never reach trial. They end in plea agreements or dismissals.

Why grand juries exist: The grand jury system is meant to serve as a check on prosecutorial power. The idea is that ordinary citizens, not just government lawyers, should have a say in whether someone faces serious criminal charges. In practice, grand juries indict in the vast majority of cases presented to them, which has led some critics to question how effective this safeguard really is.

State differences: Not all states require grand jury indictments. Some allow prosecutors to file charges directly through a document called an information or a complaint. Federal cases and serious state felonies usually require grand jury indictments, but the rules vary significantly across jurisdictions.

Felony vs. Misdemeanor

Criminal offenses in the United States are generally divided into two main categories: felonies and misdemeanors. The difference matters enormously.

A misdemeanor is a less serious criminal offense. Typical examples include minor theft, simple assault, disorderly conduct, and some first-time DUI offenses. Penalties usually include fines, probation, community service, or short jail sentences (often up to one year, typically served in a local jail).

A felony is a more serious crime, such as robbery, serious assault, large-scale fraud, or drug trafficking. Felony convictions can lead to long prison sentences, substantial fines, and permanent loss of certain civil rights, such as the right to vote or possess firearms, depending on the state.

Some crimes can be charged as either misdemeanors or felonies based on circumstances, prior offenses, or prosecutorial discretion. These are often called "wobblers." The same conduct can lead to very different outcomes depending on how it is charged.

Understanding this distinction is critical because the long-term consequences of a felony conviction often extend far beyond the sentence itself.

The collateral consequences of a felony: A felony conviction can follow you for life. It can disqualify you from professional licenses, federal student aid, public housing, and many jobs. Employers routinely conduct background checks, and a felony conviction often appears permanently. Some states allow felony convictions to be expunged or sealed under certain conditions, but the process is complicated and not always available.

What makes a crime a felony? Generally, any crime punishable by more than one year in prison is classified as a felony. The severity can be further divided into classes or degrees. For example, a state might classify felonies as Class A, B, C, or D, with Class A being the most serious. Murder, for instance, is typically a Class A or first-degree felony.

Misdemeanors still matter: Even though misdemeanors are less serious, they are still criminal convictions. They can show up on background checks, affect employment, and in some cases lead to jail time. Multiple misdemeanor convictions can also influence sentencing if you are later charged with another crime. Do not dismiss a misdemeanor charge as trivial. It can still have real consequences.

Infractions: Some jurisdictions recognize a third category called infractions or violations. These are minor offenses like traffic tickets or jaywalking. They typically result in fines but no jail time and are not considered criminal convictions in most states.

Probable Cause

Probable cause is one of the most misunderstood legal standards, yet it plays a central role in criminal law.

Probable cause means there is a reasonable basis to believe that a crime has been committed and that a particular person is involved. It is not proof beyond a reasonable doubt. It does not require certainty. It is a lower threshold based on facts, observations, and reasonable inferences.

Police officers generally need probable cause to:

- Make an arrest
- Conduct a search (unless an exception applies)
- Obtain a warrant

Courts later review whether probable cause actually existed. If it did not, evidence obtained as a result may be excluded. This is why the concept matters even after an arrest has already occurred.

Probable cause is designed to balance two competing interests: protecting individual rights and allowing law enforcement to do its job. It is intentionally flexible, which is also why it is frequently contested in court.

What does probable cause look like in practice? Imagine an officer pulls over a car and smells marijuana. The officer sees small bags and a scale on the passenger seat. These observations, taken together, create probable cause to believe drugs are present and to conduct a search. Now imagine the officer only smells something vaguely suspicious but sees nothing else. That might not be enough. Probable cause depends heavily on context.

Probable cause is not a hunch: An officer cannot arrest or search you based purely on a gut feeling. There must be specific, articulable facts that support the belief that a crime has occurred. Generalizations, stereotypes, or vague suspicions do not meet the standard.

Probable cause vs. reasonable suspicion: These are different standards. Reasonable suspicion is a lower bar and allows an officer to briefly stop and question someone. Probable cause is higher and is required for arrests and most searches. For example, an officer might have reasonable suspicion to stop you if you are walking near a burglary scene at 3 a.m., but they would need probable cause to arrest you or search your backpack.

When evidence gets thrown out: If a court finds that an arrest or search was made without probable cause, the evidence obtained may be suppressed. This is known as the exclusionary rule. Evidence that was discovered as a direct result of an illegal search cannot usually be used against you in court. This is a powerful protection, but it only applies if you challenge the search properly and the court agrees.

Civil Liability

Not all legal responsibility involves crimes. Civil liability refers to legal responsibility for causing harm to another person or entity in a civil (non-criminal) context.

A person or business is civilly liable when they are legally required to compensate someone else for injury, loss, or damage. Common examples include car accidents, medical malpractice, breach of contract, defamation, and landlord-tenant disputes.

Civil liability does not mean someone is morally wrong or criminally guilty. It means the law assigns responsibility for a loss. The standard of proof is lower than in criminal cases, and the consequences are usually financial or corrective, not punitive.

This is why someone can be found civilly liable even if they are never charged with (or are acquitted of) a crime. Civil law focuses on repairing harm, not punishing wrongdoing.

How civil cases are different from criminal cases: In a criminal case, the government prosecutes someone for breaking the law. The stakes are high: jail time, fines, a criminal record. In a civil case, one private party sues another. The goal is usually money damages or an order to do (or stop doing) something. You cannot be sent to prison for losing a civil case.

Preponderance of the evidence: In most civil cases, the standard of proof is preponderance of the evidence. This means the plaintiff (the person suing) must show that their version of events is more likely true than not. Think of it as 51% versus 49%. This is much easier to prove than beyond a reasonable doubt, the standard used in criminal trials.

Types of civil liability: There are several main categories. Negligence involves carelessness that causes harm, like a distracted driver causing an accident. Strict liability holds someone responsible regardless of fault, such as a manufacturer whose defective product injures someone. Intentional torts involve purposeful harmful acts, like assault, fraud, or defamation.

Why you can lose a civil case even after being acquitted: Consider a famous example. A person is charged with murder and acquitted in criminal court because the jury found reasonable doubt. The victim's family then sues that same person in civil court for wrongful death. The civil jury finds the person liable because they believe, by a preponderance of the evidence, that the person caused the death. Same facts, different outcomes. This happens because the standards of proof are different.

Damages and remedies: If you lose a civil case, you might be ordered to pay compensatory damages (to cover the plaintiff's actual losses), punitive damages (to punish particularly bad conduct), or be required to take specific actions (like fulfilling a contract or stopping certain behavior). The court's goal is to make the injured party whole, not to punish you with jail time.

Statute of Limitations

The statute of limitations is a legal deadline. It sets the maximum amount of time someone has to file a lawsuit or bring criminal charges after an event occurs.

Once the statute of limitations expires, the claim is usually barred forever, regardless of its merits. This rule exists to promote fairness and finality. Evidence deteriorates over time, memories fade, and it becomes harder to defend against old allegations.

Statutes of limitations vary widely:

- By state
- By type of case
- By whether the case is civil or criminal

Some serious crimes, such as murder, have no statute of limitations in many states. Others may have deadlines ranging from one year to decades. Civil cases often have shorter time limits, sometimes as little as one or two years.

Missing a statute of limitations is one of the most common (and most devastating) legal mistakes people make. It is also one of the easiest to avoid once you know it exists.

When does the clock start? For most civil cases, the statute of limitations starts running on the date the injury or harm occurred. For example, if you were injured in a car accident on January 1, 2024, and your state has a two-year statute of limitations for personal injury cases, you generally must file your lawsuit by January 1, 2026. In criminal cases, the clock usually starts on the date the crime was committed.

Discovery rule: Some jurisdictions use a discovery rule, which means the clock does not start until the injured party knew or reasonably should have known about the harm. This often applies in cases involving medical malpractice, fraud, or latent injuries (like asbestos exposure), where the harm may not be immediately obvious.

Tolling: In certain situations, the statute of limitations can be paused or extended. This is called tolling. Common reasons include the plaintiff being a minor, the defendant leaving the state, or the defendant fraudulently concealing their wrongdoing. Each state has its own rules about when and how tolling applies.

Examples of common deadlines: Personal injury claims often have statutes of limitations ranging from one to three years. Medical malpractice claims may have even shorter windows. Breach of contract cases might give you three to six years, depending on whether the contract was written or oral. Criminal charges for misdemeanors might have a one- to three-year limit, while many felonies have longer windows. Murder, as mentioned, often has no deadline at all.

Why these deadlines exist: The law recognizes that as time passes, evidence disappears, witnesses forget details or become unavailable, and documents are lost. Defending against a claim from ten years ago is inherently unfair. Statutes of limitations force people to act promptly and protect defendants from stale claims. They also encourage closure and finality, which benefits society as a whole.

What if you miss the deadline? If you file a lawsuit after the statute of limitations has expired, the defendant can file a motion to dismiss based on that fact alone. The court will almost always grant it. It does not matter if you have a strong case or overwhelming evidence. The deadline is absolute in most situations. This is why consulting a lawyer as soon as possible after an injury or dispute is critical.

Arraignment

An arraignment is often the first time a person formally appears in court after being arrested or charged with a crime. It is a critical step in the criminal justice process, yet many people do not know what it is or what to expect.

At an arraignment, the judge informs the defendant of the charges against them, explains their rights, and asks them to enter a plea: guilty, not guilty, or no contest. In many cases, bail or release conditions are also set at this hearing.

Why arraignments matter: This is where the defendant officially learns what they are accused of and has the opportunity to respond. It is also when a lawyer is appointed if the defendant cannot afford one. Missing an arraignment can result in a bench warrant for your arrest.

What happens if you plead not guilty? Most defendants plead not guilty at arraignment, even if they believe they may eventually take a plea deal. Pleading not guilty keeps all options open. It allows time for your lawyer to review the evidence, negotiate with prosecutors, and develop a defense strategy.

Bail decisions: The judge may set bail, release you on your own recognizance (a promise to return to court), or in rare cases, deny bail entirely. Factors include the seriousness of the charges, your criminal history, ties to the community, and whether you are considered a flight risk or danger to others.

Plea Bargain

A plea bargain is an agreement between the defendant and the prosecutor in which the defendant agrees to plead guilty to a charge (often a reduced charge) in exchange for a more lenient sentence or other concessions.

The vast majority of criminal cases in the United States are resolved through plea bargains, not trials. Some estimates suggest that more than 90% of cases end this way.

Why prosecutors offer plea deals: Trials are expensive, time-consuming, and unpredictable. Plea bargains allow prosecutors to secure convictions efficiently and manage heavy caseloads. They also provide certainty for both sides.

Why defendants accept plea deals: Even if you believe you are innocent or have a strong defense, going to trial is a gamble. Trials can result in harsher penalties if you lose. A plea deal offers predictability and often reduces the severity of the charges or sentence. In some cases, accepting a deal is simply the least bad option.

Are plea bargains fair? This is a hotly debated question. Critics argue that plea bargains pressure innocent people to plead guilty and that they allow prosecutors to wield excessive power. Supporters argue that they are a practical necessity in an overburdened system. What is clear is that you should never accept a plea deal without fully understanding it and consulting with a lawyer.

Appeal

An appeal is not a new trial. It is a legal process in which a higher court reviews the decision of a lower court to determine whether legal errors were made that affected the outcome.

Appeals are based on the record from the original trial. That means the appellate court reviews transcripts, evidence, and legal arguments but does not hear new testimony or consider new evidence. The question is whether the law was applied correctly, not whether the jury made the right factual decision.

Grounds for appeal: Common reasons for appeals include errors in jury instructions, improper admission or exclusion of evidence, ineffective assistance of counsel, or prosecutorial misconduct. Simply disagreeing with the verdict is not enough.

Appeals take time: The appeals process can take months or even years. It involves written briefs, legal research, and sometimes oral arguments. Success is not guaranteed. In many cases, appellate courts affirm the lower court's decision.

Not everyone can appeal: In criminal cases, defendants have the right to appeal a conviction. Prosecutors generally cannot appeal an acquittal due to double jeopardy protections. In civil cases, either party can appeal, though there are limits and procedural rules.

Subpoena

A subpoena is a legal order requiring someone to do something, usually to testify in court or produce documents. Ignoring a subpoena can result in serious consequences, including fines or even jail time for contempt of court.

There are two main types. A subpoena ad testificandum orders a person to appear and give testimony. A subpoena duces tecum orders a person to produce documents, records, or other physical evidence.

Who can issue a subpoena? In most cases, attorneys can issue subpoenas as part of the litigation process. Courts can also issue them directly. Subpoenas can be used in both civil and criminal cases.

Can you refuse a subpoena? In some circumstances, yes. You might have a valid legal reason to challenge a subpoena, such as if it requests privileged information (like communications with your lawyer or doctor), is overly broad, or is intended to harass. You generally need to file a motion with the court to quash (cancel) the subpoena.

What if you ignore it? Do not ignore a subpoena. If you fail to comply without a valid legal reason, the court can hold you in contempt, which can result in fines or jail time. If you receive a subpoena and have concerns, consult a lawyer immediately.

Warrant

A warrant is a legal document issued by a judge or magistrate that authorizes law enforcement to take a specific action. The most common types are arrest warrants and search warrants.

Arrest warrant: This authorizes police to arrest a specific person. It is issued when a judge finds probable cause to believe the person has committed a crime. Police usually need an arrest warrant to enter your home to arrest you (though exceptions exist).

Search warrant: This authorizes police to search a specific location and seize specific items. The warrant must describe the place to be searched and the things to be seized with reasonable specificity. Searches conducted without a warrant are presumed unconstitutional unless an exception applies, such as consent, exigent circumstances, or a search incident to arrest.

How do you know if there is a warrant for you? You can often check with your local courthouse or police department. Some jurisdictions have online databases. If you learn there is a warrant, do not ignore it. Consult a lawyer and consider turning yourself in voluntarily, which often looks better than being arrested unexpectedly.

Miranda Rights

You have probably heard the phrase "You have the right to remain silent" in movies or TV shows. These are Miranda rights, named after a Supreme Court case called Miranda v. Arizona.

Miranda rights are warnings that police must give to suspects before conducting a custodial interrogation. The warnings typically include:

- You have the right to remain silent.

- Anything you say can and will be used against you in a court of law.
- You have the right to an attorney.
- If you cannot afford an attorney, one will be provided for you.

When do police have to read you your rights? Only when two conditions are met: you are in custody (not free to leave) and you are being interrogated (questioned about a crime). If either condition is not met, police do not have to give Miranda warnings. This is why an officer can ask you questions during a traffic stop without reading you your rights.

What happens if police do not read you your rights? If Miranda rights are not given when required, any statements you made during the interrogation may be suppressed and cannot be used against you in court. However, this does not mean your case is automatically dismissed. Other evidence can still be used.

Invoking your rights: If you are being questioned by police and want to exercise your rights, be clear. Say something like, "I am invoking my right to remain silent" or "I want a lawyer." Simply staying quiet without explicitly invoking your rights may not be enough. Once you invoke, questioning should stop.

Why These Words Matter

Legal terms are not just labels. They are gateways to rights, risks, and consequences. Misunderstanding a single word can lead someone to ignore a deadline, underestimate a charge, or misunderstand their legal exposure.

These are the words people search for in moments of stress because they signal that something serious is happening. Knowing what they actually mean provides clarity, reduces fear, and allows people to respond rationally rather than react emotionally.

Understanding these terms is the first step. The next step is knowing when and how to act on that knowledge. In some situations, you can handle things yourself. In others, you need a lawyer. The key is recognizing the difference before it is too late.

The legal system is complex, but it is not incomprehensible. With the right information, you can navigate it more confidently and protect your rights more effectively. The following chapters will build on these definitions, applying them to real-world situations where these terms stop being abstract and start shaping lives.

PART II: Criminal Law & Your Rights

3

What Happens If You're Arrested

An arrest is one of the most stressful interactions most people will ever have with the legal system. Even individuals who have never been in trouble before can suddenly find themselves confused, frightened, and unsure of what to say or do. What happens in the minutes and hours after an arrest can have long-lasting consequences.

This chapter explains what an arrest actually is, what rights you have during police encounters, and how searches, seizures, and Miranda warnings really work, without legal jargon or courtroom drama.

Your Rights During Police Encounters

Not every interaction with police is the same, and your rights depend on the type of encounter. Understanding these distinctions can help you respond appropriately and protect yourself.

Consensual Encounters

A consensual encounter occurs when an officer approaches you and asks questions, but you are free to leave. This might happen on the street, in a public place, or even at your door. In these situations, you generally do not have to answer questions, and you can ask whether you are being detained. If the answer is no, you are free to walk away.

During a consensual encounter, the officer has no legal power to stop you or force you to stay. You can politely decline to answer questions and continue on your way. However, many people do not realize they have this option and answer questions out of habit or a desire to be helpful. While there is nothing wrong with speaking to police voluntarily, remember that anything you say can be documented and potentially used later.

If you are unsure whether an encounter is consensual, you can simply ask: "Am I free to leave?" or "Am I being detained?" The officer's answer will clarify your legal status.

Detentions (Terry Stops)

A detention happens when an officer temporarily stops you because they have reasonable suspicion that a crime may be occurring or has occurred. Reasonable suspicion is a lower standard than probable cause, but it still requires specific facts that would lead a reasonable officer to believe criminal activity is taking place.

During a detention, you are not free to leave, but the stop must be limited in scope and duration. The officer can ask you questions and may request identification. In some states, you are legally required to provide your name when detained. This is sometimes called a "stop and identify" statute.

Officers may also conduct a limited pat-down search of your outer clothing if they have reasonable suspicion that you are armed and dangerous. This is known as a "Terry frisk" or "stop and frisk." The search is supposed to be limited to checking for weapons, not searching for evidence of other crimes.

Detentions should be brief. If the officer does not develop probable cause to arrest you or determine that no crime has occurred, they must let you go. However, the line between a detention and an arrest can sometimes be unclear, especially if the stop becomes prolonged.

Arrests

An arrest occurs when you are taken into custody based on probable cause. Probable cause means the officer has enough facts and circumstances to believe that a crime has been committed and that you committed it. This is a higher standard than reasonable suspicion but does not require absolute certainty.

An arrest can happen with or without handcuffs, and it does not require the officer to use the word "arrest." What matters is whether a reasonable person in your situation would feel free to leave. If you are placed in a police car, told you cannot leave, or restrained in a way that significantly limits your freedom, you are likely under arrest, regardless of what words are used.

Arrests can occur with a warrant or without one. When police have a warrant, it means a judge has reviewed the evidence and determined that probable cause exists. Warrantless arrests are also legal in many situations, such as when a crime occurs in the officer's presence or when there is not enough time to obtain a warrant without risking public safety.

Your Core Rights During Any Police Encounter

During any police encounter, whether consensual, a detention, or an arrest, you have important constitutional protections:

You have the right to remain silent. You do not have to answer questions about where you are going, where you have been, what you are doing, or anything else. The Fifth Amendment protects you from being compelled to incriminate yourself. Politely saying "I am exercising my right to remain silent" is usually sufficient.

You have the right to refuse consent to searches. If an officer asks to search your person, your belongings, your car, or your home, you can say no. This does not mean they will not search anyway if they have legal authority to do so, but refusing consent protects your rights if the search turns out to be illegal. Simply say, "I do not consent to any searches."

You have the right to ask for a lawyer if you are arrested. Once you are in custody, you can request an attorney at any time. Questioning should stop once you make this request, though police may try to continue the conversation in subtle ways.

You generally should not physically resist, even if you believe the arrest is unlawful. Resisting arrest, even an unlawful one, can lead to additional charges and can escalate the situation dangerously. If you believe an arrest is improper, the time to challenge it is in court, not on the street.

Remaining calm and respectful while asserting your rights clearly is often the safest approach. Silence cannot legally be used as evidence of guilt, but statements can. Many people talk themselves into far worse legal trouble by trying to explain or justify their actions during an arrest.

Searches, Seizures, and Warrants

The Fourth Amendment to the U.S. Constitution protects people from unreasonable searches and seizures. In practice, this means police usually need a warrant or a recognized exception to conduct a search.

What Is a Warrant?

A warrant is a court order authorizing law enforcement to search a specific place or seize specific items. To obtain a warrant, police must present evidence to a judge showing probable cause that a crime has been committed and that evidence of that crime will be found in the place to be searched.

Warrants must be specific. A search warrant for a home, for example, should describe the address and the items being sought. A general warrant allowing police to search wherever they want or seize whatever they find is unconstitutional.

When police execute a search warrant, they are generally required to knock and announce their presence before entering, unless the warrant specifically authorizes a no-knock entry. If you are present when a search warrant is executed, you have the right to see the warrant and verify that it appears valid. You do not have to answer questions, and you can ask for a lawyer.

Exceptions to the Warrant Requirement

Despite the general rule that searches require a warrant, courts have recognized numerous exceptions where police may search without one. These exceptions have expanded significantly over the years, and understanding them is important.

Search incident to a lawful arrest. When police lawfully arrest someone, they can search that person and the area within their immediate control without a warrant. The purpose is to ensure officer safety and to prevent the destruction of evidence. For example, if you are arrested in your living room, police can search your pockets and the area around you, but they generally cannot search your entire house without a warrant or additional justification.

Plain view doctrine. If an officer is lawfully in a position to observe an item and it is immediately apparent that the item is evidence of a crime, they can seize it without a warrant. For instance, if police are in your home with your consent and see illegal drugs on your kitchen table, those drugs can be seized.

Consent searches. If you voluntarily consent to a search, police do not need a warrant or probable cause. Consent must be given freely and not under coercion. You can limit the scope of your consent or withdraw it at any time. For example, you might consent to a search of your living room but not your bedroom.

Automobile exception. Cars have less Fourth Amendment protection than homes. If police have probable cause to believe a vehicle contains evidence of a crime, they can search it without a warrant. They can search any area of the car where the evidence might be found, including the trunk and closed containers.

Exigent circumstances. Police may enter a home or conduct a search without a warrant if there is an emergency, such as someone inside calling for help, the imminent destruction of evidence, or a fleeing suspect. The scope of the search must be limited to addressing the emergency.

Inventory searches. When a car is impounded or a person is arrested and booked into jail, police can conduct an inventory search to document belongings. These searches are supposed to be routine and not pretexts for investigating crimes, though the line is often blurry.

A Critical Point About Consent

You can refuse consent to a search. This is one of the most important protections you have. If police have a legal basis to search anyway, they will do so regardless of your refusal. But if they do not, consent can eliminate your ability to challenge the search later.

Police may try various tactics to obtain consent. They might say things like, "You don't have anything to hide, do you?" or "We can just get a warrant, so you might as well let us search now." Do not be intimidated. Politely say, "I do not consent to any searches." You are not required to explain or justify your refusal.

Consent can be given by others who share authority over a space. For example, if you share an apartment with a roommate, your roommate can consent to a search of common areas. If police have permission from one person who has authority over a space, items found in plain view can often be used against you, even if you did not consent.

Seizures of People and Property

Seizure does not only mean taking property. It also includes restraining a person's movement. A seizure occurs anytime police stop you from leaving, whether through physical force, a command, or other means that make you feel you must comply.

Whether a seizure was lawful often becomes a central issue in criminal cases. If police lacked reasonable suspicion to detain you or lacked probable cause to arrest you, any evidence found as a result may be excluded from court. This is called the exclusionary rule, and it is designed to discourage illegal searches and seizures.

For property, a seizure occurs when police take control of your belongings. Even if the seizure is lawful, you may have the right to get your property back once the case is resolved, depending on the circumstances.

Miranda Rights Explained Plainly

Miranda rights are among the most widely known and most misunderstood legal protections. These rights come from a 1966 Supreme Court case called Miranda v. Arizona, which established that suspects must be informed of certain rights before custodial interrogation.

When Miranda Warnings Are Required

- Police are required to read Miranda warnings when two conditions are met:
- You are in custody
- You are being interrogated

Custody generally means you are under arrest or your freedom of movement is restricted in a significant way. Interrogation means police are asking questions designed to elicit incriminating responses.

If both conditions are present and police fail to read you your Miranda rights, your statements may be excluded from evidence. However, this does not automatically make an arrest illegal or require the case to be dismissed. Physical evidence found as a result of the illegal interrogation may still be admissible, depending on the circumstances.

What the Miranda Warning Includes

The warnings inform you that:

You have the right to remain silent. You do not have to say anything. Silence cannot be used against you as evidence of guilt in most situations.

Anything you say can be used against you in court. This is not an exaggeration. Statements made to police can and often will be introduced as evidence during trial or plea negotiations.

You have the right to an attorney. You can have a lawyer present during questioning. If you cannot afford one, an attorney will be provided for you. This does not mean one will appear immediately, but the questioning should stop until you have the opportunity to consult with counsel.

Common Misconceptions About Miranda

One common misconception is that police must always read Miranda rights at the time of arrest. They do not. The warnings are tied to interrogation, not arrest itself. If police arrest you but do not ask you questions, they do not need to read you your rights.

Another misconception is that if police fail to read Miranda warnings, the case will be thrown out. That is not true. Only the statements you made during the unwarned interrogation will be excluded. The charges and other evidence remain.

People also often believe that volunteering information before police ask questions is protected. It is not. If you start talking on your own, your statements can be used against you, even if you have not been read your Miranda rights.

How to Invoke Your Rights

To invoke your rights, you must clearly say so. Vague or ambiguous statements may not be enough. Saying "I think I want a lawyer" or "Maybe I should talk to a lawyer" has been found insufficient by some courts.

A clear statement such as "I am invoking my right to remain silent and I want a lawyer" is far more effective. Once you invoke your right to an attorney, police must stop questioning you. If you invoke only your right to silence, police may try again later, though they should give you time to reconsider.

You can also invoke your rights at any time during questioning. Even if you have been answering questions, you can stop and request a lawyer. Do not feel pressured to continue simply because you have already started talking.

Waiving Your Rights

Police will often ask you to waive your Miranda rights and speak with them. They might say things like, "If you cooperate, things will go easier for you," or "We just want to hear your side of the story." These statements are tactics to encourage you to talk.

You can waive your Miranda rights, but the waiver must be voluntary, knowing, and intelligent. This means you must understand what rights you are giving up and choose to do so without coercion. However, once you waive your rights and start talking, anything you say can be used against you.

There is rarely any advantage to speaking to police without a lawyer present. Even if you believe you are innocent or that you can explain away the situation, statements made under stress and without legal advice often create more problems than they solve.

After the Arrest

After an arrest, the process typically includes booking, fingerprinting, photographing, and possible detention until bail or a court appearance. What happens next depends on the charge, jurisdiction, and individual circumstances.

The Booking Process

Booking is the administrative process of recording your arrest. You will be asked for personal information, including your name, address, date of birth, and other identifying details. Your fingerprints and photograph will be taken. You will be searched, and your personal belongings will be inventoried and stored.

During booking, police may try to ask additional questions. You still have the right to remain silent and request a lawyer. Just because the arrest has already happened does not mean you must answer questions.

Detention and Bail

After booking, you may be held in jail until your first court appearance, or you may be released on bail or on your own recognizance. Bail is money paid to the court to ensure you will return for future court dates. If you cannot afford bail, you remain in custody.

Some jurisdictions use risk assessment tools to determine whether someone should be released before trial. Factors include the seriousness of the charge, criminal history, ties to the community, and flight risk.

If you are detained, you have the right to contact someone, such as a family member or lawyer. Many jails allow one or more phone calls, though these calls are often recorded.

What You Say Matters Most

What matters most is what you say and what you do not say. Many cases are significantly shaped by statements made before a lawyer is present. People often believe that explaining their side of the story will help, but the legal system does not work that way during the arrest phase.

Officers are trained to ask questions that seem friendly or helpful but are designed to gather evidence. A question like, "Where were you tonight?" seems innocent but can lock you into a timeline that conflicts with other evidence. Even truthful statements can be misinterpreted or used out of context.

Silence is not an admission of guilt. It is a constitutional right. Judges and juries are instructed not to draw negative inferences from a defendant's decision to remain silent. Using this right does not make you look guilty. It makes you smart.

Getting Legal Representation

If you cannot afford a lawyer, one will be appointed to represent you. This usually happens at your first court appearance. Public defenders are real lawyers who handle criminal cases full-time, and many are highly experienced.

If you can afford to hire a private attorney, it is often wise to do so as soon as possible. A lawyer can advise you on what to say, help secure your release, and begin working on your defense immediately.

Do not rely on advice from cellmates, friends, or online forums. Criminal law is complex, and every case is different. Only a licensed attorney who knows the facts of your case can give you reliable legal advice.

Why This Chapter Matters

Most people who are arrested did not plan for it. They react instinctively, often believing that cooperation and explanation will resolve the situation. Sometimes it does. Often, it does not.

Understanding your rights does not mean being uncooperative or hostile. It means protecting yourself within the legal system as it exists. Knowledge at this stage can prevent small problems from becoming much larger ones.

The legal system is not designed to be forgiving of mistakes made in the moment. Statements given during arrest are often the strongest evidence against a defendant. By knowing your rights and exercising them calmly and clearly, you give yourself the best chance of a fair outcome.

You do not have to be a legal expert to protect yourself. You simply need to remember a few key principles: stay calm, remain silent, do not consent to searches, ask for a lawyer, and do not physically resist. These steps can make an enormous difference in how your case unfolds.

The next chapter explores what happens after charges are filed and how cases move through the courts once the arrest is over.

4

Charges, Courts, and Consequences

An arrest is only the beginning of a criminal case. What follows is often slower, more complex, and far more consequential than people expect. Many individuals assume that once they are charged, the outcome is fixed, or that a charge itself is the same as a conviction. Neither is true.

This chapter explains what happens after an arrest: how charges work, how cases move through the courts, and how outcomes can affect a person long after the case is closed. It also covers practical steps you can take to protect your rights and your future.

Charged vs. Convicted: A Crucial Difference

Being charged with a crime means the government has formally accused someone of violating the law. Charges are based on probable cause, not proof beyond a reasonable doubt. They represent allegations, not conclusions. Think of charges as the government's opening claim in a legal dispute, not the final answer.

A conviction, on the other hand, occurs only after guilt has been legally established, either through a guilty plea or a verdict at trial. This distinction is essential. People are legally presumed innocent until proven guilty, even after charges are filed. This presumption is a bedrock principle of American law, though it can feel abstract when facing the stress of pending charges.

What Can Happen to Charges

Charges are not permanent. They can be:

Reduced: Prosecutors may agree to charge a lesser offense, often as part of plea negotiations. For example, a felony charge might be reduced to a misdemeanor, significantly changing the potential penalties and long-term consequences.

Dismissed: If evidence is weak, witnesses are unavailable, or legal procedures were violated, charges can be dismissed before trial. Dismissals can happen at various stages: at arraignment, during preliminary hearings, or even on the eve of trial.

Resolved through diversion programs: Some jurisdictions offer alternatives to prosecution, especially for first-time offenders or low-level charges. These programs may require counseling, community service, or treatment. Successful completion often results in charges being dropped.

Proven or disproven at trial: If a case goes to trial, the jury or judge decides guilt or innocence based on the evidence presented.

The Hidden Impact of Charges

Yet charges alone can carry immediate consequences, even before any legal determination of guilt. Employers, landlords, licensing boards, and immigration authorities may react to pending charges. A background check showing an arrest can cost someone a job offer or an apartment, regardless of whether the case is still pending or the person is ultimately found innocent.

This reality often pressures defendants to act quickly and carefully. Waiting for the system to work itself out can mean losing opportunities in the meantime. Understanding your options early is critical.

The First Court Appearance: Arraignment

After an arrest and formal charging, the first court appearance is typically an arraignment. This is a brief hearing where several important things happen:

The charges are formally read: You hear exactly what the government is accusing you of.

You enter a plea: Most people plead not guilty at arraignment, which simply preserves the right to challenge the charges. Pleading not guilty does not mean the case must go to trial. It means you are not ready to accept responsibility at this early stage.

Bail is addressed: The court decides whether you will be released or held in custody while the case proceeds.

Your next court date is set: Criminal cases involve multiple court appearances. The arraignment sets the schedule in motion.

At arraignment, you have the right to an attorney. If you cannot afford one, the court must appoint a public defender or other counsel to represent you. Never waive this right without fully understanding what you are giving up.

Bail: Freedom While a Case Is Pending

After charges are filed, courts must decide whether a person will remain in custody or be released while the case proceeds. This decision is known as bail or pretrial release.

The Purpose of Bail

Bail is not a punishment. Its purpose is to ensure the defendant returns to court and does not pose a danger to the community. The idea is that people should not be jailed before trial simply because they have been accused. Detention before conviction contradicts the presumption of innocence.

Courts may consider several factors when setting bail:

- **The seriousness of the charge:** More serious allegations, especially violent felonies, often result in higher bail or no bail at all.
- **Prior criminal history:** A record of past convictions or failures to appear in court can influence the decision.
- **Risk of flight:** Does the person have strong community ties, a stable job, and family in the area? Or do they lack local connections and have the means to leave the jurisdiction?
- **Community safety:** Is there evidence the person poses a danger to specific individuals or the public generally?

Types of Release Conditions

Release conditions can vary widely and may include:

Cash bail or bond: The defendant (or someone on their behalf) posts money as security. If the defendant appears at all court dates, the money is returned. If not, it is forfeited. Bail can range from hundreds to hundreds of thousands of dollars depending on the charge and circumstances.

Supervised release: The defendant is monitored by a pretrial services agency, which may include regular check-ins, drug testing, or electronic monitoring.

Travel restrictions: The court may prohibit leaving the state or county.

No-contact orders: If the alleged offense involves a specific victim, the court may order no communication or contact.

Surrender of passport: In cases involving flight risk, the court may require the defendant to surrender travel documents.

Own recognizance (OR): In some cases, defendants are released on their own recognizance, meaning no money is required. The person simply promises to return to court.

The Bail Problem

In other cases, bail may be set so high that release is effectively impossible. Someone facing a $50,000 bail may need to pay a bail bondsman $5,000 (typically 10 percent, which is not refundable) or come up with the full amount themselves. For many people, these sums are insurmountable.

This has led to a troubling reality: people who are legally presumed innocent can spend weeks, months, or even years in jail simply because they cannot afford bail. During this time, they may lose jobs, housing, and custody of children. The pressure to resolve the case quickly, even through an unfavorable plea deal, becomes enormous.

Bail practices vary widely by state and have become a major focus of legal reform. Some jurisdictions have eliminated cash bail for certain offenses or adopted risk assessment tools to make detention decisions more equitable.

What You Can Do About Bail

If bail is set at an amount you cannot pay, you have options:

- **Request a bail reduction hearing:** Your attorney can argue that the bail is excessive and request a lower amount.
- **Explore bail funds:** Some nonprofit organizations pay bail for people who cannot afford it, especially in cases involving low-level charges.
- **Negotiate conditions:** Even if you cannot afford cash bail, you may be able to secure release through other conditions like supervision or electronic monitoring.

Never ignore bail simply because you cannot pay it. Work with your attorney to explore every available option.

Public Defenders and Private Attorneys

One of the first decisions you will face is who will represent you. If you cannot afford an attorney, the court will appoint a public defender. Public defenders are real lawyers, often highly experienced in criminal law, but they typically carry overwhelming caseloads. This can limit the time they have for each client.

If you can afford to hire a private attorney, you gain more control over who represents you and potentially more personalized attention. However, private attorneys can be expensive, often requiring thousands of dollars upfront.

Regardless of who represents you, your attorney's job is to:

- Investigate the facts of your case
- Challenge weak or illegally obtained evidence
- Negotiate with prosecutors
- Advise you on plea deals
- Represent you at trial if the case proceeds that far

Your relationship with your attorney matters. You should feel comfortable asking questions, expressing concerns, and understanding the strategy. If communication breaks down, address it directly. Your future may depend on this relationship.

Preliminary Hearings and Grand Juries

Before a felony case proceeds to trial, there is often an intermediate step to determine whether sufficient evidence exists. This step varies by state.

Preliminary Hearings

In a preliminary hearing, the prosecutor must present evidence to a judge showing probable cause that a crime occurred and that the defendant committed it. This is not a full trial. The standard is low, and the defense typically does not present its own case. However, preliminary hearings offer valuable opportunities:

- The defense can see some of the prosecution's evidence early
- Witnesses can be cross-examined under oath
- Weak cases can sometimes be dismissed
- If the judge finds probable cause, the case moves forward. If not, charges may be reduced or dismissed.

Grand Juries

In federal cases and in some states, prosecutors present evidence to a grand jury instead of a judge. A grand jury is a group of citizens who hear evidence in secret and vote on whether to issue an indictment (a formal charge). Grand jury proceedings are one-sided. The defense is not present, and the defendant does not testify unless they choose to (which is rare and risky).

Critics argue that grand juries are too heavily influenced by prosecutors, leading to the saying that a prosecutor could "indict a ham sandwich." Still, grand juries do occasionally refuse to indict, effectively ending a case.

Discovery: Learning the Prosecution's Case

Discovery is the process by which the defense learns what evidence the prosecution has. In criminal cases, prosecutors have a constitutional duty to disclose certain information, including:

Exculpatory evidence: Any evidence that tends to show the defendant is innocent or that undermines the prosecution's case. This is required under Brady v. Maryland, a landmark Supreme Court decision.

Witness lists: Who the prosecution plans to call at trial.

Police reports and investigative materials: Documents describing how the case was built.

Physical evidence: Items like surveillance video, forensic analysis, or seized property.

Discovery is rarely as complete or as smooth as it should be. Prosecutors sometimes withhold information, accidentally or intentionally. Defense attorneys must be vigilant in demanding disclosure and challenging gaps in what is provided.

As a defendant, your role in discovery is to be honest with your attorney about the facts. Even details that seem embarrassing or unhelpful may be critical to building a defense. Your attorney cannot be blindsided at trial by facts you chose not to share.

Plea Deals: The Most Common Outcome

Despite popular portrayals of dramatic courtroom battles, most criminal cases do not go to trial. The vast majority, upwards of 90 percent in many jurisdictions, are resolved through plea agreements.

What Is a Plea Deal?

A plea deal is an agreement in which the defendant pleads guilty, often to a reduced charge or in exchange for a lighter sentence. For example, someone charged with aggravated assault might plead guilty to simple assault. Someone facing 10 years might plead in exchange for a sentence of 2 years.

Why Plea Deals Happen

For prosecutors, plea deals conserve resources and reduce uncertainty. Trials are expensive and time-consuming, and there is always a chance the government will lose. A plea guarantees a conviction.

For defendants, plea deals can limit risk and provide faster resolution. Trials are unpredictable. Even with a strong defense, a jury might convict, and post-trial sentences are often harsher than what was offered in a plea. Accepting a deal can mean avoiding the worst-case scenario.

However, plea deals involve significant trade-offs. By pleading guilty, a defendant gives up the right to trial and the opportunity to challenge the government's evidence in court. Even a reduced charge can still carry long-term consequences. A misdemeanor conviction can affect employment, housing, and professional licenses just as a felony can, though usually less severely.

The Pressure to Plead

The pressure to accept a plea can be intense. Defendants held in jail pretrial may feel desperate to resolve the case and get out. Prosecutors may offer deals that expire if not accepted quickly, creating artificial urgency. Public defenders with limited time may encourage pleas even when a trial might be winnable.

This pressure is compounded by what is known as the "trial penalty." Defendants who reject plea deals and are convicted at trial often face significantly harsher sentences than they would have under the plea. This disparity is intended to reward those who plead guilty and save the system resources, but it can feel like punishment for exercising the constitutional right to trial.

Should You Accept a Plea?

Deciding whether to accept a plea is one of the most significant choices in a criminal case. It depends on multiple factors:

Evidence strength: How strong is the prosecution's case? Are there witnesses, video, forensic evidence, or confessions? Or is the case based on shaky testimony or circumstantial evidence?

Potential penalties: What is the maximum sentence if convicted at trial, and how does that compare to the plea offer?

Collateral consequences: What are the long-term effects of a conviction, even a reduced one? Will it affect your job, professional license, immigration status, or custody of your children?

Individual priorities: Are you willing to accept responsibility to move forward, or is fighting the charge a matter of principle? How much risk are you willing to take?

Your attorney should explain these factors in detail and provide a clear recommendation, but the decision is ultimately yours. Never plead guilty to something you did not do simply because you feel pressured. At the same time, refusing a reasonable plea out of pride or fear can lead to far worse outcomes.

Alford and Nolo Contendere Pleas

In some jurisdictions, defendants can enter special types of pleas:

Alford plea: You plead guilty while maintaining your innocence. This acknowledges that the prosecution has enough evidence to likely convict you, even though you deny wrongdoing.

Nolo contendere (no contest): You do not admit guilt but accept the conviction and punishment. This can be useful in cases where a guilty plea might be used against you in a related civil lawsuit.

Both types of pleas result in convictions but offer slight strategic advantages in specific situations.

Trials: When Cases Are Fully Litigated

When a case goes to trial, the government must prove guilt beyond a reasonable doubt. This is the highest standard of proof in the legal system, far higher than the probable cause needed to charge someone or the preponderance of evidence used in civil cases.

Types of Trials

Defendants have the right to choose between a jury trial and a bench trial:

Jury trial: A group of citizens (typically 12 in felony cases, sometimes 6 in misdemeanors) hears the evidence and decides guilt or innocence.

Bench trial: The judge alone decides the case. Bench trials are faster and may be preferable in highly technical cases where a judge's expertise is advantageous.

In most cases, defendants choose jury trials, believing that a group of peers is more likely to sympathize with the defense.

The Trial Process

Trials involve several stages:

Jury selection: Attorneys question potential jurors to identify biases and select a panel. Both sides can exclude certain jurors for cause (clear bias) or through peremptory challenges (no reason needed, with some limits).

Opening statements: Each side outlines what they expect the evidence to show. These are roadmaps, not arguments.

Presentation of evidence: The prosecution goes first, calling witnesses and introducing physical evidence. The defense can cross-examine each witness. After the prosecution rests, the defense may present its own witnesses or evidence, though it is not required to do so.

Witness testimony and cross-examination: This is often the most dramatic part of a trial. Attorneys ask questions designed to support their theory of the case while undermining the other side's.

Legal arguments: Throughout the trial, attorneys may make motions to exclude evidence, dismiss charges, or clarify legal standards.

Closing arguments: Each side summarizes the evidence and argues why the jury should rule in their favor.

Jury instructions: The judge explains the law the jury must apply.

Jury deliberation: The jury discusses the case in private and attempts to reach a unanimous verdict (in most states). If they cannot agree, the result is a hung jury and a mistrial, meaning the case could be retried.

Verdict: The jury announces whether the defendant is guilty or not guilty. A not guilty verdict is final and cannot be appealed by the prosecution.

The Risks of Trial

Trials are unpredictable. They can result in acquittals, convictions, or mistrials. Even strong cases can fall apart due to witness credibility issues, procedural errors, or jury sympathy. However, trials also carry the risk of harsher penalties if a defendant is convicted after rejecting a plea.

Because of these risks, trials are often reserved for cases where the defense believes the evidence is weak, the law is unclear, or the stakes justify the gamble. Some defendants also proceed to trial on principle, unwilling to plead guilty to something they did not do, regardless of the risk.

Your Role at Trial

If your case goes to trial, your attorney will handle the legal strategy, but you still have an important role:

- Dress appropriately and behave respectfully in court
- Do not react visibly to testimony, even if it is false or upsetting
- Decide whether to testify (your attorney will advise you, but the choice is yours)
- Testifying allows you to tell your story, but it also opens you to cross-examination
- Many defendants choose not to testify, and the jury is instructed not to hold this against them. However, jurors are human, and some may wonder why the defendant stayed silent.

Sentencing and Consequences

If a conviction occurs, whether through a plea or trial, the court imposes a sentence. Sentencing can happen immediately or at a separate hearing weeks later.

Types of Sentences

Sentences may include:

Jail or prison time: Jail is typically for sentences under one year and is run by local authorities. Prison is for longer sentences and is run by the state or federal government.

Probation: Instead of incarceration, the defendant is supervised in the community under specific conditions. Violating probation can result in jail time.

Fines and fees: Courts often impose financial penalties, which can range from hundreds to thousands of dollars. Failure to pay can lead to additional legal trouble.

Community service: The defendant must complete unpaid work for the public benefit.

Mandatory programs or treatment: Courts may require anger management classes, drug treatment, or other programs.

Restitution: If the offense caused financial harm to a victim, the defendant may be ordered to pay compensation.

Factors Influencing Sentencing

Sentencing is influenced by statutory guidelines, judicial discretion, and aggravating or mitigating factors:

Statutory guidelines: Laws specify sentencing ranges for different offenses. Some states have mandatory minimums, meaning judges must impose at least a certain sentence.

Aggravating factors: These increase the severity of the sentence. Examples include prior convictions, use of a weapon, or victim vulnerability.

Mitigating factors: These reduce the severity. Examples include lack of criminal history, accepting responsibility, or evidence of rehabilitation.

Judicial discretion: Judges have significant leeway within statutory limits. Two defendants convicted of the same crime in the same courthouse might receive very different sentences based on how the judge views their individual circumstances.

Sentences can vary dramatically for similar offenses depending on jurisdiction and circumstances. A drug possession charge might result in probation in one county and years in prison in another.

Collateral Consequences

Beyond formal punishment, convictions carry collateral consequences. These are legal penalties or restrictions that follow automatically from a conviction, often without being mentioned at sentencing. They may affect:

Employment: Many employers conduct background checks and refuse to hire people with criminal records. Certain professions, like healthcare, education, and law, may be entirely off-limits.

Housing: Landlords often deny applications from people with criminal histories. Public housing may also be unavailable.

Professional licenses: Doctors, lawyers, nurses, contractors, and others may lose their licenses or be barred from obtaining them.

Voting rights: Some states permanently disenfranchise people with felony convictions, while others restore voting rights after sentence completion.

Firearm ownership: Federal law prohibits people convicted of felonies or domestic violence misdemeanors from possessing firearms.

Immigration status: Noncitizens can face deportation, denial of naturalization, or bars to reentry even for relatively minor convictions.

Public benefits: Some convictions make people ineligible for student loans, food assistance, or housing subsidies.

Often, these consequences last far longer than the sentence itself. A person who serves six months in jail may face decades of employment barriers and housing discrimination.

Before accepting a plea or going to trial, it is essential to understand not just the sentence you might face, but these hidden consequences. Your attorney should explain them, but if they do not, ask.

Appeals: Challenging Convictions

If you are convicted at trial, you have the right to appeal. An appeal is not a new trial. Instead, an appellate court reviews the trial record to determine whether legal errors occurred that affected the outcome.

Grounds for Appeal

Common grounds include:

- **Insufficient evidence:** The prosecution did not prove guilt beyond a reasonable doubt.
- **Legal errors:** The judge made mistakes in admitting evidence, instructing the jury, or applying the law.
- **Constitutional violations:** Your rights were violated, such as through an unlawful search or ineffective assistance of counsel.
- **Prosecutorial misconduct:** The prosecutor engaged in improper behavior that prejudiced the trial.

Appeals are difficult to win. Appellate courts give trial judges substantial deference and will not reverse convictions unless the error was significant.

However, successful appeals can result in convictions being overturned or new trials being ordered.

Time Limits

Appeals must be filed within strict deadlines, often just 30 days after sentencing. Missing this deadline generally means losing the right to appeal forever. If you are convicted, talk to your attorney immediately about whether an appeal makes sense.

Appeals from Guilty Pleas

If you pleaded guilty, your right to appeal is much more limited. You typically can only challenge the voluntariness of the plea or the legality of the sentence, not the evidence against you. This is another reason to think carefully before pleading guilty.

Criminal Records and Expungement

A criminal case does not simply disappear when it ends. Arrests, charges, and convictions often remain on a person's criminal record, accessible to employers, landlords, and background check companies.

What Appears on a Criminal Record

Records can include:

- **Arrests:** Even if charges were dropped or you were found not guilty, the arrest itself may appear.
- **Charges:** Pending or dismissed charges may remain visible.
- **Convictions:** These are almost always included, along with details of the sentence.
- **Court records:** Documents filed in your case are typically public.

How Records Affect Your Life

Criminal records can appear on background checks used for employment, housing, education, and more. Even old or minor offenses can disqualify someone from opportunities.

Many people assume their record will clear automatically over time. In most states, it does not. Records remain indefinitely unless you take legal action to remove them.

Sealing and Expungement

Some records can be:

Sealed: Hidden from public view. Government agencies may still be able to access sealed records, but most employers and landlords cannot.

Expunged: Legally erased or destroyed. Expunged records are treated as though they never existed, though some government agencies may still know about them.

Eligibility for expungement or sealing depends on state law, the type of offense, and how the case was resolved. Generally, minor offenses, cases that resulted in acquittals or dismissals, and first-time offenses are more likely to qualify.

Waiting periods: Many states require you to wait a certain number of years after completing your sentence before applying.

Filing requirements: You typically must file a petition with the court, provide documentation, and sometimes attend a hearing.

Legal assistance: The process can be complex, and hiring an attorney may improve your chances, though some legal aid organizations offer free help.

Why Expungement Matters

Taking action to clear your record can open doors that have been closed for years. It can mean the difference between getting a job or being rejected, securing housing or facing denial.

If you are eligible, do not wait. The sooner you act, the sooner you can move forward.

Probation and Parole: Supervised Release

Many people convicted of crimes do not go to prison or serve only a portion of their sentence behind bars. Instead, they are placed on probation or parole.

Probation

Probation is a sentence served in the community under supervision. Conditions typically include:

- Regular meetings with a probation officer
- Drug testing
- Employment or education requirements
- Travel restrictions
- Payment of fines, fees, and restitution
- Avoiding new criminal conduct

Violating probation can result in the original sentence being imposed. For example, if you were sentenced to five years with probation, violating probation could mean serving those five years in prison.

Parole

Parole is supervised release after serving part of a prison sentence. It functions similarly to probation but applies to people who have already been incarcerated. Parole boards decide whether inmates are ready for release and under what conditions.

Both probation and parole require strict compliance. What may seem like minor violations (missing an appointment, traveling without permission) can have serious consequences.

The Bigger Picture: How the System Works

Understanding the criminal justice system means recognizing how its parts fit together. Prosecutors have enormous power to decide who gets charged, with what, and whether to offer deals. Judges have discretion in sentencing. Defense attorneys must navigate heavy caseloads and limited resources. And defendants must make life-altering decisions under intense pressure with incomplete information.

The system is not designed for speed or simplicity. Cases can drag on for months or years. Uncertainty is constant. And outcomes often feel arbitrary, depending on who your prosecutor is, who your judge is, and whether you can afford a good attorney.

But the system is also filled with opportunities to challenge, negotiate, and advocate. Charges can be reduced. Cases can be dismissed. Sentences can be minimized. Records can be cleared.

Why This Chapter Matters

The period between arrest and resolution is where most legal damage or protection occurs. Decisions made during this time can determine not only the outcome of a case, but the shape of a person's future.

Understanding the difference between being charged and convicted, knowing how bail and plea deals work, recognizing the long-term impact of criminal records, and knowing when to fight and when to negotiate allows individuals to navigate the system with intention rather than fear.

The stakes are too high to rely on assumptions or hope. Knowledge is the most powerful tool you have.

The next chapters turn from criminal law to the legal issues that arise in everyday life: work, family, housing, and money, where the law shapes outcomes just as powerfully, though often less visibly.

PART III: Work, Wages, and Employment Law

5

Pay, Hours, and Worker Rights

For many Americans, the most frequent legal questions have nothing to do with courtrooms or police. They arise at work: on paydays, in scheduling disputes, or when a job suddenly ends. Because employment laws are complex and vary by state, workers often sense something is wrong without knowing whether it is illegal.

This chapter explains the basic legal rules governing pay, hours, and worker classification, and why understanding them can protect both income and job security.

Minimum Wage Laws

Minimum wage laws set the lowest hourly pay an employer may legally offer. In the United States, minimum wage operates on two levels: federal and state.

Federal law establishes a nationwide minimum wage, but states and cities are free to set higher rates. When multiple minimum wages apply, employees are entitled to the highest applicable rate, not the lowest. For example, if the federal minimum wage is $7.25 per hour but your state has set a minimum of $15.00 per hour, your employer must pay you at least $15.00. The same principle applies if your city or county has set an even higher local minimum wage.

Minimum wage rules apply to most workers, but there are exceptions. Certain categories, such as tipped employees, some agricultural workers, and trainees, may be subject to different standards. Tipped employees, for instance, may receive a lower base wage if their tips bring their total earnings up to at least the regular minimum wage. Employers must still follow specific rules about tip credits, training wages, and recordkeeping. If your tips do not bring your hourly earnings up to the minimum wage, your employer is required to make up the difference.

Violations are common. Employers may:

- Pay below the legal minimum
- Require unpaid work "off the clock"
- Misclassify workers to avoid wage laws
- Deduct expenses from wages in ways that push pay below minimum wage
- Fail to properly calculate the regular rate for tipped workers

Minimum wage violations can entitle workers to back pay, penalties, and sometimes double damages. Yet many workers never recover unpaid wages because they do not realize the law was violated. If you believe your pay falls below the minimum wage, you can file a complaint with your state labor department or the U.S. Department of Labor's Wage and Hour Division. In many cases, you can also pursue a private lawsuit to recover what you are owed.

Overtime and Exempt Employees

Overtime pay is one of the most misunderstood areas of employment law.

In general, non-exempt employees are entitled to overtime pay, usually one and a half times their regular rate, for hours worked beyond a set threshold, often 40 hours per week. This rule applies regardless of whether the employee is paid hourly or by salary. For example, if your regular hourly rate is $20, your overtime rate would be $30 per hour for any hours over 40 in a workweek.

Being paid a salary does not automatically eliminate overtime rights. This is one of the most important misconceptions to understand. Many salaried workers assume that receiving a fixed weekly or monthly salary means they are not entitled to overtime, but this is often incorrect. The key question is whether an employee is legally exempt or non-exempt.

To be exempt from overtime requirements, an employee must usually meet both:

- A minimum salary requirement (which is set by federal law and updated periodically)
- Specific job duty criteria

Common exemptions include certain executive, administrative, and professional roles. However, job titles alone do not determine exemption status. What matters is the actual work performed day to day. An employer cannot simply call you a "manager" or "administrator" to avoid paying overtime if your actual duties do not meet the legal standards for exemption.

For example, to qualify for the executive exemption, you typically must have management as your primary duty, regularly direct the work of at least two full-time employees, and have genuine input into hiring and firing decisions. Simply having "manager" in your job title while spending most of your time doing the same work as the employees you supervise does not make you exempt.

Misclassification is widespread. Employers may label employees as "managers" or "professionals" while assigning duties that do not meet exemption standards. When this happens, employees may be owed significant unpaid overtime, sometimes going back several years. If you work more than 40 hours per week on a salary and are unsure whether you should be receiving overtime, it is worth reviewing the actual duties test for exemptions or consulting with your state labor department.

Independent Contractor vs. Employee

One of the most important, and frequently abused, distinctions in employment law is whether a worker is an employee or an independent contractor.

Employees are entitled to legal protections such as:

- Minimum wage and overtime
- Workers' compensation if injured on the job
- Unemployment benefits if laid off

- Anti-discrimination protections under federal and state civil rights laws
- Family and medical leave in certain circumstances
- Protection under workplace safety regulations

Independent contractors generally are not entitled to any of these protections. They are considered to be running their own business, even if they work for only one client.

The label an employer uses is not controlling. Just because your employer calls you an independent contractor, gives you a 1099 tax form instead of a W-2, or has you sign an independent contractor agreement does not make you one in the eyes of the law. Courts and government agencies look at the reality of the working relationship, not just the paperwork. Key factors often include:

Degree of control over the work: Does the company control when, where, and how you work? Do they set your schedule, require you to work on-site, or dictate the methods you use to complete tasks? The more control they exercise, the more likely you are an employee.

Whether the worker can make a profit or loss: Do you have the opportunity to earn more by working efficiently or investing in your own tools and methods? Can you lose money on a project? Independent contractors typically have this potential; employees generally do not.

Who provides tools and equipment: Do you use your own computer, vehicle, tools, or equipment, or does the company provide them? Employees typically use employer-provided resources.

Whether the work is integral to the business: Is the work you do central to the company's operations? For example, if you drive for a ride-sharing company, that work is core to their business. If you are called in occasionally to fix the company's plumbing, that is not. The more integral your work, the more likely you are an employee.

Permanency of the relationship: Do you work for this company indefinitely, or is your work limited to a specific project or time period? Ongoing relationships suggest employee status.

Investment in the business: Have you made a significant investment in facilities, tools, or other resources independent of the company? True independent contractors usually have.

Different tests apply depending on whether the question arises under wage laws, tax laws, or unemployment insurance, but the fundamental inquiry is similar: who bears the risk and who has control?

Misclassifying employees as contractors can save employers money, but it shifts risk onto workers. Those workers may lose wages, benefits, and legal protections without realizing it. They may also face unexpected tax bills, since independent contractors are responsible for paying self-employment taxes that would otherwise be split with an employer. If you suspect you have been misclassified, you can file a complaint with the IRS, your state labor department, or the Department of Labor. You may be entitled to back pay, overtime, and other compensation you should have received as an employee.

Why These Rules Matter

Pay and classification issues are not technicalities. They determine whether workers are fairly compensated, protected from exploitation, and able to support themselves and their families.

Because employment laws are enforced primarily through complaints, many violations persist simply because workers do not know their rights. Employers are not required to inform you of all the protections you are entitled to, and many do not. Understanding minimum wage rules, overtime eligibility, and worker classification empowers employees to recognize problems early and seek remedies before losses accumulate.

If you believe your rights have been violated, you have options. You can file a complaint with your state labor department or the U.S. Department of Labor. In many cases, you can also file a private lawsuit. Some violations carry penalties that go beyond simple back pay, which means you may recover more than just the wages you lost. There are also protections against retaliation: it is illegal for an employer to fire you or punish you for asserting your rights under wage and hour laws.

Knowing your rights is the first step. The second is recognizing when those rights have been violated. The third is taking action before it is too late. Many wage and hour claims are subject to statutes of limitations, meaning you may lose the right to recover unpaid wages if you wait too long.

The next chapter builds on these foundations by addressing what happens when employment relationships break down through termination, layoffs, or discrimination, and what legal protections may still apply.

6

Getting Fired, Laid Off, or Discriminated Against

Few legal events feel as personal, or as destabilizing, as losing a job. Termination can affect income, housing, healthcare, immigration status, and family stability. Many people assume that being fired automatically means something illegal occurred, while others believe employers can do whatever they want. The truth lies between those extremes.

This chapter explains how job loss works under U.S. law, when termination is lawful, and when it crosses the line into illegality.

At-Will Employment Explained

Most jobs in the United States are governed by at-will employment. This means that, in general, an employer can terminate an employee at any time, for any reason, or for no reason at all, and the employee can quit under the same terms. The employer does not need to provide advance notice, does not need to give you a warning, and does not need to explain why you are being let go.

At-will employment often sounds harsh, but it has limits. Employers may not terminate workers for illegal reasons, even in at-will states. These illegal reasons include firing someone based on their race, religion, or other protected characteristics, firing someone in retaliation for reporting illegal activity, or firing someone in violation of an employment contract. In addition, written contracts, union agreements, company policies, or employee handbooks can modify at-will status. For example, if your employee handbook states that employees can only be terminated "for cause" after progressive discipline, your employer may be required to follow that process.

Common misconceptions include:

"At-will means I can be fired for anything." This is not true. While at-will employment gives employers broad discretion, there are still many illegal reasons for termination. You cannot be fired for discriminatory reasons, for exercising legal rights, or in retaliation for protected activities.

"My employer must give me a reason." Usually not. In most at-will situations, your employer can simply tell you that your employment is ending without providing any explanation. However, if you apply for unemployment benefits, your employer may need to state a reason to the unemployment office.

"Being laid off is the same as being fired." These are legally different. Being fired typically suggests termination for cause or performance issues, while being laid off usually means your position was eliminated for business reasons. This distinction can matter for unemployment benefits, references, and eligibility for rehire.

Understanding at-will employment helps clarify what protections still exist when a job ends. Just because your employment is at-will does not mean you have no rights. It simply means the baseline rule is flexible, subject to important exceptions.

Wrongful Termination

Wrongful termination occurs when an employer fires an employee for a reason prohibited by law or in violation of an agreement. Despite the name, not every termination that feels wrong or unfair qualifies as legally wrongful.

Examples of potentially wrongful termination include firing an employee:

For reporting illegal conduct (whistleblowing): If you report that your employer is violating environmental laws, committing fraud, endangering public safety, or breaking other laws, you are generally protected from retaliation. This protection applies whether you report internally to management or externally to a government agency. For example, if you report safety violations to OSHA and are fired a week later, that termination may be wrongful.

For filing a workers' compensation claim: If you are injured on the job and file a workers' compensation claim, your employer cannot legally fire you in retaliation. This protection exists because workers' compensation is a right guaranteed by law, and employers cannot punish employees for exercising legal rights.

For taking legally protected leave: Federal and state laws, such as the Family and Medical Leave Act (FMLA), protect your right to take unpaid leave for certain medical and family reasons. If you take FMLA leave to care for a sick family member and are terminated upon your return, that may constitute wrongful termination. The same applies to other forms of protected leave, such as military leave or leave to serve on a jury.

In retaliation for complaining about harassment or wage violations: If you complain to your employer or a government agency about sexual harassment, unpaid wages, or other legal violations, you are protected from retaliation. Employers cannot fire you, demote you, cut your pay, or otherwise punish you for making these complaints, even if the complaint turns out to be unfounded, as long as it was made in good faith.

In violation of an employment contract or company policy: If you have a written employment contract that specifies you can only be terminated for cause, your employer must have a valid reason and may need to follow certain procedures. Similarly, if your employee handbook promises progressive discipline or a specific termination process, firing you without following that process may be wrongful, depending on your state's laws.

Wrongful termination claims are highly fact-specific. Timing, documentation, and employer behavior matter. An employer may cite one reason for termination while the real motivation is unlawful retaliation. For example, your employer might say you were fired for poor performance, but if you were fired just days after filing a discrimination complaint, and your performance reviews had always been positive, this timing may suggest the real reason was retaliation.

This is why documentation is so important. If you believe you may face retaliation, keep copies of positive performance reviews, emails showing you reported problems, and any communications about the issues you raised. If you are fired, write down what was said, who was present, and when it happened. This evidence can be critical in proving wrongful termination.

Importantly, unfair treatment is not always illegal. The law does not prohibit poor management, favoritism, or arbitrary decisions, unless they intersect with protected rights. Your boss can fire you because they do not like your personality, because they favor another employee, or even for a reason that is completely irrational. As long as the decision is not based on a protected characteristic and does not violate any other law or agreement, it is generally legal, even if it feels deeply unjust.

Workplace Discrimination and Harassment

Employment discrimination laws prohibit adverse treatment based on certain protected characteristics. At the federal level, these typically include:

Race or color: It is illegal to treat employees or job applicants differently because of their race or skin color. This includes decisions about hiring, firing, pay, promotions, and assignments.

Sex, gender identity, or sexual orientation: Federal law prohibits discrimination based on sex, which courts have interpreted to include discrimination based on pregnancy, gender identity, and sexual orientation. This means you cannot be fired, demoted, or harassed because you are a woman, because you are transgender, or because you are gay or lesbian.

Religion: Employers cannot discriminate based on religious beliefs or practices. They must also provide reasonable accommodations for religious practices, such as time off for religious observances or permission to wear religious attire, unless doing so would create an undue hardship.

National origin: Discrimination based on where you or your ancestors are from is illegal. This includes discrimination based on accent, ethnicity, or association with people of a particular national origin.

Disability: Employers cannot discriminate against qualified individuals with disabilities and must provide reasonable accommodations, such as modified work schedules or assistive equipment, unless doing so would impose an undue hardship on the business.

Age (over a certain threshold): The Age Discrimination in Employment Act protects workers who are 40 years old or older from discrimination based on age. This means employers cannot refuse to hire, fire, or demote someone simply because they are older.

Many states and cities provide additional protections beyond federal law. Some states prohibit discrimination based on marital status, political affiliation, criminal history, or other characteristics. Check your state and local laws to understand the full scope of protections available to you.

Discrimination can take many forms, including:

- Hiring decisions: Refusing to hire someone because of a protected characteristic
- Promotions: Passing over qualified employees for advancement based on discriminatory reasons
- Pay disparities: Paying employees less because of their sex, race, or other protected status
- Discipline: Imposing harsher discipline on employees in a protected class
- Termination: Firing someone because of a protected characteristic
- Job assignments: Giving less desirable work or limiting opportunities based on stereotypes

Harassment becomes illegal when it is severe or pervasive enough to create a hostile work environment or when it involves quid pro quo demands. A hostile work environment exists when unwelcome conduct based on a protected characteristic is so severe or frequent that it makes the workplace intimidating, hostile, or abusive. This does not mean every rude comment or isolated incident is illegal. The conduct must be serious enough that a reasonable person would find the environment hostile, and it must actually affect your ability to do your work.

Quid pro quo harassment occurs when someone in authority, such as a supervisor, demands sexual favors or other actions in exchange for job benefits or threatens adverse consequences if you refuse. For example, if your manager says you will be promoted only if you go on a date with them, or that you will be fired if you refuse, that is quid pro quo harassment.

Sexual harassment is only one category. Harassment based on race, religion, disability, or other protected traits is equally unlawful. Racial slurs, jokes about someone's religion, mocking someone's accent, or making fun of a person's disability can all create a hostile work environment if the behavior is severe or pervasive.

Employees generally must report discrimination or harassment internally before pursuing legal claims, unless reporting would be futile or unsafe. This means you typically need to follow your company's complaint procedure, which is usually outlined in your employee handbook. Reporting gives your employer the opportunity to investigate and stop the conduct. If your employer takes appropriate action, that may resolve the problem without the need for a lawsuit.

However, if reporting internally would be dangerous, pointless, or if the harasser is the owner or CEO with no one above them, you may be able to skip internal reporting and go directly to a government agency. You should also report externally if your employer ignores your complaint or retaliates against you for making it.

Deadlines for filing complaints with government agencies are strict and vary by jurisdiction. For federal claims, you generally must file a charge with the Equal Employment Opportunity Commission (EEOC) within 180 days of the discriminatory act, or within 300 days if your state has its own anti-discrimination agency. Some states have even shorter deadlines. Missing these deadlines can mean losing your right to sue, so it is important to act quickly if you believe you have been discriminated against.

If you file a charge with the EEOC or your state agency, they will investigate and may try to resolve the dispute through mediation. If that does not work, the agency may sue on your behalf or issue you a "right to sue" letter, which allows you to file your own lawsuit. You typically have 90 days from receiving the right to sue letter to file in court.

Layoffs and Reductions in Force

Being laid off is different from being fired for cause. Layoffs usually result from business decisions such as restructuring, downsizing, closing a facility, or financial hardship. When you are laid off, it generally means your position was eliminated, not that you did anything wrong.

While layoffs are often lawful, they can still be illegal if:

Selection is discriminatory: Employers cannot use layoffs as a cover for getting rid of employees in protected classes. For example, if a company lays off all of its oldest employees while keeping younger workers in similar positions, that may be age discrimination. Similarly, if women or racial minorities are disproportionately selected for layoff without a legitimate business reason, that may violate discrimination laws.

Required notices are not given: The federal WARN Act (Worker Adjustment and Retraining Notification Act) requires certain employers to provide 60 days' advance notice before mass layoffs or plant closings. This law applies to employers with 100 or more employees if the layoff affects at least 50 workers at a single site. If your employer violates the WARN Act, you may be entitled to back pay and benefits for the period you should have received notice. Some states have similar laws with different thresholds.

Contracts or collective bargaining agreements are violated: If you are covered by a union contract, that contract may specify the process for layoffs, such as requiring that layoffs be done in order of seniority. If your employer violates these terms, the union can file a grievance on your behalf. Similarly, if you have an individual employment contract that limits the circumstances under which you can be laid off, violating that contract may give you grounds for a lawsuit.

Even in a legitimate layoff, you may be entitled to severance pay, continuation of health benefits under COBRA, or unemployment compensation. Some employers offer severance packages in exchange for signing a release of legal claims. Before signing such a release, consider whether you may have legal claims worth pursuing and whether the severance offer is fair. You may want to consult with an attorney, especially if you are over 40, since the law gives you extra time to consider releases in age discrimination cases.

Why This Chapter Matters

Job loss can happen suddenly, and misinformation spreads quickly in moments of stress. Knowing whether a termination is lawful affects how, and how quickly, someone should respond.

Understanding at-will employment, wrongful termination, and discrimination law allows workers to distinguish between unfairness and illegality, to preserve evidence, and to meet deadlines that cannot be extended. If you are fired and believe it may have been illegal, act quickly:

Document everything: Write down what happened, when, and who was involved. Save emails, text messages, performance reviews, and any other relevant documents.

File for unemployment: Even if you were fired, you may still be eligible for unemployment benefits, especially if the reason given was not misconduct.

Know your deadlines: Discrimination claims, WARN Act claims, and other employment claims have strict filing deadlines. Missing a deadline can mean losing your rights permanently.

Seek advice: Consider consulting with an employment attorney, especially if you believe your termination was discriminatory or retaliatory. Many employment lawyers offer free initial consultations.

Even if your termination was legal, you still have rights. You are entitled to your final paycheck according to your state's laws, continuation of health insurance under COBRA if you were covered, and unemployment benefits if you qualify. Understanding these rights can help you move forward and protect your financial stability during a difficult transition.

The next section turns to family law, another area where legal decisions intersect deeply with personal life and long-term stability.

PART IV: Family Law & Relationships

7

Marriage, Prenups, and Legal Partnerships

Marriage is often discussed as an emotional or cultural milestone, but in legal terms it is also a powerful contract. The moment two people marry, their legal rights and responsibilities change, sometimes in ways they did not expect or intend. Many of the most common family law disputes arise not because people made bad choices, but because they did not understand the legal effects of the choices they made.

This chapter explains what marriage actually does under the law, how prenuptial agreements work, and the misconceptions that frequently cause confusion and conflict.

What Marriage Legally Changes

When two people marry, the law begins to treat them as a single economic and legal unit in many respects. This does not eliminate individual rights, but it does create shared obligations and benefits that begin immediately upon marriage.

Marriage can affect:

Property ownership: Income and assets acquired during marriage may be considered jointly owned, depending on state law. In community property states (such as California, Texas, Arizona, and several others), most income earned and property acquired during the marriage is automatically owned equally by both spouses, regardless of whose name is on the title or who earned the money. In equitable distribution states (the majority of states), property is not automatically split equally, but the court will divide marital property fairly, though not necessarily 50/50, if the marriage ends in divorce. Property you owned before marriage typically remains yours individually, as do gifts and inheritances you receive during the marriage, though this can become complicated if assets are commingled or improved with marital funds.

Debt: Some debts incurred during marriage can become shared obligations, even if only one spouse's name is on the account. In community property states, debts incurred during marriage for family purposes are generally considered community debts that both spouses are responsible for paying. Even in equitable distribution states, debts taken on for the benefit of the family, such as a mortgage, car loan, or credit card used for household expenses, may be treated as joint obligations. However, debts one spouse brings into the marriage usually remain that person's individual responsibility, unless the other spouse cosigns or benefits from the debt.

Taxes: Married couples may file joint or separate tax returns, with significant financial consequences. Filing jointly often results in lower taxes because of higher standard deductions and more favorable tax brackets, but it also means both spouses are jointly liable for any taxes owed, including penalties and interest. If one spouse underreports income or claims improper deductions, the other spouse can be held responsible unless they qualify for innocent spouse relief. Filing separately may protect you from your spouse's tax problems but typically results in higher taxes and the loss of certain tax credits and deductions. The choice between filing jointly or separately should be made carefully, especially if there are concerns about your spouse's financial honesty or tax compliance.

Healthcare and decision-making: Spouses often gain automatic authority to make medical decisions if one partner becomes incapacitated. In most states, if you are unable to make medical decisions for yourself due to illness or injury, your spouse is automatically recognized as your legal next of kin and can make healthcare decisions on your behalf. This includes decisions about surgery, life support, and end-of-life care. Spouses also typically have automatic hospital visitation rights and access to medical records. Without marriage, unmarried partners may be excluded from medical decisions and even denied the right to visit their partner in the hospital unless specific legal documents, such as a healthcare power of attorney, are in place.

Inheritance: Marriage affects inheritance rights, even when no will exists. If you die without a will (called dying intestate), state law determines who inherits your property. In most states, your spouse automatically inherits a significant portion or all of your estate, even if you have children or other family members. The exact share depends on state law and whether you have children. Importantly, in many states, you cannot completely disinherit your spouse even if you have a will. Most states give surviving spouses the right to claim a portion of the estate regardless of what the will says, often called an elective share or statutory share. This protection exists to prevent one spouse from leaving the other with nothing.

Benefits and protections: Spouses may qualify for insurance, retirement benefits, and legal privileges unavailable to unmarried partners. These include the ability to be covered under your spouse's health insurance plan, the right to receive Social Security benefits based on your spouse's work record, the ability to inherit your spouse's pension or retirement accounts, protection under the Family and Medical Leave Act to care for a sick spouse, and the right to bring wrongful death claims if your spouse is killed due to someone else's negligence. Married couples also enjoy certain legal privileges, such as spousal privilege in court (the right not to testify against your spouse in criminal cases) and immigration benefits that allow citizens to sponsor their spouses for green cards.

These changes happen automatically at marriage. They do not depend on intent or awareness. You do not need to take any additional legal steps or sign any papers beyond the marriage license. The moment you are legally married, all of these rights and obligations take effect. Understanding them in advance can prevent serious disputes later and help you make informed decisions about protecting assets, planning your estate, and structuring your finances.

Prenuptial Agreements

A prenuptial agreement, or prenup, is a contract entered into before marriage that defines how certain matters will be handled if the marriage ends in divorce or if one spouse dies. It allows couples to make their own rules about financial matters rather than relying on default state laws that may not fit their situation.

Prenups can address:

Division of property: You can specify which assets will remain separate and which will be considered marital property subject to division. For example, you might agree that any property owned before marriage remains separate, or that a business one spouse owns will not be divided in a divorce. You can also address how assets acquired during marriage, such as retirement accounts or real estate, will be divided.

Treatment of income and assets: You can define whether income earned during the marriage will be considered separate or marital property. This can be especially important if one spouse earns significantly more than the other or if one spouse will leave the workforce to raise children or support the other's career.

Responsibility for debts: A prenup can protect one spouse from being held responsible for the other's debts, whether those debts existed before marriage or are incurred during the marriage. For example, if one spouse has significant student loans or credit card debt, the prenup can specify that this remains their sole responsibility.

Spousal support or its limitation: You can agree in advance whether spousal support (also called alimony or maintenance) will be paid if the marriage ends, how much will be paid, and for how long. Some couples agree to waive spousal support entirely, while others set a formula or cap on the amount and duration.

Protection of family businesses or inheritances: If you own a family business or expect to inherit property or assets, a prenup can ensure these remain your separate property and will not be subject to division in a divorce. This can be crucial for protecting a business that has been in your family for generations or ensuring that inherited property stays within your family.

Contrary to popular belief, prenups are not only for the wealthy. They are often used by people who:

Own businesses: Even a small business can be at risk in a divorce. A prenup can protect your ownership and prevent a court from forcing you to sell or divide the business.

Have children from prior relationships: If you want to ensure that certain assets pass to your children from a previous marriage, a prenup can protect those assets and clarify your inheritance intentions.

Expect inheritances: If you expect to receive family property, money, or heirlooms, a prenup can keep these items separate and ensure they remain in your family.

Earn significantly different incomes: When one partner earns substantially more than the other, a prenup can clarify financial expectations and prevent disputes about standard of living or spousal support.

Are entering a second or later marriage: People who have been through divorce before often want more clarity and control over the financial aspects of their next marriage.

Have significant student loan debt or other pre-marriage obligations: A prenup can protect the debt-free spouse from becoming responsible for their partner's pre-existing financial obligations.

For a prenup to be enforceable, it generally must be entered into voluntarily, with full financial disclosure, and without coercion. This means several things:

First, both parties must enter the agreement willingly. If one person is pressured, threatened, or forced to sign, the prenup can be invalidated. Presenting a prenup for the first time on the eve of the wedding, when invitations have been sent and deposits are non-refundable, may be considered coercive. It is best to discuss and negotiate a prenup months before the wedding to ensure both parties have adequate time to consider it.

Second, both parties must fully disclose their assets, debts, income, and financial obligations. If one person hides bank accounts, property, or debts, the prenup can be thrown out. Full disclosure means providing detailed information about everything you own and owe, often including documentation like bank statements, tax returns, and property deeds.

Third, both parties should have the opportunity to consult with independent legal counsel. While it is not always legally required, having separate lawyers review the agreement makes it much more likely to be enforced. Each attorney can explain what the agreement means, whether it is fair, and what rights are being waived.

Fourth, the agreement must not be unconscionable, meaning it cannot be so one-sided or unfair that no reasonable person would agree to it. For example, a prenup that leaves one spouse with nothing while the other keeps everything might be struck down, especially if the disadvantaged spouse gave up a career or made other sacrifices for the marriage.

A prenup does not signal distrust. Legally, it is a planning tool, similar to insurance or estate planning, that clarifies expectations and reduces uncertainty. Many couples find that discussing a prenup actually strengthens their relationship because it forces them to have honest conversations about money, values, and expectations that they might otherwise avoid. It can prevent the kind of misunderstandings and assumptions that lead to conflict during marriage and bitter disputes during divorce.

Common Misconceptions

Misunderstandings about marriage and prenups are widespread and can lead to serious problems.

One common misconception is that marriage automatically means "everything is split 50/50" in divorce. In reality, outcomes depend on state law, timing of asset acquisition, and individual circumstances. In community property states, marital property is generally split equally, but separate property (owned before marriage or received as a gift or inheritance) is not divided. In equitable distribution states, courts divide marital property fairly based on factors like the length of the marriage, each spouse's income and earning capacity, contributions to the marriage (including homemaking and child-rearing), and each spouse's financial needs. Fair does not always mean equal. One spouse might receive 60% or 70% of the marital assets if the court determines that division is more equitable based on the circumstances.

Another misconception is that staying unmarried avoids legal entanglement entirely. Unmarried partners may still face property disputes, support claims, or parenting obligations, often with fewer protections than married couples have. If an unmarried couple buys a house together and breaks up, they may face a complicated partition lawsuit to divide the property. If they have children together, they will need to establish custody, visitation, and child support arrangements just like divorcing couples, but without the established framework that divorce law provides. Some states recognize common-law marriage or palimony claims, which can create obligations even without a formal marriage. In many ways, long-term cohabitation without clear legal agreements can be riskier than marriage because the rules are less clear and the protections are weaker.

Some people believe prenups are invalid or easily thrown out. While poorly drafted agreements can be challenged, well-prepared prenups are regularly enforced by courts. The key is to follow proper procedures: negotiate the agreement well in advance of the wedding, ensure full financial disclosure, give both parties time to review it with independent attorneys, make sure the terms are reasonable, and execute the agreement properly according to state law. A prenup prepared this way is just as enforceable as any other contract.

Finally, many assume marriage law is uniform across the country. It is not. States differ significantly in how they treat marital property, spousal support, and legal partnerships. For example, community property rules in California are very different from equitable distribution rules in New York. Some states recognize common-law marriage while others do not. The requirements for a valid prenup vary from state to state. Spousal support laws differ widely in terms of how support is calculated and how long it lasts. If you marry in one state and later move to another, or if you and your spouse live in different states when you divorce, understanding which state's laws apply can be crucial. This is why it is important to consult with an attorney in your state when considering marriage, a prenup, or divorce.

Domestic Partnerships and Civil Unions

In addition to marriage, some states offer legal statuses called domestic partnerships or civil unions. These were originally created to provide legal recognition to same-sex couples before marriage equality was established nationwide, but some states still offer them and some opposite-sex couples choose them instead of marriage.

The rights and responsibilities of domestic partnerships and civil unions vary significantly by state. In some states, they provide nearly all the same rights as marriage under state law, including property rights, inheritance rights, and medical decision-making authority. In other states, they provide only limited rights, such as hospital visitation or health insurance coverage.

However, domestic partnerships and civil unions are not recognized by the federal government, which means partners do not receive federal benefits like Social Security survivor benefits, federal tax filing status, or immigration sponsorship rights. They may also not be recognized if you move to another state.

If you are considering a domestic partnership or civil union instead of marriage, it is important to understand exactly what rights you will and will not have under your state's law and how your status will be treated if you travel or relocate.

Why This Chapter Matters

Marriage creates legal consequences that extend far beyond the wedding day. Understanding those consequences allows individuals to make informed choices, protect themselves and their families, and avoid conflicts that arise from misplaced assumptions.

Whether you are considering marriage for the first time, entering a second marriage, or evaluating whether a prenup makes sense for your situation, knowledge is power. Taking the time to understand what marriage means legally, what rights and obligations it creates, and what protections you can put in place can save you from costly disputes and heartbreak later.

Marriage should be entered into with both emotional commitment and legal awareness. The two are not in conflict. In fact, understanding the legal side of marriage allows you to build a stronger foundation for your relationship by ensuring that both partners have clear expectations and that important matters like finances, property, and future planning are discussed openly before they become sources of conflict.

The next chapter addresses what happens when marriages end, through separation or divorce, and how the law resolves the financial and personal questions that follow.

8

Divorce, Alimony, and Property

Divorce is both a legal process and a life transition. While the emotional aspects often dominate attention, the legal structure of divorce determines financial stability, housing, and long-term security. Many people are surprised to learn how much of the outcome is shaped not by personal fairness, but by state law and procedural rules.

This chapter explains how divorce works in practice, how spousal support is decided, and how property and debt are divided when a marriage ends. Understanding these fundamentals can help you navigate one of life's most challenging transitions with greater clarity and confidence.

Divorce Processes by State

Divorce law is primarily governed by state law, which means the process can look very different depending on where a case is filed. However, most divorces follow a similar general framework.

Filing and Notification

A divorce typically begins when one spouse files a petition requesting that the marriage be legally dissolved. This document is filed with the appropriate court, usually in the county where one or both spouses live. The petition includes basic information about the marriage, any children, and what the filing spouse is requesting in terms of property division, support, and custody.

The other spouse must be formally notified and given an opportunity to respond. This notification, called service of process, ensures that both parties have a fair chance to participate in the proceedings. The responding spouse typically has a set period, often 20 to 30 days, to file an answer or response to the petition.

Residency Requirements and Waiting Periods

Some states impose residency requirements before a divorce can be filed. You may need to have lived in the state for six months or a year before the court will accept your case. This prevents people from shopping for favorable divorce laws by filing in states where they have no real connection.

Many states also require waiting periods between filing and finalization. These cooling-off periods, which can range from a few weeks to several months, are designed to give couples time to reconsider or work out agreements. However, they can also prolong a difficult situation for those who are certain about ending the marriage.

No-Fault vs. Fault-Based Divorce

Most states allow no-fault divorce, meaning a spouse does not need to prove wrongdoing. Common no-fault grounds include "irreconcilable differences," "irretrievable breakdown," or simply stating that the marriage cannot be saved. No-fault divorces tend to be faster, less expensive, and less emotionally draining than fault-based cases.

Fault-based divorces still exist in some states, but they are less common and often more complex. Grounds for fault may include adultery, abandonment, cruelty, substance abuse, or imprisonment. Proving fault typically requires evidence and may involve testimony or documentation. In some states, proving fault can affect decisions about alimony or property division, but in others, it has little to no impact on the outcome.

Contested vs. Uncontested Divorce

Divorces may be uncontested, where both spouses agree on major issues like property division, support, and custody, or contested, where disputes require negotiation or court intervention. Uncontested divorces are generally faster, cheaper, and less stressful. Some can be completed in a few months with minimal court appearances.

Contested divorces involve more time, legal fees, and court involvement. When spouses cannot agree, they may go through discovery (exchanging financial documents and information), mediation (working with a neutral third party), or ultimately a trial where a judge makes the final decisions. The more issues the parties can resolve cooperatively, the faster and less expensive the process usually is.

Spousal Support (Alimony)

Spousal support, commonly known as alimony, is financial assistance one spouse may be required to pay the other after separation or divorce. It is not automatic and does not exist to punish or reward behavior. Rather, it is intended to address economic imbalances and help a lower-earning spouse maintain a reasonable standard of living.

When Alimony Is Awarded

Courts consider many factors when deciding whether alimony is appropriate. The length of the marriage is often significant. Short marriages (typically under five years) rarely result in alimony, while longer marriages are more likely to include support, especially if one spouse sacrificed career opportunities to support the family or care for children.

Each spouse's income and earning capacity matter greatly. If one spouse earns significantly more than the other, or if one spouse left the workforce and would struggle to reenter it, alimony becomes more likely. Courts look at current income, future earning potential, education, work history, and job skills.

The standard of living during the marriage serves as a reference point. Courts often try to help both spouses maintain a lifestyle reasonably similar to what they enjoyed while married, though this is not always possible, especially in cases with limited resources.

Contributions to the household, including unpaid labor, are considered. A spouse who stayed home to raise children, manage the household, or support the other spouse's career made valuable contributions even without earning a paycheck. Courts recognize this when evaluating support.

The age and health of each spouse also factor in. An older spouse or one with health problems may have difficulty becoming self-sufficient, making alimony more appropriate. Conversely, a young, healthy spouse with good job prospects may receive little or no support.

Types of Alimony

Alimony can take different forms depending on the circumstances.

Temporary support is provided during divorce proceedings to maintain stability while the case is ongoing. This ensures that a lower-earning spouse can pay bills and legal fees during what can be a lengthy process. Temporary support ends when the divorce is finalized and is replaced by whatever final support arrangement the court orders.

Short-term or rehabilitative support helps a spouse become self-sufficient, often through education or job training. For example, a spouse who left college to get married might receive support while completing a degree. Or someone who has been out of the workforce might receive support while gaining new skills or certifications. This type of support typically lasts a few years and ends once the recipient is able to support themselves.

Long-term or permanent support exists in limited circumstances, typically after very long marriages or when one spouse cannot reasonably become financially independent due to age, health, or other factors. Despite the name "permanent," this support can still be modified or terminated if circumstances change significantly. In some states, permanent support is becoming less common as courts favor rehabilitative approaches.

Reimbursement alimony is awarded in cases where one spouse supported the other through school or training with the expectation of future benefit. If the couple divorces soon after the education is complete, the supporting spouse may be compensated for their investment.

How Alimony Is Calculated

State laws vary widely in how alimony is calculated and how long it lasts. Some states use formulas or guidelines, while others give judges broad discretion. Factors typically include the duration of the marriage, income disparity, and the recipient's needs versus the payer's ability to pay.

Alimony payments may be made monthly or in a lump sum, though monthly payments are more common. The amount and duration should be clearly specified in the divorce decree or separation agreement.

Modifying or Terminating Alimony

Changes in income or life circumstances may allow support orders to be modified. For example, if the paying spouse loses their job or experiences a significant pay cut, they can petition the court to reduce the payment amount. Similarly, if the paying spouse gets a substantial raise, the receiving spouse might request an increase.

Remarriage of the receiving spouse typically ends alimony automatically in most states. Cohabitation with a new partner may also affect support, though the rules vary. Courts reason that if the receiving spouse has a new source of financial support, the former spouse's obligation should be reduced or eliminated.

If either spouse dies, alimony obligations generally end, though this can be addressed differently in divorce agreements. Some agreements require life insurance to protect the recipient if the payer dies.

Dividing Assets and Debts

One of the most contentious aspects of divorce is dividing property and debt. What couples accumulated together must now be separated, and the process is rarely simple or emotionally neutral. State law plays a central role in determining how assets and debts are split.

Community Property vs. Equitable Distribution

States generally follow one of two systems for property division.

In **community property states** (Arizona, California, Idaho, Louisiana, Nevada, New Mexico, Texas, Washington, and Wisconsin), most assets and debts acquired during marriage are divided equally between spouses. The assumption is that both spouses contributed equally to the marriage, regardless of who earned more money or whose name is on the title. Community property states start with a 50-50 split, though deviations are possible in certain circumstances.

In **equitable distribution states** (the majority of states), property is divided fairly, but not necessarily equally. The court considers multiple factors like each spouse's financial contribution to the marriage, future earning potential, the length of the marriage, and the needs of any children. One spouse might receive 60% of the assets while the other receives 40%, depending on what the court deems fair. Equitable distribution gives judges more flexibility but also more discretion, making outcomes less predictable.

Marital Property vs. Separate Property

Courts distinguish between marital property and separate property. Understanding this distinction is critical because it determines what gets divided.

Marital property typically includes income and assets acquired during the marriage. This includes salaries, bonuses, homes purchased during the marriage, vehicles, furniture, bank accounts funded with marital income, and investments made during the marriage. It also includes increases in value of assets during the marriage, even if the asset itself was owned before marriage.

Separate property may include assets owned before marriage, gifts given to only one spouse, inheritances received by one spouse, and personal injury settlements awarded to one spouse. Property acquired after separation but before divorce may also be considered separate, depending on state law.

However, separate property can sometimes become marital property through a process called commingling. If you deposit an inheritance into a joint bank account and use it for household expenses, it may lose its separate character. If you use marital funds to renovate a home you owned before marriage, the increased value might be considered marital property. Keeping clear records and maintaining separate accounts can help preserve the separate nature of certain assets.

How Debts Are Divided

Debts are treated similarly to assets. Who incurred the debt, when it was incurred, and how it was used all matter.

Marital debts typically include credit card balances for household expenses, car loans for family vehicles, mortgages on the marital home, medical bills incurred during marriage, and business debts if the business supported the family. These debts are usually divided between spouses according to state law, whether equally or equitably.

Separate debts might include student loans from before the marriage, credit card debt for personal expenses unrelated to the marriage, and debts incurred after separation. However, if separate debt benefited the marriage (for example, student loans that led to a higher income used to support the family), courts may treat it differently.

One critical point that surprises many people: one spouse may still be legally responsible for joint debts even if the divorce decree assigns payment responsibility to the other spouse. This is because creditors are not bound by divorce orders. If your name is on a credit card or mortgage, you remain liable to the creditor regardless of what the divorce agreement says. If your ex-spouse stops paying a joint credit card, the creditor can pursue you for payment, and your credit score will suffer.

To protect yourself, consider paying off joint debts before finalizing the divorce, refinancing loans to remove one spouse's name, or closing joint accounts as soon as possible.

Specific Assets and How They Are Handled

Common assets that must be divided include the family home, retirement accounts, investments, vehicles, and business interests. Each type of asset may require special handling.

The Family Home

The marital home is often the most valuable and emotionally charged asset. Options include selling the home and dividing the proceeds, one spouse buying out the other's share, or continuing to co-own the property (usually temporarily, such as until children graduate from high school).

If one spouse keeps the home, they typically must refinance the mortgage in their name alone to release the other spouse from liability. If refinancing is not possible, the couple might defer the decision or negotiate other terms.

Retirement Accounts

Retirement accounts like 401(k)s, pensions, and IRAs are often substantial assets. Dividing them requires careful attention to avoid tax penalties.

A Qualified Domestic Relations Order (QDRO) is a specialized court order that allows retirement funds to be divided between spouses without triggering early withdrawal penalties or immediate taxes. The QDRO must be properly drafted and approved by both the court and the retirement plan administrator. Each type of retirement account has specific rules, so professional assistance is usually necessary.

Investments and Bank Accounts

Stocks, bonds, mutual funds, and savings accounts are divided according to state law. The division might involve liquidating investments and splitting the proceeds, or transferring ownership of specific assets to each spouse.

Tax consequences should be considered. Selling investments may trigger capital gains taxes. Transferring assets incident to divorce is usually tax-free, but future sales or withdrawals will have tax implications.

Vehicles

Cars, trucks, motorcycles, boats, and RVs are divided based on value, need, and equity. If a vehicle is financed, the spouse who keeps it should ideally refinance the loan in their name alone.

Business Interests

If one or both spouses own a business, valuing and dividing it can be complex. Options include one spouse buying out the other's interest, selling the business and dividing proceeds, or continuing to co-own the business (though this is rare and often impractical).

Business valuation typically requires expert analysis. Factors include current revenue, profit margins, assets, liabilities, market conditions, and future earning potential.

Other Assets

Do not overlook other valuable items like collectibles, artwork, jewelry, intellectual property (such as royalties from books or patents), and even frequent flyer miles or loyalty points. Make a comprehensive list of everything you own to ensure nothing is forgotten.

Protecting Your Interests During Property Division

Several steps can help you navigate property division more effectively.

Gather financial documents. Collect bank statements, tax returns, pay stubs, retirement account statements, mortgage documents, credit card statements, and loan agreements. The more complete your financial picture, the better positioned you are.

Get appraisals. For valuable assets like real estate, businesses, or collections, professional appraisals provide objective valuations that courts will respect.

Understand tax implications. Some assets are worth less than they appear once taxes are considered. A $100,000 retirement account that will be taxed upon withdrawal is worth less than $100,000 in cash.

Consider liquidity. Receiving the house might seem appealing, but can you afford the mortgage, taxes, insurance, and maintenance? Cash or liquid investments might provide more financial flexibility.

Think long-term. Do not focus only on immediate needs. Consider how each asset will serve you in five, ten, or twenty years, especially regarding retirement security.

Why This Chapter Matters

Divorce outcomes shape financial futures. Decisions made, or avoided, during divorce can affect housing stability, retirement security, and long-term financial independence.

Understanding how divorce works by state, how alimony is determined, and how property is divided helps people approach the process with realistic expectations rather than assumptions or fear. It also highlights the importance of seeking legal advice early, keeping thorough financial records, and understanding that what feels fair emotionally may differ from what the law requires.

The laws are complex and vary significantly by jurisdiction. What applies in one state may not apply in another. Consulting with a qualified family law attorney in your state is essential to understanding your rights and obligations.

Divorce is rarely easy, but knowledge reduces uncertainty. When you understand the legal framework, you can make informed decisions, advocate for your interests, and move forward with greater confidence.

The next chapter turns to one of the most sensitive areas of family law: children, custody, and support, where legal decisions have lasting impacts on entire families.

9

Custody, Support, and Parental Rights

When children are involved, family law becomes less about dividing the past and more about shaping the future. Custody and support decisions affect children's stability, education, and emotional well-being long after a case ends. Because emotions often run high, misunderstandings about how the law views parents and children are common and costly.

This chapter explains how custody works, how child support is calculated, and what parental rights and responsibilities mean in practice. Whether you are navigating divorce, separation, or establishing parental rights for the first time, understanding these legal frameworks will help you make informed decisions that serve your child's best interests.

Understanding Custody Types

In legal terms, custody refers to the authority to make decisions for a child and the responsibility for the child's day-to-day care. Custody is not a measure of parental love or worth. It is a legal framework designed to serve the child's best interests.

Many parents assume custody is a single, all-or-nothing designation. In reality, there are two main types of custody that work independently of each other. You can have one type without the other, and understanding this distinction is crucial for navigating custody arrangements.

Legal Custody: Decision-Making Authority

Legal custody involves decision-making authority over major aspects of a child's life, such as education, healthcare, and religious upbringing. Legal custody can be shared (joint) or held by one parent (sole).

When parents share joint legal custody, they must consult with each other and agree on major decisions, even if the child lives primarily with one parent. This means both parents have equal say in choosing schools, authorizing medical procedures, deciding on mental health treatment, and determining religious education. Joint legal custody requires cooperation and communication. Parents who cannot work together on important decisions may find joint legal custody frustrating and unworkable.

What counts as a "major decision" requiring consultation? Generally, this includes enrolling a child in a new school or changing schools, agreeing to non-emergency medical procedures or ongoing treatment, choosing or changing a child's religion, and decisions about extracurricular activities that significantly impact the child's schedule or the other parent's time. Routine decisions like daily meals, bedtimes, homework help, or permission for a playdate do not require joint consultation.

Sole legal custody means one parent has the final say on these important matters, though this does not prevent the other parent from staying informed or giving input. The parent with sole legal custody can make major decisions independently, though courts encourage parents to communicate and consider the other parent's perspective when appropriate. Sole legal custody might be awarded if one parent has been absent from the child's life, if there is a history of domestic violence, if one parent has consistently undermined the other's decisions, or if parents simply cannot communicate effectively enough to make joint decisions.

Physical Custody: Where the Child Lives

Physical custody refers to where the child lives and who provides daily care. Physical custody can also be joint or sole, and it does not always mean equal time.

Joint physical custody might mean the child splits time evenly between two homes, or it might mean the child lives primarily with one parent but spends regular, substantial time with the other. There is no universal formula for what constitutes joint physical custody. In some states, spending at least 30 percent of nights with each parent qualifies as joint physical custody. In others, the threshold is higher. What matters is that both parents have significant periods of physical responsibility for the child.

Joint physical custody arrangements vary widely. Some families use a week-on, week-off schedule. Others alternate every few days. Some split the week, with the child staying with one parent during the school week and the other parent on weekends and school breaks. The key is finding an arrangement that minimizes disruption to the child's routine while allowing both parents meaningful time.

Sole physical custody means the child lives with one parent, though the other parent typically has visitation rights. The noncustodial parent might see the child every other weekend, one evening per week, and during school breaks and holidays. Visitation schedules are enforceable court orders, not suggestions. Both parents must follow the schedule unless they mutually agree to changes or seek a court modification.

Common Custody Arrangements

Understanding the practical options available can help you envision what might work for your family:

Equal or near-equal parenting time. The child spends approximately half their time with each parent. This works best when parents live relatively close to each other, can communicate effectively, and both have flexible work schedules. Children benefit from substantial time with both parents but may struggle with frequent transitions between homes.

Primary physical custody with regular visitation. The child lives primarily with one parent and visits the other parent on a regular schedule, such as alternating weekends and one weeknight. This provides stability and consistency for the child while ensuring the noncustodial parent remains actively involved.

Split custody. In rare cases involving multiple children, siblings may be divided between parents, with each parent having primary custody of at least one child. Courts generally disfavor splitting siblings unless there are compelling reasons, such as a significant age gap, different needs, or the children's own strong preferences.

Bird's nest custody. An uncommon but creative arrangement where the children stay in one home and the parents rotate in and out. This minimizes disruption for children but requires parents to maintain three residences (the shared family home and separate homes for each parent), which is often financially impractical.

How Courts Decide Custody

Courts focus on the best interests of the child, a standard that sounds simple but encompasses many factors. Judges consider the totality of circumstances, weighing evidence and testimony to determine what arrangement will best serve the child's needs.

Key Factors Courts Consider

The child's relationship with each parent. Courts look at the quality and history of each parent's bond with the child. Which parent has been more involved in day-to-day care? Who helps with homework, attends school events, takes the child to doctor appointments, and manages the child's social life? A parent who has been actively engaged in these activities typically has a stronger case for custody.

Stability and continuity in the child's life. Courts prefer to minimize disruption. If a child has lived primarily with one parent, attended the same school, and maintained friendships and routines, judges are reluctant to upend that stability without good reason. The parent who can maintain continuity in the child's education, community connections, and peer relationships has an advantage.

Each parent's ability to provide care. Courts assess practical caregiving capacity. Does the parent have stable housing with adequate space for the child? Can the parent's work schedule accommodate the child's needs, or is reliable childcare available? Is the parent physically and mentally healthy enough to meet the demands of parenting? Financial resources matter, but a wealthier parent does not automatically win custody. A parent with modest means who provides love, attention, and stability may be favored over a wealthier but less involved parent.

Any history of abuse or neglect. Evidence of domestic violence, child abuse, substance abuse, or neglect weighs heavily against a parent. Courts take allegations seriously and may order investigations, appoint guardians ad litem to represent the child's interests, or require supervised visitation until safety concerns are resolved. Even if abuse was directed at the other parent rather than the child, courts recognize that children are harmed by witnessing violence.

The child's needs and, in some cases, preferences. Every child is different. A child with special educational needs, medical conditions, or mental health challenges may benefit from living with the parent better equipped to address those needs. Courts may also consider a child's extracurricular commitments, relationships with siblings, and connections to extended family.

Older children may have their preferences considered, though the weight given to their wishes varies by state and the child's age and maturity. Some states allow children as young as 12 to express a preference, while others wait until the child is 14 or older. Even when a child's preference is heard, it is not controlling. Judges recognize that children may be influenced by a parent's manipulation, loyalty conflicts, or short-term desires that do not align with their long-term best interests.

Each parent's willingness to foster a relationship with the other parent. Courts favor parents who encourage and support the child's relationship with the other parent. A parent who badmouths the other parent, interferes with visitation, or undermines the other parent's authority may lose custody or have their parenting time reduced. Cooperative co-parenting is seen as essential to the child's emotional health.

Dispelling Common Custody Myths

Gender alone is not supposed to determine custody outcomes. While outdated stereotypes once favored mothers, especially for young children, modern courts increasingly favor arrangements that allow children to maintain meaningful relationships with both parents when it is safe and appropriate. Courts evaluate each parent's involvement in the child's life, work schedules, living arrangements, and ability to cooperate with the other parent.

The "tender years doctrine," which presumed that young children should be with their mothers, has been largely abandoned. Fathers have equal rights to seek custody and are increasingly successful when they can demonstrate active involvement and caregiving ability.

Similarly, being the higher earner does not guarantee custody. Financial stability matters, but courts prioritize emotional bonds, caregiving history, and the child's day-to-day needs over income disparities.

Modifying Custody Arrangements

It is important to understand that custody arrangements can be modified if circumstances change significantly. A parent who relocates, experiences a major change in work schedule, or faces new concerns about safety may request a modification. Courts generally require proof that the change serves the child's best interests and that circumstances have changed substantially since the original order.

Substantial changes might include a parent's remarriage or new partnership that affects the child's living situation, a parent developing substance abuse problems or mental health issues, a significant change in the child's needs as they grow older, job loss or a major promotion that alters a parent's availability, or evidence of abuse or neglect that was not previously known.

Minor inconveniences or dissatisfaction with the current arrangement are not enough. The parent seeking modification bears the burden of proof and must show that the proposed change would materially improve the child's situation.

Child Support Basics

Child support is financial support paid by one parent to the other to help cover the costs of raising a child. It is the child's right, not the receiving parent's. This means parents cannot agree to waive child support without court approval, and even informal agreements are not legally binding.

This principle has important implications. Even if you trust your co-parent and believe you can work out support informally, verbal agreements have no legal force. If the paying parent stops paying, the receiving parent has no recourse. Worse, a parent who accepts an informal agreement waiving support might later find that they cannot retroactively claim support for periods when no formal order was in place.

How Child Support Is Calculated

Most states use formula-based guidelines that consider each parent's income, the amount of time spent with the child, the number of children, and healthcare and childcare costs. These formulas are designed to ensure consistency and fairness while accounting for each family's financial reality.

Income shares model. Many states use an income shares model, which estimates the total amount both parents would have spent on the child if they lived together, then divides that amount between parents based on their incomes. For example, if the combined parental income is $100,000 and the guidelines estimate that parents at this income level spend $20,000 annually on one child, each parent's share is proportional to their income. If one parent earns $60,000 and the other earns $40,000, the higher earner would be responsible for 60 percent of the support obligation.

The income shares model accounts for the fact that both parents contribute to the child's expenses. The custodial parent's contribution is presumed to be the direct costs of housing, feeding, and caring for the child, while the noncustodial parent's contribution is the support payment.

Percentage of income model. Other states use a percentage of income model, where the noncustodial parent pays a set percentage of their income based on the number of children. The percentage typically increases with each additional child. For instance, a state might require 20 percent of net income for one child, 28 percent for two children, and 32 percent for three children.

This model is simpler to calculate but does not account for the custodial parent's income, which can lead to disparities in situations where the custodial parent earns significantly more or less than the noncustodial parent.

What Child Support Covers

Support is designed to cover basic needs such as housing, food, clothing, education, and medical care. It may also include contributions toward extracurricular activities, childcare expenses, and health insurance premiums.

Courts recognize that children living in two households incur duplicative costs. The child may need clothes, toys, and school supplies at both homes. Support payments help equalize the financial burden and ensure the child's needs are met regardless of which parent they are with.

Medical expenses are often addressed separately. Many support orders require one or both parents to provide health insurance for the child. Unreimbursed medical expenses, such as co-pays, prescriptions, dental work, and orthodontia, are typically split between parents in proportion to their incomes or on a 50-50 basis.

Extracurricular activities, special educational needs, and childcare costs may be added to the base support amount. If a child participates in expensive sports, music lessons, or tutoring, courts can allocate these costs between parents.

Income Considered for Child Support

The amount is typically based on gross income, though some deductions (like support for other children) may be considered. Gross income includes wages, salaries, bonuses, commissions, self-employment income, rental income, investment income, pensions, and unemployment benefits.

Courts look beyond pay stubs to assess a parent's true earning capacity. If a parent is voluntarily unemployed or underemployed, meaning they are capable of earning more but choose not to, courts may impute income based on their potential earnings. A parent who quits a well-paying job to avoid support obligations or who refuses to seek employment commensurate with their education and experience may have income attributed to them anyway.

Self-employed parents sometimes attempt to hide income or inflate business expenses to reduce their apparent earnings. Courts can examine tax returns, bank statements, and business records to determine actual income.

Duration of Child Support

Support obligations typically continue until the child reaches the age of majority (usually 18), graduates from high school (often extended to age 19 if still in high school), becomes emancipated (such as by joining the military, getting married, or becoming self-supporting), or, in some states, completes college.

Some states allow courts to order parents to contribute to college expenses. This varies widely. In states that permit it, courts consider the parents' financial resources, the child's academic performance and commitment to education, and the availability of financial aid and scholarships.

Enforcing and Modifying Child Support

Support is not optional. It must be paid as ordered, even if visitation is denied or the custodial parent refuses to communicate. Support obligations and visitation rights are separate legal issues. Withholding support because of visitation disputes can result in serious legal consequences.

Parents sometimes mistakenly believe they can stop paying support if the custodial parent violates the visitation order. This is incorrect. If you are being denied access to your child, the appropriate remedy is to file a motion for contempt or enforcement with the court, not to withhold support payments.

Consequences of Nonpayment

Failure to pay support can result in serious penalties. Enforcement mechanisms include:

Wage garnishment. Support is automatically deducted from paychecks and sent directly to the custodial parent or a state disbursement unit. This ensures consistent payment and creates a clear record.

Interception of tax refunds. Federal and state tax refunds can be seized to satisfy child support arrears.

Suspension of driver's licenses or professional licenses. A parent who falls significantly behind on support may lose the ability to drive legally or practice their profession, which can create a difficult cycle where inability to work leads to further nonpayment.

Reporting to credit agencies. Unpaid child support is reported to credit bureaus, damaging the noncustodial parent's credit score and ability to obtain loans, rent housing, or finance major purchases.

Contempt of court. Willful nonpayment can result in fines or jail time. Courts distinguish between parents who cannot pay due to genuine financial hardship and those who refuse to pay despite having the means. Incarceration is typically reserved for parents who deliberately avoid their obligations.

Denial of passport. The federal government can deny or revoke passports for parents who owe significant child support arrears.

The government has extensive enforcement tools and takes child support obligations seriously. State child support enforcement agencies actively pursue nonpaying parents, and interstate enforcement mechanisms ensure that parents cannot escape obligations by moving to another state.

Modifying Child Support Orders

Support orders can be modified if circumstances change significantly, such as job loss, substantial income increase, changes in custody arrangements, or the child's needs changing. However, modifications are not automatic. A parent must petition the court and prove the change in circumstances.

Examples of substantial changes include:

Job loss or significant income reduction. If a parent loses their job or experiences a substantial, involuntary pay cut, they can request a modification. However, courts will scrutinize whether the job loss was voluntary or in bad faith. Quitting without another job lined up or being fired for misconduct may not qualify.

Significant income increase. If the paying parent receives a major promotion, bonus, or new high-paying job, the receiving parent can request an increase in support.

Changes in custody. If parenting time shifts significantly, such as moving from sole physical custody to joint physical custody, support obligations may be recalculated.

Changes in the child's needs. A child who develops special medical or educational needs may require increased support.

Changes in other financial obligations. If the paying parent has additional children from a new relationship, courts may consider this when recalculating support, though existing obligations typically take priority.

The key is to act promptly. If your circumstances change, file for modification immediately. Support modifications typically take effect only from the date of filing, not retroactively. If you wait months to seek a modification, you remain responsible for the original support amount during that period, even if you were unemployed or unable to pay.

Support Arrears: What You Need to Know

Support arrears (past-due support) generally cannot be erased and continue to accrue interest until paid. Unlike some debts, child support arrears survive bankruptcy and cannot be discharged.

Parents who fall behind often find themselves in a deep hole. Arrears accumulate quickly, interest compounds, and enforcement actions create additional financial stress. If you are struggling to pay support, do not ignore the problem. Contact your state child support enforcement agency or seek a modification as soon as possible. Communicating proactively with the court and the other parent demonstrates good faith and may result in more lenient treatment than simply disappearing or refusing to pay.

Parental Rights and Responsibilities

Parents have both rights and obligations toward their children. These exist in tandem. You cannot claim parental rights without accepting parental responsibilities, and the law enforces both.

Fundamental Parental Rights

Custody and visitation. Parents have the right to spend time with their children and participate in their lives. Even noncustodial parents have legally protected visitation rights that cannot be arbitrarily denied.

Decision-making authority. Parents with legal custody have the right to make important decisions about their child's education, healthcare, and upbringing.

Access to information. Even parents without legal custody typically have the right to access their child's school records, medical records, and other important information. Schools and healthcare providers must respect this right unless a court order explicitly restricts it.

Protection from interference. Third parties, including grandparents and extended family, cannot interfere with a parent's rights without legal justification.

Core Parental Responsibilities

Financial support. Parents must provide financial support for their children, whether through direct care or child support payments.

Ensuring safety. Parents are legally obligated to protect their children from harm, provide a safe living environment, and ensure adequate supervision.

Meeting basic needs. This includes food, clothing, shelter, education, and medical care.

Protecting the child from harm. Parents must not expose children to dangerous situations, abusive relationships, or neglectful care.

Failing to meet these responsibilities can result in legal consequences ranging from loss of custody to criminal charges for neglect or endangerment.

Establishing Parentage

For unmarried parents, establishing legal parentage is often the first step in securing custody and support rights. When a child is born to married parents, both spouses are automatically considered legal parents. For unmarried parents, the process varies.

Mothers and Automatic Legal Recognition

Mothers are typically recognized automatically. The woman who gives birth is presumed to be the legal mother in all states. This presumption can be challenged in rare cases, such as surrogacy arrangements, but generally holds.

Fathers and Establishing Paternity

Unmarried fathers must establish paternity to gain legal rights. This can be done voluntarily through an acknowledgment of paternity signed at the hospital or later, or through a court order if paternity is disputed.

Voluntary acknowledgment of paternity. Many hospitals offer unmarried parents the opportunity to sign an Acknowledgment of Paternity (AOP) form shortly after the child's birth. This legal document, signed by both parents, establishes the father's legal relationship to the child. It has the same legal effect as a court order and allows the father's name to be added to the birth certificate.

Signing an AOP is simple and free, but it carries significant legal consequences. Once signed and filed with the state, it can be difficult to rescind. Most states allow a brief window (often 60 days) during which either parent can rescind the acknowledgment. After that, the acknowledgment can only be challenged in court by proving fraud, duress, or material mistake of fact.

Court-ordered paternity. If paternity is disputed, either parent can file a petition with the court to establish parentage. DNA testing may be required if there is disagreement. Modern genetic testing is highly accurate, with results typically showing a 99.9 percent probability of paternity or conclusively excluding a man as the father.

Courts can order alleged fathers to submit to DNA testing. Refusing to comply can result in a default judgment establishing paternity. Once paternity is established, the court can issue orders for custody, visitation, and child support.

Why establishing paternity matters. Without legal recognition, an unmarried father has no legal rights to custody or visitation, even if he is actively involved in the child's life and providing financial support. He cannot make decisions about the child's education or healthcare, cannot access school or medical records, and has no legal standing if the mother moves away with the child or denies him contact.

Establishing paternity protects both the father's rights and the child's interests. Children benefit from having two legal parents who can provide financial support, health insurance, inheritance rights, and access to government benefits like Social Security or veterans' benefits.

When Parental Rights Can Be Limited

Parental rights can be limited or terminated in extreme cases involving abuse, neglect, or abandonment, but courts generally aim to preserve parental relationships whenever possible. The constitutional right to parent one's children is among the most protected rights in American law, and courts are reluctant to sever the parent-child relationship.

Temporary Restrictions on Parental Rights

Supervised visitation. If there are safety concerns, such as a history of domestic violence, substance abuse, or mental health crises, courts may order that visitation occur only in the presence of a neutral third party. Supervision can be provided by a professional agency, a mutually agreed-upon family member, or a court-appointed supervisor.

Supervised visitation is intended to be temporary. The goal is to ensure the child's safety while allowing the parent to maintain a relationship and demonstrate that they can interact with the child appropriately. Parents subject to supervised visitation can petition to have restrictions lifted once they address the underlying concerns, such as completing substance abuse treatment or anger management classes.

Restrictions on decision-making. A parent may lose legal custody or have their decision-making authority limited if they have consistently made harmful choices for the child, such as refusing necessary medical treatment, exposing the child to dangerous situations, or undermining the child's education.

Temporary loss of custody. In emergencies, such as credible allegations of abuse, courts can issue temporary orders removing a child from a parent's care while investigations proceed. These orders typically last only until a full hearing can be held.

Termination of Parental Rights

Complete termination of parental rights is reserved for the most serious situations and permanently severs the legal relationship between parent and child, including all rights and obligations. Once parental rights are terminated, the parent has no legal relationship with the child, no right to visitation, and no obligation to pay child support. The child can be adopted without the terminated parent's consent.

Grounds for termination vary by state but generally include:

Severe or chronic abuse or neglect. Physical, sexual, or emotional abuse that causes significant harm, or ongoing neglect that endangers the child's health or safety.

Abandonment. A parent who has had no contact with the child for an extended period (often six months to a year) without good cause may be found to have abandoned the child.

Failure to support. Willful failure to provide financial support for an extended period can contribute to termination, though this is rarely the sole basis.

Incarceration. Long-term imprisonment, especially for crimes involving violence against children, may result in termination if the parent will be unavailable for a substantial portion of the child's minority.

Substance abuse. Chronic addiction that prevents a parent from safely caring for the child, particularly if the parent refuses treatment or repeatedly relapses.

Mental illness. Severe, untreated mental illness that renders a parent unable to care for the child, though courts require evidence that the condition is unlikely to improve.

Termination proceedings are serious and require clear and convincing evidence. Parents facing termination have the right to legal representation, and courts often appoint attorneys for indigent parents. The state bears the burden of proving that termination is warranted and in the child's best interests.

Grandparents and Extended Family Rights

Grandparents and other relatives may petition for visitation rights in some states, particularly if they have had a significant relationship with the child. However, parental rights generally take priority, and courts will not override a fit parent's decisions without compelling reasons.

The U.S. Supreme Court has held that parents have a fundamental right to make decisions about their children's upbringing, including deciding who the child spends time with. This means that grandparents seeking visitation face a high burden. They must typically show that visitation serves the child's best interests and that denying visitation would harm the child.

Grandparent visitation laws vary widely by state. Some states allow grandparents to petition only if the parents are divorced, separated, or if one parent is deceased. Others allow petitions in intact families but require proof of a substantial pre-existing relationship between the grandparent and child.

In rare cases, grandparents or other relatives may seek custody if both parents are unfit, deceased, or have abandoned the child. Courts evaluate these petitions using the same best interests standard applied in custody disputes between parents, but the relative must show that placing the child with them, rather than with a parent, serves the child's welfare.

Why This Chapter Matters

Custody and support cases are not about winning or losing. They are about creating legal structures that allow children to thrive despite changes in family circumstances.

Understanding custody types, child support rules, and parental responsibilities helps parents focus on solutions rather than conflict and protects children from becoming collateral damage in legal disputes. Children benefit most when parents can cooperate, communicate effectively, and prioritize stability over scoring points against each other.

Alternatives to Courtroom Battles

Many parents find that mediation or collaborative law approaches work better than courtroom battles. These alternatives allow parents to craft creative solutions tailored to their children's needs rather than accepting a one-size-fits-all court order.

Mediation involves a neutral third party who helps parents negotiate agreements on custody, visitation, and support. The mediator does not make decisions but facilitates communication and helps parents find common ground. Mediation is typically less expensive, faster, and less adversarial than litigation. Many courts require parents to attempt mediation before proceeding to trial.

Collaborative law involves both parents and their attorneys signing an agreement to resolve disputes without going to court. The process is cooperative rather than adversarial, with all parties working together to reach mutually acceptable solutions. If the process fails and the case proceeds to litigation, the collaborative attorneys must withdraw, and the parents must hire new counsel.

Both approaches offer significant advantages. They give parents more control over outcomes, reduce the emotional and financial costs of litigation, preserve co-parenting relationships, and model constructive conflict resolution for children.

When Court Intervention Is Necessary

When conflict is unavoidable, understanding the legal framework helps parents advocate effectively while keeping their children's best interests at the center. Some situations require judicial intervention:

Safety concerns. If abuse, neglect, or substance abuse is involved, court orders may be necessary to protect the child.

Fundamental disagreements. When parents cannot agree on basic issues like where the child will live or attend school, a judge must decide.

Enforcement issues. If one parent repeatedly violates court orders or refuses to follow agreements, legal enforcement may be the only remedy.

Even in contentious cases, parents can take steps to make the process less harmful to their children. Avoid speaking negatively about the other parent in front of the child. Shield children from legal proceedings and adult conflicts. Follow court orders scrupulously, even when you disagree with them. Document interactions and communications in case disputes arise. Focus on the child's needs rather than your grievances with the other parent.

Looking Ahead

Family law recognizes that children's needs evolve as they grow. What works for a toddler may not work for a teenager. Custody arrangements, support obligations, and parental roles will likely change over time. Staying flexible, maintaining open communication with your co-parent, and revisiting agreements as circumstances change will serve your child far better than rigid adherence to outdated arrangements.

The legal system provides a framework for resolving disputes, but it works best when parents approach it with honesty, good faith, and a genuine commitment to their children's well-being. Courts cannot mandate love, cooperation, or effective co-parenting. They can only enforce legal obligations and set boundaries. The rest is up to you.

The next chapter shifts from family law to housing, exploring tenant rights, landlord obligations, and the legal rules that govern where people live.

PART V: Housing, Property, and Landlords

10

Landlords and Tenants

Housing is one of the most basic human needs, and renting is how millions of Americans meet it. Yet landlord-tenant law is an area filled with confusion, fear, and misinformation. Many renters assume they have no rights, while some landlords assume they have unlimited authority over their property. Neither assumption is correct.

The relationship between landlord and tenant is a legal one, governed by state and local laws that create obligations and protections for both sides. These laws exist because housing is not just another consumer transaction. Where you live affects your safety, your health, your ability to work, and your family's stability. The law recognizes this by imposing specific duties on landlords and granting specific rights to tenants, regardless of what a lease agreement might say.

This chapter explains the core legal rules that govern renting a home, what tenants are entitled to, what landlords can and cannot do, and what must happen before a renter can legally be forced to leave. Whether you are renting an apartment, a house, or a room, understanding these basics can mean the difference between being taken advantage of and standing on solid legal ground.

Understanding Your Tenant Rights

Tenants have legal rights the moment they move into a rental unit, whether or not there is a written lease. While the specifics vary by state and city, certain protections are widely recognized across the country. These rights exist to ensure that renters have safe, stable housing and are treated fairly by those who profit from providing it.

The Right to a Habitable Home

One of the most important tenant rights is the implied warranty of habitability. This legal principle requires landlords to maintain rental properties in a condition fit for human living. It applies even if your lease says nothing about repairs or maintenance, and in most states, landlords cannot waive this obligation through a lease clause. You cannot be forced to sign away your right to a safe home, even if you agree to it in writing.

What does habitability mean in practice? It generally includes working heat during cold months, functional plumbing and hot water, safe electrical systems, structurally sound walls and ceilings, adequate weatherproofing to keep out rain and cold, functioning locks on doors and windows, and freedom from serious pest infestations like rats or bedbugs. It also means the property must be free from dangerous conditions such as exposed wiring, broken stairs, mold caused by leaks, or lead paint hazards in units where children live.

The requirement goes beyond just the four walls of your unit. Common areas like hallways, stairways, entrances, and parking areas must also be maintained in safe condition. Broken exterior lighting that creates a safety hazard, collapsed stairs, or unsecured entry doors that allow unauthorized access can all be habitability violations.

Minor issues like a dripping faucet or a small crack in the wall typically do not violate habitability standards. The standard is whether the condition makes the home unfit or unsafe to live in, not whether it is perfect or aesthetically pleasing. A worn carpet or outdated appliances, while not ideal, usually do not rise to the level of a habitability violation unless they create actual safety or health hazards.

However, seemingly minor issues can become major ones. A small leak that the landlord ignores can turn into mold growth that makes the unit uninhabitable. A malfunctioning smoke detector is a serious safety issue even though it costs little to fix. The test is always whether the condition poses a genuine risk to health or safety.

When Repairs Are Needed

If something breaks or stops working in your rental unit, the first step is to notify your landlord in writing. While a phone call or text might seem easier, written notice creates a paper trail that can be critical if the problem is not fixed. Your notice should describe the problem clearly, explain why it needs repair, and request that it be fixed within a reasonable timeframe.

What counts as reasonable depends on the severity of the problem. No heat in winter is an emergency requiring immediate attention. A broken cabinet hinge can wait a few weeks. If the landlord does not respond or refuses to make necessary repairs, you have several options, but the best choice depends on your state's laws.

Some states allow rent withholding, which means you can stop paying rent until the repairs are made. However, this is risky if not done correctly. Most states that allow rent withholding require you to deposit the rent money in an escrow account or with the court to show you are not just refusing to pay. You typically cannot withhold rent for minor issues, and you must follow specific procedures or risk eviction.

Other states permit repair and deduct, allowing you to hire someone to make the repairs yourself and subtract the cost from your rent. Again, there are usually limits on how much you can spend (often one month's rent or less) and requirements that you give the landlord proper notice and a chance to fix the problem first.

A safer option in most cases is to report the violation to your local housing or health department. Most cities have inspectors who can visit the property, document code violations, and order the landlord to make repairs. This puts the pressure on the landlord without putting you at risk of eviction. Landlords who fail to comply with official repair orders can face fines, and in extreme cases, the property can be declared uninhabitable and tenants can be released from their leases.

In situations where the unit is truly unfit to live in, such as no running water, no heat in freezing weather, or serious safety hazards, you may have the right to break your lease without penalty. Some states also allow you to move out temporarily and withhold rent until repairs are made, though you should get legal advice before taking this step.

The key in all repair situations is documentation. Take photos or videos of the problem. Keep copies of all written requests you send to the landlord. Save emails and texts. If you call the landlord, follow up with an email or letter confirming what you discussed. If an inspector visits, get a copy of the inspection report. This evidence can protect you if the landlord claims you never reported the problem or tries to evict you for withholding rent.

The Right to Privacy

Tenants also have a right to privacy in their rental homes. Just because a landlord owns the property does not mean they can enter whenever they want. When you rent a home, you have what the law calls the right to quiet enjoyment, which means the right to live in your home without unreasonable interference from the landlord.

Most states require landlords to give advance notice before entering a rental unit, typically 24 to 48 hours, except in emergencies like a fire, flood, gas leak, or other situation requiring immediate entry to prevent harm. The notice must usually be in writing and must state the reason for entry and the approximate time the landlord plans to enter.

Entry is usually permitted only for legitimate reasons such as making necessary repairs, showing the unit to prospective tenants or buyers, or inspecting for damage. Some states also allow periodic inspections to check on the condition of the property, but these must still be done with proper notice and at reasonable times.

What counts as reasonable? Generally, landlords should enter during normal business hours, not late at night or very early in the morning. Weekends may be acceptable for showings but should still be scheduled in advance. Landlords cannot use their right of entry to harass tenants, monitor their activities, or retaliate for complaints.

If your landlord repeatedly enters without proper notice, shows up at unreasonable hours, or enters for invalid reasons (such as just checking up on you), they may be violating your privacy rights. In some states, you can change the locks if the landlord is abusing their entry rights, though you usually must provide the landlord with a key. In more serious cases, you may be able to sue for invasion of privacy, break your lease without penalty, or even call the police if the landlord refuses to leave when asked.

There are limits to privacy rights, however. If there is a genuine emergency, the landlord does not need to wait for notice. If the landlord has reason to believe you have abandoned the property, they may be able to enter to verify. And if you have refused to allow entry for legitimate repairs after proper notice, the landlord may be able to obtain a court order for access.

Landlords also cannot install cameras or recording devices inside your rental unit, even in common areas of the interior, without your consent. Security cameras in building hallways, parking lots, or building exteriors are generally permissible, but cameras that monitor the inside of your home are not.

Protection from Discrimination

Federal and state fair housing laws prohibit landlords from discriminating against tenants based on certain protected characteristics. Under federal law, it is illegal to discriminate based on race, color, national origin, religion, sex, familial status (meaning having children under 18 or being pregnant), or disability. Many states and cities add additional protected categories such as sexual orientation, gender identity, source of income (such as housing vouchers), marital status, age, or veteran status.

Discrimination can take many forms, and it is often subtle. It includes refusing to rent to someone because of their protected status, charging higher rent or deposits to certain groups, imposing different lease terms or rules, providing inferior maintenance or services, harassing tenants, advertising in ways that exclude certain groups, or retaliating against someone who complains about discrimination.

Examples of housing discrimination include a landlord who tells a family with children that no units are available but then shows units to a couple without children. A landlord who charges higher deposits to applicants with accents or foreign-sounding names. A landlord who refuses to make reasonable accommodations for a tenant with a disability, such as allowing a service animal despite a no-pets policy or installing a wheelchair ramp. A landlord who discourages applicants from certain racial backgrounds from applying by making comments about the neighborhood not being right for them.

Discrimination also includes refusing to rent to someone because they receive housing assistance, such as Section 8 vouchers, though this protection varies by state. Some landlords try to avoid voucher holders by claiming they do not accept vouchers or by setting income requirements that effectively exclude them. In jurisdictions with source-of-income protections, these practices are illegal.

If you believe you have been discriminated against, you have several options. You can file a complaint with the U.S. Department of Housing and Urban Development (HUD) or your state's fair housing agency. These agencies will investigate and can order remedies such as requiring the landlord to rent to you, pay damages, or take fair housing training. You can also file a lawsuit in federal or state court seeking damages and other relief.

Fair housing complaints must usually be filed within one year of the discriminatory act, so it is important to act promptly. You do not need a lawyer to file an administrative complaint, and many fair housing organizations provide free assistance.

Proving discrimination can be challenging because landlords rarely admit their true reasons. Evidence can include statements the landlord made, differences in how you were treated compared to others, patterns of renting only to certain groups, or sudden changes in availability when the landlord meets you in person after speaking with you by phone.

It is important to know that these protections apply at every stage of the rental process, from advertising and applications through the entire tenancy and even when you move out. A landlord cannot legally refuse to rent to you because of your race, but they also cannot harass you during your tenancy for the same reason or retaliate when you complain about it.

Protection from Retaliation

In many jurisdictions, tenants are protected from retaliation if they exercise their legal rights. This means a landlord cannot evict you, raise your rent, reduce services, or otherwise punish you for actions like reporting code violations to the health department, requesting necessary repairs, joining a tenants' union, organizing other tenants, filing a discrimination complaint, or testifying against the landlord in court.

Retaliation laws typically create a presumption that any negative action taken by a landlord within a certain period after a tenant asserts their rights (often 90 to 180 days) is retaliatory. The landlord then has the burden of proving they had a legitimate, non-retaliatory reason for their action.

For example, if you report your landlord to the building inspector for lack of heat, and two weeks later the landlord serves you with an eviction notice for a supposed lease violation that has existed for months, that looks like retaliation. The law presumes it is retaliation, and the landlord would have to prove otherwise.

However, these protections do not give tenants unlimited immunity. If you stop paying rent or violate your lease in other ways, a landlord can still take action against you even if you recently complained about repairs. The key question is whether the landlord's action was motivated by your protected activity or by a legitimate business reason.

If you believe you are being retaliated against, document everything. Keep records of when you made complaints, what the landlord's response was, and when the retaliatory action occurred. The timing and sequence of events is often the strongest evidence of retaliation.

If you can prove retaliation, the consequences for the landlord can be serious. Courts can stop an eviction, award you damages, reduce your rent, or order other remedies. Some states allow you to recover attorney's fees if you win a retaliation case, which makes it easier to find a lawyer willing to take your case.

Lease Terms and Fair Treatment

Whether you have a written lease or a month-to-month oral agreement, you are entitled to fair treatment under the terms you agreed to. A lease is a contract, and both sides must follow it. Landlords cannot unilaterally change the lease during its term (such as suddenly requiring additional fees, changing rules about guests or pets, or eliminating services like parking) unless the lease specifically allows it.

If you have a fixed-term lease (such as one year), the landlord generally cannot raise your rent or evict you without cause until the lease expires. This is one of the main benefits of a lease compared to month-to-month tenancy. You have security knowing that as long as you pay rent and follow the lease terms, you can stay for the agreed period.

Month-to-month tenants have less protection but are still entitled to proper notice before rent increases or termination of tenancy. The notice period varies by state but is typically 30 days for the tenant to give notice they are leaving, and 30 to 60 days for the landlord to raise rent or end the tenancy. Some cities with rent control have additional protections limiting when and by how much rent can be raised.

When reading a lease, pay close attention to provisions about rent increases, lease renewal, maintenance responsibilities, guest policies, pet policies, and what happens if you need to break the lease early. Many leases include clauses that favor the landlord, such as automatic renewal, broad rules about what constitutes damage, or requirements that you pay the landlord's attorney's fees if there is a dispute.

Some lease terms may not be enforceable even if you sign them. For example, a clause saying you waive your right to a habitable home, or that you cannot report code violations, or that the landlord can enter anytime without notice, is likely unenforceable because it violates your legal rights. However, fighting unenforceable lease terms usually requires going to court, so it is better to negotiate or avoid problematic leases in the first place if possible.

It is worth noting that enforcement of tenant rights often depends on tenants knowing those rights exist and acting within required procedures. Many violations go unchallenged simply because tenants do not realize they have legal recourse or fear retaliation. Understanding your rights is the first step toward being able to assert them.

Security Deposits: Your Money, Your Rights

A security deposit is money paid at the start of a tenancy, typically equal to one or two months' rent, to cover potential damage to the unit or unpaid rent at the end of the lease. It is one of the most regulated aspects of landlord-tenant law, yet also one of the most misunderstood and one of the most common sources of disputes between landlords and tenants.

What Landlords Can Charge

State laws regulate how much a landlord can charge for a security deposit. Some states cap it at one or two months' rent, while others have no limit. A few states require landlords to pay interest on deposits held for longer than a certain period, typically at a rate set by law or tied to bank interest rates.

Landlords may also charge additional deposits for pets or require renters insurance, though some jurisdictions limit these practices as well. It is important to understand what you are paying upfront and what it covers. A pet deposit may be labeled as non-refundable, meaning the landlord keeps it regardless of whether your pet causes damage, while a security deposit must be returned if you leave the property in good condition. Some states prohibit non-refundable fees altogether, requiring that all deposits be refundable unless used for legitimate deductions.

Last month's rent is different from a security deposit. If you pay last month's rent upfront, the landlord must apply it to your final month of tenancy and cannot use it to cover damages. If you pay both a security deposit and last month's rent, make sure the lease clearly distinguishes between the two.

Be wary of landlords who ask for cash deposits without providing a receipt. Always get written documentation of any money you pay, including the amount, the date, what it is for, and where it will be held. This receipt is your proof that you paid the deposit and protects you if the landlord later claims you never paid it or paid a different amount.

How Deposits Must Be Held

Many states require landlords to hold security deposits in a separate bank account, not mix them with their personal funds. Some states also require landlords to provide tenants with information about where the deposit is being held, the name and address of the bank, and the account number. A few states require this information to be provided within a certain number of days after you move in.

These rules exist to protect tenants from landlords who spend deposit money and then cannot return it when the tenant moves out. Landlords who fail to properly hold deposits in some states forfeit their right to keep any portion of it, even for legitimate damage, and may be liable for penalties.

If your state requires deposits to earn interest, the landlord must either pay you the interest annually or credit it when you move out. The interest rates are usually small, but over several years in the same rental, they can add up to a meaningful amount.

Some states allow landlords to post a bond instead of holding deposits in a bank account. The bond serves the same protective function, ensuring that money will be available to return deposits to tenants.

Normal Wear and Tear vs. Damage

When you move out, the landlord must return your security deposit within a time period set by state law, usually between 14 and 60 days. If the landlord intends to keep any portion of the deposit, they must provide an itemized written statement explaining what the deductions are for, along with receipts or estimates for the work in many states.

Here is where many disputes arise. Landlords can deduct for actual damage beyond normal wear and tear, but not for routine deterioration that happens from ordinary use of the property over time. Normal wear and tear includes things like minor scuffs on walls from moving furniture, worn carpet in high-traffic areas like hallways and living rooms, faded or discolored paint from sunlight and age, small nail holes from hanging pictures or mirrors, worn finish on countertops or cabinet handles from regular use, or minor scratches on hardwood floors.

Damage, on the other hand, means things like large holes punched in walls, carpet stained or burned beyond cleaning, broken windows or doors, broken appliances caused by misuse or neglect, excessive filth requiring professional cleaning beyond normal move-out cleaning, unapproved alterations like painting walls unauthorized colors or installing fixtures, or damage caused by pets beyond what a pet deposit covers.

The distinction is not always clear-cut, but the general rule is that landlords cannot charge you for making the unit look new again if the wear is consistent with normal living over the lease period. If you lived in the unit for five years, the carpet will be more worn than if you lived there for six months, and the landlord cannot expect the same condition.

The age and quality of items also matters. If the carpet was already eight years old when you moved in and had a ten-year expected lifespan, the landlord cannot charge you the full cost of replacing it when you move out. They can only charge for the remaining useful life you used up. Some states have specific formulas or depreciation schedules for calculating this.

Landlords also cannot deduct for repairs that were needed before you moved in or for pre-existing damage, which is why documenting the condition of the unit at move-in is so important. If there was already a stain on the carpet or a crack in the tile when you moved in, the landlord cannot charge you for it when you leave.

Cleaning is a gray area. You are expected to leave the unit reasonably clean, meaning swept, mopped, with appliances cleaned and trash removed. However, landlords cannot charge you for professional deep cleaning or carpet shampooing unless the unit is left excessively dirty or the lease specifically requires professional cleaning at move-out. Some states have ruled that normal cleaning between tenants is a cost of doing business that landlords must cover, not something tenants pay for through their deposits.

Documenting Condition to Protect Yourself

The single most effective way to protect yourself in a security deposit dispute is to thoroughly document the condition of the rental unit when you move in and when you move out. This creates evidence that can prove what damage existed before you arrived and what condition you left the property in.

When you move in, take photographs or videos of every room from multiple angles. Photograph walls, floors, ceilings, windows, doors, appliances, countertops, cabinets, bathroom fixtures, closets, and any other features. Take close-ups of any existing damage, stains, scratches, holes, or wear.

Make sure your photos are dated, either through the camera's automatic date stamp or by including that day's newspaper in a photo.

Many landlords provide a move-in checklist or inspection form. Fill it out carefully and completely, noting everything you observe, even small items. Be specific. Instead of writing "carpet is worn," write "carpet in living room has dark stain near window and worn area by door." Instead of "wall has mark," write "bedroom wall has 4-inch scratch above light switch."

Ask the landlord or property manager to sign the checklist and give you a copy. If they refuse or if no checklist is provided, create your own and send it to the landlord by certified mail or email so you have proof they received it.

When you move out, do the same process in reverse. Clean the unit thoroughly before taking your move-out photos. Document that you left it in good condition. Again, photograph everything from multiple angles and take close-ups showing that damage you were accused of at move-in still exists but you created no new damage.

If you made any repairs yourself during your tenancy, photograph those repairs and keep receipts. If you replaced a broken towel rack or patched a hole, that works in your favor.

Keep all of this evidence in a safe place, backed up digitally. If a landlord withholds part of your deposit unfairly, this evidence can be critical in small claims court or in negotiations to get your money back. Without documentation, it often becomes your word against the landlord's, and landlords have the advantage of still holding your money while you try to get it back.

What to Do If Your Deposit Is Not Returned

If your landlord does not return your deposit within the legal time frame, or provides an itemized statement you believe is inaccurate or inflated, you have options. Do not simply accept an unfair deduction. Many landlords count on tenants not fighting back, and many unjustified deductions would not hold up if challenged.

Start by sending a written demand letter to the landlord. Explain specifically why you believe you are entitled to a full or partial refund of your deposit. Reference the law in your state about security deposits and deadlines. Attach copies of your move-in and move-out photos if relevant. Give the landlord a deadline to refund the disputed amount, typically 7 to 14 days.

Send the letter by certified mail with return receipt requested so you have proof the landlord received it. Keep a copy for your records. Many disputes are resolved at this stage because landlords realize the tenant knows their rights and has documentation.

If the demand letter does not work, you can file a case in small claims court. Small claims court is designed to be accessible without a lawyer and to resolve disputes quickly. The filing fee is usually under $100, and you can often recover it if you win. Many states allow you to file online or by mail.

In your small claims case, bring all your evidence: photos, the lease, the move-in checklist, copies of letters or emails to the landlord, receipts, and any other documentation. Explain clearly what you believe you are owed and why. Many judges are familiar with security deposit disputes and are skeptical of landlords who make excessive or poorly documented claims.

Many states allow tenants to recover not just the deposit but also penalties (such as double or triple the amount withheld) and court costs if the landlord's withholding was in bad faith. Bad faith typically means the landlord knew they were not entitled to keep the money but did it anyway, or failed to follow required procedures like providing an itemized statement or returning the deposit within the legal deadline.

Even if you do not win the full amount you sought, you will often win at least a partial refund. Security deposit disputes are among the most common landlord-tenant conflicts, but they are also among the most winnable for tenants who have done their homework and kept good records.

One final tip: some landlords use security deposits as a profit center, routinely overcharging tenants for minor wear or inflating repair costs. If you encounter this, consider reporting the landlord to your local housing authority or tenant advocacy organization. Patterns of abuse can lead to investigations and penalties for landlords who systematically violate the law.

Evictions and Tenant Removal: Know Your Rights

A landlord cannot simply lock a tenant out, shut off utilities, or remove belongings to force them to leave. Eviction is a formal legal process, and it must follow strict rules set by state law. These rules exist to protect tenants from being unfairly or arbitrarily thrown out of their homes without due process. Violating these rules can result in serious penalties for landlords, including liability for damages.

Why Landlords Evict

Landlords can seek to evict tenants for several specific reasons, and the reason matters because it determines what kind of notice must be given, how much time you have to respond, and what defenses you might be able to raise.

The most common reason is nonpayment of rent. If you fail to pay rent when it is due, the landlord can begin eviction proceedings. However, even for nonpayment, they must follow the legal process and cannot simply lock you out.

Other common reasons include violating lease terms, such as having unauthorized occupants living in the unit, keeping pets in violation of a no-pets policy, using the property for illegal purposes, subletting without permission, or causing significant damage to the property beyond normal wear and tear.

Landlords can also evict for engaging in illegal activity on the property, such as drug dealing, manufacturing drugs, or other criminal conduct. Some states have expedited eviction procedures for criminal activity.

In month-to-month tenancies, landlords can terminate the rental agreement without giving a reason, though they must still provide proper notice (usually 30 to 60 days). Similarly, when a fixed-term lease expires, the landlord can choose not to renew it, though some cities with just-cause eviction protections limit this.

In rent-controlled cities or jurisdictions with just-cause eviction laws, landlords can only evict for specific reasons listed in the law. These typically include nonpayment, lease violations, owner move-in, substantial renovations, or removing the unit from the rental market. Landlords in these areas cannot evict simply because they want a different tenant or want to raise the rent beyond legal limits.

Notice Requirements: The First Step in Eviction

Before filing an eviction case in court, landlords are almost always required to give the tenant written notice. This is called a notice to quit, pay-or-quit notice, cure-or-quit notice, or notice to vacate, depending on the reason and the state. The type and length of notice depend on the reason for eviction and the laws of the state.

Pay or Quit Notices

For nonpayment of rent, many states require a pay or quit notice, giving the tenant a short period (often three to five days, though it can be as little as one day or as long as 14 days) to pay the overdue rent in full or move out. If the tenant pays the full amount owed within that time period, the eviction generally cannot proceed. The landlord must accept the payment and allow the tenant to stay.

The notice must typically state exactly how much rent is owed, how it should be paid, and by what date. It must usually include only rent, not other fees, though this varies by state. If the notice demands more than what you actually owe or includes improper charges, it may be invalid, and you may be able to fight the eviction on that basis.

Cure or Quit Notices

For lease violations other than nonpayment, landlords typically must give a cure or quit notice, allowing the tenant time to fix the violation (such as removing an unauthorized pet or having an unauthorized occupant move out) or leave. The time period is often longer than for pay-or-quit notices, ranging from 3 to 30 days depending on the state and the severity of the violation.

Some violations are considered incurable, meaning they cannot be fixed. These typically include serious lease violations, illegal activity, or repeated violations of the same term after previous warnings. For incurable violations, the notice may simply demand that the tenant vacate by a certain date without any opportunity to fix the problem.

Termination of Tenancy Notices

For month-to-month tenancies or situations where a lease is simply ending and not being renewed, landlords must give a longer notice period, typically 30 or 60 days depending on how long the tenant has lived there. Some states require 60 days' notice if the tenant has lived in the unit for a year or more.

These notices do not need to give a reason unless the jurisdiction has just-cause eviction protections. They simply inform the tenant that the tenancy will end on a specific date and the tenant must move out by then.

Proper Service of Notice

The notice must be delivered properly according to state law. Methods typically include personal service (handing it directly to the tenant), substitute service (leaving it with another adult at the residence), or posting it on the door and mailing a copy. Some states allow service by certified mail or regular mail.

The specific rules vary by state, but improper notice can invalidate the entire eviction case. If you receive an eviction notice, check whether it was served correctly. If it was not, that may be a defense you can raise in court.

The time period in the notice does not start until it is properly served. If the notice says you have three days to pay or quit, and it is served by posting and mailing, you may have additional time because of mail delivery delays. Read your state's law carefully or consult with a legal aid organization to understand your exact deadline.

The Eviction Court Process

If the tenant does not comply with the notice by either fixing the problem, paying the rent, or moving out, the landlord's next step is to file an eviction lawsuit. This is often called an unlawful detainer, forcible entry and detainer, or summary possession case, depending on the state. It is filed in a local court, usually a district, county, or housing court.

Once the lawsuit is filed, you will receive a summons and complaint. The summons tells you when and where the court hearing will be held and how much time you have to file a response. This time period is very short compared to other types of lawsuits, often only 5 to 10 days in some states. Read the summons carefully to understand your deadlines.

Responding to the Eviction Complaint

In many states, you must file a written answer or response to the eviction complaint within the deadline stated in the summons. The answer is your opportunity to admit or deny the landlord's claims and to raise any defenses you have. Defenses might include that the landlord failed to give proper notice, that you already paid the rent, that the eviction is retaliatory or discriminatory, that the landlord failed to maintain the property in habitable condition, or that the landlord breached the lease.

If you fail to file an answer, the landlord can request a default judgment, meaning they win automatically without you having a chance to present your side. This is one of the most common reasons tenants lose eviction cases. They receive the paperwork, do not understand it or think there is nothing they can do, fail to respond, and lose by default.

Even if you think you will probably lose, filing an answer and showing up to court can buy you time, allow you to negotiate, or raise defenses the landlord was not expecting.

The Eviction Hearing

Eviction hearings are usually brief, often lasting only a few minutes to half an hour. Both sides have the opportunity to present evidence and testimony. You can bring witnesses, documents, photos, and other evidence to support your case.

The landlord must prove they have grounds for eviction and followed all required procedures. You can challenge their evidence or present defenses. For example, if the eviction is for nonpayment, you can show receipts proving you paid. If it is for a lease violation, you can show you cured the violation within the notice period or that the violation never occurred.

Common tenant defenses in eviction cases include:

- The landlord failed to give proper notice or the notice was defective
- The rent was paid or tendered within the required time
- The eviction is retaliatory for exercising tenant rights
- The eviction is discriminatory based on a protected characteristic
- The landlord failed to maintain the property in habitable condition, justifying rent withholding
- The landlord accepted rent after the notice period, waiving the eviction
- The lease violation was cured within the allowed time
- The landlord breached the lease first, excusing the tenant's performance

If you raise a habitability defense, having evidence like photos of the conditions, copies of repair requests you sent, inspection reports from the housing authority, or testimony from witnesses can be critical.

The Judge's Decision

If the landlord wins, the court will issue a judgment for possession, also called a writ of possession or writ of restitution. This gives you a final deadline to vacate the property, often just a few days to a week. The judgment may also include a money judgment for back rent, damages, court costs, and attorney's fees if the lease allows it.

If you win, the eviction case is dismissed, and you can stay. You may also be entitled to your court costs or attorney's fees in some cases.

If you lose, you can sometimes appeal, but appeals in eviction cases are difficult because you often must post a bond and continue paying rent into the court while the appeal is pending. The time to file an appeal is very short, usually less than two weeks.

The Final Step: Physical Eviction

Even if the landlord wins in court, they still cannot physically remove you themselves. If you do not leave by the deadline in the judgment, the landlord must request a writ of eviction from the court. This authorizes law enforcement (usually a sheriff or marshal) to remove you and your belongings from the property.

You will typically receive a final notice from the sheriff giving you a specific date and time when the eviction will occur, often 24 to 72 hours' notice. On that date, the sheriff will arrive, require you to leave, and oversee the removal of your belongings. In some jurisdictions, your belongings will be placed on the curb. In others, they may be stored for a short period, though you will have to pay storage fees to retrieve them.

Once a physical eviction occurs, you cannot simply move back in. The landlord can change the locks, and you will have no legal right to re-enter the property.

Illegal Evictions: What Landlords Cannot Do

Landlords who try to evict tenants without going through the court process are engaging in illegal self-help eviction. This includes changing the locks to prevent you from entering, shutting off utilities like heat, water, electricity, or gas to make the unit uninhabitable, removing or disposing of your belongings from the property, threatening or harassing you to force you out, physically blocking you from entering the property, or removing doors or windows to make the unit unlivable.

These actions are illegal in every state, and they remain illegal even if you owe rent, violated your lease, or the landlord has a legitimate reason to evict you. The landlord must still follow the legal process. There are no shortcuts, no matter how justified the landlord believes their case to be.

If you are subjected to an illegal eviction, you have powerful legal remedies. You can sue the landlord for damages, which may include the cost of temporary housing in a hotel or with family, the value of belongings that were damaged or lost, lost wages if you missed work because of the lockout, emotional distress, and in some cases punitive damages meant to punish the landlord for their illegal conduct. These damages can add up to thousands of dollars, far more than the rent that might have been owed.

In some jurisdictions, you can also call the police to report an illegal lockout. Police may order the landlord to let you back into the property immediately. You can also seek an emergency court order requiring the landlord to restore your access.

Some tenants are afraid to assert their rights against illegal evictions because they fear the landlord will just evict them legally afterward. However, an illegal eviction may give you defenses in a later legal eviction, such as retaliation. It also gives you leverage to negotiate, and the damages you can recover may help you afford to move and start over somewhere else.

Document everything if you experience an illegal eviction. Take photos of changed locks, shut-off utilities, or removed belongings. Save any threatening messages or communications from the landlord. Get witness statements if anyone saw what happened. This evidence will be essential if you sue.

What Tenants Should Do When Facing Eviction

If you receive an eviction notice, do not ignore it. This is one of the most critical pieces of advice in this entire chapter. The timelines in eviction cases are extremely short, and once a judgment is entered against you, it is very difficult to undo. Many tenants lose simply because they do not respond in time or do not show up to court.

Read the notice carefully to understand what you are being accused of, what your options are, and what deadline you face. Is it for nonpayment of rent? A lease violation? Termination of tenancy? The reason determines your options.

If the eviction is for nonpayment of rent:

If you can pay the amount demanded within the time allowed, do so immediately. You usually must pay the full amount, in the form specified (often cashier's check or money order), by the deadline. Keep proof of payment. If you pay within the notice period, the landlord must accept it and cannot proceed with the eviction.

If you cannot pay in full, contact the landlord immediately to see if you can work out a payment plan. Some landlords will agree to this, especially if you have been a good tenant and this is your first missed payment. However, they are not required to accept partial payment or a payment plan.

Look for emergency rental assistance. Many cities and counties have programs that can help with back rent, especially in the wake of COVID-19. Contact local nonprofits, churches, or government agencies that provide assistance. Getting help quickly can stop the eviction before it reaches court.

If you are withholding rent because of habitability issues, you may have a defense, but you must be able to prove it. Gather evidence of the problems, your requests for repairs, and if possible, an inspection report from the housing authority. Consult with a legal aid organization about whether rent withholding is allowed in your state and whether you followed the proper procedures.

If the eviction is for a lease violation:

Determine whether the violation is something you can fix. If you can cure it within the time allowed (such as removing an unauthorized pet or having an unauthorized occupant move out), do so immediately and document that you did. Take photos, save moving receipts, or get statements from witnesses.

If the alleged violation did not actually occur, gather evidence proving that. For example, if you are accused of having a pet but do not have one, gather statements from neighbors or other evidence showing you are in compliance with the lease.

If the violation is something that happened in the past and has already been resolved, you may have a defense. For example, if you had a brief unauthorized guest who has since left, that may not justify eviction depending on your state's law.

If the eviction is for termination of tenancy or non-renewal:

If you are a month-to-month tenant or your lease is expiring, you may have fewer options. However, you can still check whether the landlord gave proper notice and whether it complies with state law. If the notice period is too short or was not properly served, you may be able to challenge it.

In jurisdictions with just-cause eviction laws, check whether the landlord has stated a valid reason for terminating your tenancy. If they have not, you may have a defense.

Even if the eviction is legally valid, you may be able to negotiate more time to move out. Many landlords would rather give you an extra month than go through a full eviction, which costs them time and money.

Get legal help:

Eviction cases are complicated, and the stakes are high. If you are facing eviction, contact a legal aid organization, tenant rights group, or lawyer who handles landlord-tenant cases. Many areas have free or low-cost legal help available for low-income tenants.

Even a brief consultation can help you understand your rights, identify possible defenses, and learn what to expect in court. Some legal aid organizations will represent you in court at no cost if you qualify.

Many cities have eviction prevention or diversion programs that help mediate between landlords and tenants to work out solutions before going to court. These programs can help you negotiate a payment plan, access rental assistance, or get more time to move.

Attend your court hearing no matter what:

Even if you think you will lose, showing up gives you a chance to explain your situation, present any defenses, possibly negotiate a move-out date that works better for you, or raise legal issues the landlord was not expecting.

Judges in eviction cases have some discretion. They can sometimes give you more time to move if you ask, especially if you can show you are actively looking for a new place or waiting for rental assistance to come through. If you do not show up, you automatically lose and get no consideration.

Bring all relevant documents to court: your lease, rent receipts, photos, letters or emails with the landlord, repair requests, inspection reports, or anything else that supports your case. Dress respectfully and be polite to the judge. Explain your situation clearly and honestly.

If you lose, ask the judge if you can have additional time to move out. Even a few extra weeks can make a huge difference in finding a new place and avoiding homelessness.

Understand the consequences:

An eviction on your record can make it extremely difficult to rent in the future. Most landlords run background checks that will show eviction cases, even if you won or the case was dismissed. Many landlords have policies against renting to anyone with an eviction history.

This is why fighting an unjust eviction or negotiating an outcome that avoids a formal judgment can protect your ability to find housing later. Some options to consider:

Negotiate a move-out agreement where you leave voluntarily by a certain date and the landlord agrees not to file the eviction case. This keeps the eviction off your record.

If an eviction case has been filed, negotiate a settlement where the case is dismissed in exchange for you moving out. A dismissal looks much better than an eviction judgment.

If you have to go to court, raise any valid defenses you have. Even if you ultimately lose, you may be able to negotiate a dismissal as part of a settlement.

After an eviction, be prepared to explain the situation to future landlords. Having a good rental history before and after the eviction, references from other landlords, or documentation showing the eviction was resolved can help.

Some tenant advocates recommend being upfront about an eviction when applying for new housing and explaining the circumstances. Others recommend not volunteering the information unless asked directly. This is a personal decision based on your situation and the rental market in your area.

Special Protections for Certain Tenants

Some tenants have additional protections against eviction based on their circumstances.

Domestic violence victims: Many states prohibit eviction based on domestic violence incidents or allow victims to break leases early without penalty. If you are a victim of domestic violence, check your state's law or contact a domestic violence advocacy organization for help.

People with disabilities: Tenants with disabilities are entitled to reasonable accommodations under fair housing law. If your disability contributed to a lease violation (such as a noise complaint related to a mental health condition), you may be entitled to an accommodation rather than eviction. You must request the accommodation and provide documentation of your disability and the need for accommodation.

Section 8 and subsidized housing tenants: Tenants receiving housing assistance have additional procedural protections. Landlords must follow HUD regulations, provide specific notices, and in some cases can only evict for certain reasons. If you have a housing voucher or live in subsidized housing, contact your housing authority or a legal aid organization if you face eviction.

Tenants in foreclosed properties: If the property you rent is foreclosed, you may have rights to remain for a certain period even after the foreclosure sale. Federal law provides a minimum of 90 days' notice, and some state laws provide longer protections.

Senior citizens and families with children: Some jurisdictions provide additional protections or longer notice periods for eviction of elderly tenants or families with young children, especially during winter months or the school year.

If you fall into any of these categories and are facing eviction, seek legal help to understand your additional protections.

Why This Chapter Matters

Housing disputes move fast, and mistakes can result in homelessness, damaged credit, eviction records that follow you for years, or long-term rental barriers that make it nearly impossible to find decent housing. The consequences of not knowing your rights as a tenant can be devastating and long-lasting.

Many tenants lose eviction cases not because the law is against them, but because they do not know their rights, miss critical deadlines, fail to document their situation properly, or are too afraid to fight back against landlords who have more resources and experience.

Landlords typically have lawyers, property managers, and years of experience navigating the rental system on their side. They know the law, they know the procedures, and they know that most tenants do not. This imbalance of knowledge and power is exactly why tenant protection laws exist, but those laws only help if people know about them and use them.

Understanding tenant protections means knowing that you cannot be forced to live in unsafe or unhealthy conditions. It means knowing that your landlord must follow rules before entering your home and cannot discriminate against you based on who you are. It means knowing that your security deposit is your money unless the landlord can prove you damaged the property beyond normal wear and tear.

Understanding eviction procedures means knowing that you have time to respond to an eviction notice, that you have the right to go to court and be heard before being forced to leave, and that illegal shortcuts like lockouts or utility shutoffs are not just unfair but are violations you can sue over and win damages.

This knowledge does not guarantee you will win every dispute with your landlord. Sometimes landlords are in the right. Sometimes tenants do owe rent or have violated their leases in ways that justify eviction. But knowing your rights gives you a fighting chance. It allows you to protect yourself when you are being treated unfairly, assert your rights lawfully, and seek help before problems escalate into crises.

It also helps you make better decisions. Knowing what to document when you move in can save you hundreds or thousands of dollars when you move out. Knowing how to properly request repairs can get your heat fixed instead of leaving you freezing through winter. Knowing how to respond to an eviction notice can mean the difference between keeping your home and losing it.

The rental housing system can feel stacked against tenants, and in many ways it is. But tenants do have rights, and those rights are meaningful. Courts do rule in favor of tenants who have been wronged. Landlords do face consequences for violating the law. The system is not perfect, but it is not hopeless either.

If you are renting a home, you are not powerless. You are a party to a legal contract with rights and protections under the law. The landlord may own the property, but you have the right to live there safely, privately, and with dignity as long as you hold up your end of the agreement.

The more tenants who know their rights and stand up for them, the harder it becomes for unscrupulous landlords to take advantage. Every tenant who successfully challenges an illegal lockout, recovers a wrongfully withheld deposit, or defeats a retaliatory eviction makes the system a little more fair for everyone.

This chapter has covered the essential legal principles that govern renting in America. The specifics vary by state and city, so it is always worth researching the exact laws where you live or consulting with a local tenant rights organization. But the core principles apply almost everywhere: habitability, privacy, non-discrimination, proper eviction procedures, and fair treatment.

Armed with this knowledge, you can be an informed, empowered tenant. You can spot problems early, document them properly, assert your rights when necessary, and seek help when you need it. You can avoid common pitfalls that cost tenants their security deposits, their homes, and their housing stability.

The next chapter turns to homeownership and property rights, where different but equally important legal rules apply. Owning property brings its own set of responsibilities, protections, and potential conflicts with neighbors, governments, and lenders. But the foundation remains the same: knowing your rights is the first step to protecting them.

11

Owning Property

Owning property is often viewed as a major milestone: a sign of stability, independence, and long-term security. For many people, buying a home is the largest financial decision they will ever make. But property ownership is not just about pride or investment value. From a legal standpoint, owning property comes with a detailed and sometimes surprising set of rights, responsibilities, and risks.

Property law governs far more than the act of buying or selling a home. It affects how you use your property, how you interact with neighbors, how governments regulate your land, and how lenders protect their interests. Many property-related conflicts arise not because someone acted in bad faith, but because owners misunderstand what property ownership actually allows and what it requires.

This chapter explains the legal basics of owning property, the most common disputes owners face, and the responsibilities that come with having your name on the deed.

Understanding Property Ownership

What Does It Really Mean to "Own" Property?

When you own property, you actually own a "bundle of rights" rather than just the physical land and buildings. These rights include the ability to use the property, modify it, sell it, lease it, and exclude others from it. However, none of these rights are absolute.

Your ownership rights are limited by laws, regulations, and agreements that existed before you bought the property and continue after you sell it. For example, you cannot use your property in ways that violate zoning laws, even if you own it outright. You may not be able to cut down certain trees, build certain structures, or operate certain businesses from your home, regardless of your ownership status.

Types of Property Ownership

Property can be owned in several different ways, and the type of ownership affects your rights and obligations:

Sole ownership means one person holds all ownership rights. This is the simplest form but offers no automatic transfer of property if the owner dies.

Joint tenancy involves two or more owners who each own an equal share. When one owner dies, their share automatically passes to the surviving owners, regardless of what their will says.

Tenancy in common also involves multiple owners, but shares can be unequal, and each owner can leave their share to whomever they choose in their will.

Community property applies in certain states where married couples own property equally, with special rules about what happens during divorce or death.

Tenancy by the entirety is a special form of joint ownership available only to married couples in some states, offering certain protections from creditors.

The type of ownership you choose has significant legal and tax implications. Many people accept whatever ownership form is suggested without understanding the alternatives or consequences.

What's Included in Property Ownership?

Property ownership typically includes not just the land and buildings, but also:

- **Subsurface rights**, which may include minerals, oil, gas, or water beneath your property (though these are sometimes sold separately)

- **Air rights**, which govern how high you can build and whether you control the airspace above your property
- **Water rights**, which determine your ability to use rivers, streams, lakes, or groundwater on or near your property
- **Fixtures**, which are items permanently attached to the property, such as built-in appliances, lighting fixtures, or heating systems

Disputes often arise when buyers and sellers disagree about what stays with the property and what the seller can take. A chandelier might seem like personal property to the seller but a fixture to the buyer. Clear contract language prevents these disagreements.

Buying and Selling Homes

Buying a home is both a financial transaction and a legal one. While buyers often focus on price, interest rates, and monthly payments, the legal structure of the transaction is just as important. Each step in the process creates enforceable rights and obligations that can have long-term consequences.

The Purchase Agreement

The purchase agreement is the foundation of every real estate transaction. This binding contract spells out the price, deadlines, contingencies, and responsibilities of each party. Once both parties sign, they are legally obligated to perform according to its terms.

Key elements of most purchase agreements include:

- **The purchase price and deposit amount.** The deposit (often called earnest money) shows the buyer is serious and may be forfeited if the buyer backs out without a valid reason.
- **Contingencies that allow the buyer to cancel the contract** under certain conditions, such as being unable to obtain financing, discovering major defects during inspection, or failing to sell their current home.
- **The closing date and timeline** for completing inspections, obtaining financing, and finalizing the sale.
- **What's included in the sale**, such as appliances, window treatments, or outdoor structures.

- **Who pays for what**, including inspections, repairs, title insurance, and closing costs.

Many buyers sign purchase agreements without fully understanding their obligations. If you agree to waive inspections or forgo certain contingencies to make your offer more attractive, you give up important legal protections. A competitive market does not eliminate legal risks.

Seller Disclosures

In most states, sellers are legally required to reveal known defects, hazards, or past problems with the property. These disclosure requirements exist because buyers cannot possibly discover every issue during a brief inspection, and sellers have superior knowledge about their own property.

Typical disclosure requirements cover:

- **Structural issues**, such as foundation problems, roof leaks, or water damage
- **Environmental hazards**, including lead paint, asbestos, radon, mold, or contaminated soil
- **Pest infestations**, such as termites or rodents
- **Mechanical problems** with heating, cooling, plumbing, or electrical systems
- **Legal issues**, such as zoning violations, unpermitted additions, boundary disputes, or easements
- **Past insurance claims or major repairs**
- **Deaths on the property** (required in some states, particularly if recent or under certain circumstances)

The key limitation is that sellers typically must disclose only what they actually know. If a seller genuinely does not know about a problem, they usually have no duty to investigate or discover it. However, deliberately hiding known issues or lying about the property's condition can lead to lawsuits and financial liability.

Some sellers attempt to avoid disclosure obligations by selling property "as is." While this can limit certain claims, it does not eliminate the duty to disclose known material defects in most states. An "as is" sale means the buyer accepts the property in its current condition, but the seller must still be truthful about what that condition actually is.

Title and Title Insurance

Title is the legal term for ownership. When you buy property, you are buying the seller's title. But title can be complicated. Previous owners may have created claims, liens, easements, or restrictions that still affect the property even after it is sold.

A **title search** examines public records to identify any issues with the title. Common problems include:

- **Liens**, which are legal claims for unpaid debts, such as unpaid property taxes, contractor bills, or homeowners association fees
- **Easements**, which give others the right to use part of your property for specific purposes, such as utility access or shared driveways
- **Encumbrances**, such as mortgages, judgments, or restrictions on how the property can be used
- **Errors in public records**, such as incorrect property descriptions, forged signatures, or undisclosed heirs

Even a thorough title search may miss certain issues. That is why most lenders require title insurance. **Owner's title insurance** (which protects you) is separate from **lender's title insurance** (which protects the bank). Many buyers purchase only lender's insurance, leaving themselves exposed if a title problem emerges years later.

Title insurance is a one-time cost paid at closing. It protects against losses from title defects that existed before you bought the property but were not discovered until later. It does not cover issues that arise after you take ownership.

The Home Inspection

A professional home inspection is one of the most important protections available to buyers. Inspectors examine the property's structure, systems, and major components to identify existing problems or potential issues.

A thorough inspection typically covers:

- **The foundation, framing, and structural integrity**

- **The roof, gutters, and drainage systems**
- **Heating, ventilation, and air conditioning systems**
- **Plumbing and water systems**
- **Electrical systems and safety issues**
- **Insulation, ventilation, and moisture problems**
- **Doors, windows, and exterior features**

Inspections have limits. Inspectors cannot see through walls or predict when a system might fail. They identify current conditions and red flags, not every possible future problem. Specialized inspections may be needed for pests, radon, mold, septic systems, or wells.

Many buyers make the mistake of attending the inspection but not reading the written report carefully. The report contains important details and disclaimers that the inspector may not emphasize verbally. Understanding what the inspector found (and did not find) helps buyers make informed decisions about repairs, price negotiations, or whether to proceed with the purchase.

Closing the Transaction

Closing is the final step where ownership officially transfers. Both parties sign numerous legal documents, funds change hands, and the deed is recorded with the local government.

Documents you will likely sign or receive at closing include:

- **The deed**, which legally transfers ownership from seller to buyer
- **The mortgage or deed of trust** (if financing the purchase), which gives the lender a security interest in the property
- **The closing disclosure**, which itemizes all costs, credits, and financial details of the transaction
- **The promissory note**, which is your personal promise to repay the loan
- **Title insurance policies**
- **Affidavits and disclosures** required by state or local law

Many people sign these documents without reading them carefully, trusting that their attorney, real estate agent, or lender has protected their interests. While professionals play important roles, you are the one legally bound by what you sign. Taking time to review documents before closing, rather than during it, helps you understand what you are agreeing to.

After closing, the deed must be recorded with the appropriate government office. Recording provides public notice of your ownership and protects against competing claims. Your lender will typically handle recording, but you should confirm it occurred and obtain a recorded copy for your records.

Special Considerations for Sellers

Selling a home carries its own legal obligations and risks. Beyond making required disclosures, sellers must:

- **Maintain the property in its current condition** until closing. Removing fixtures or allowing the property to deteriorate can breach the contract.
- **Deliver the property as promised.** If the contract says certain appliances or features are included, they must remain.
- **Respond honestly to buyer inquiries.** Even casual conversations can create legal obligations if they contain misrepresentations.
- **Comply with fair housing laws**, which prohibit discrimination based on race, color, religion, national origin, sex, disability, or familial status.

Many sellers also face decisions about how to price their property, whether to make repairs, and how to handle multiple offers. These are business decisions, but they can have legal implications if not handled properly.

Sellers who fail to meet disclosure obligations face the greatest legal risk. Lawsuits can be filed months or even years after closing if undisclosed problems are discovered. Even honest mistakes can result in legal liability if disclosure laws are violated. Documentation is your best protection. Keep records of repairs, maintenance, insurance claims, and any issues that arose during your ownership.

Real Estate Laws Vary by Location

Real estate laws differ significantly by state, and even local practices can vary within the same state. Contract terms that are standard in one area may be ineffective or illegal in another. Some states require attorneys at closing; others do not. Some states are "disclosure states" with extensive requirements; others place more responsibility on buyers to investigate.

Understanding the rules that apply where the property is located is essential. Working with professionals who practice in that area, reading contracts carefully, and asking questions when something is unclear can prevent expensive surprises.

Property Disputes

Property ownership does not exist in isolation. Homes sit next to other homes, are subject to community rules, and are regulated by local governments and lenders. As a result, disputes are common, even among neighbors who generally get along.

Boundary Disagreements

One of the most common property disputes involves disagreement about where one property ends and another begins. Fences, driveways, gardens, and structures near property lines can all trigger boundary conflicts.

These disputes often arise because:

- **Property descriptions in old deeds are vague or inconsistent** with modern surveys
- **Fences or structures were built in the wrong location**, sometimes decades ago, and newer owners assumed they marked the true boundary
- **Natural features like trees, streams, or slopes have shifted** over time
- **Surveys from different companies produce slightly different results**

A professional survey is usually the best way to resolve boundary questions, but surveys can be expensive, and neighbors may disagree about which survey is correct. Some states recognize a legal doctrine called "adverse possession," where someone who openly uses another person's land for a certain number of years (often 10 to 20) can actually gain legal ownership of that land. This makes boundary disputes potentially very serious.

If you discover that your neighbor's fence, driveway, or shed is actually on your property, you cannot necessarily force them to remove it immediately. Depending on how long it has been there and how it was used, they may have acquired legal rights. Early legal advice can help you understand your options and the potential consequences of different approaches.

Easements

An easement is a legal right to use someone else's property for a specific purpose. Easements can be created by written agreement, by necessity, by long-term use, or by implication from past conduct.

Common types of easements include:

- **Utility easements**, which allow power, water, gas, or telecommunications companies to install and maintain lines on your property
- **Access easements**, which give someone the right to cross your property to reach their own property or a public road
- **Shared driveway easements**, where neighbors have agreed (or courts have ruled) that both can use a driveway that sits primarily on one property
- **Drainage easements**, which allow water to flow across property or give municipalities the right to manage drainage

Easements "run with the land," meaning they remain in effect even when the property is sold. You may buy a property without realizing that your neighbor has a legal right to use part of it, or that you have the right to use part of theirs.

Disputes arise when easement rights are unclear, when one party exceeds the scope of the easement, or when the burdened property owner interferes with the easement holder's rights. For example, if you have an access easement to cross your neighbor's property, they cannot block that access, but you also cannot expand your use beyond what the easement allows.

Adverse Possession

Adverse possession is a legal doctrine that allows someone to gain ownership of property by using it openly, continuously, and without permission for a specified period (typically 10 to 20 years, depending on the state).

The requirements for adverse possession vary by state but generally include:

- **Actual possession**, meaning the person physically uses the property
- **Open and notorious possession**, meaning the use is visible and obvious, not hidden
- **Exclusive possession**, meaning the person treats the property as their own, not shared with the true owner
- **Continuous possession** for the entire statutory period
- **Hostile possession**, meaning without the owner's permission (though this does not require ill will, just lack of permission)

Adverse possession exists to encourage productive use of land and to resolve long-standing ambiguities in ownership. However, it can result in unfair outcomes when property owners are unaware of encroachments or fail to take action for many years.

If you notice someone using your property without permission (even if the use seems harmless), addressing it early prevents adverse possession claims from developing. Written permission converts hostile use into permitted use, stopping the adverse possession clock.

Noise, Nuisance, and Land Use Issues

Living near other people inevitably creates some friction. Most minor annoyances are not legal issues. However, when one property owner's use of their land substantially interferes with another's ability to enjoy their property, it may constitute a legal nuisance.

Common nuisance claims involve:

- **Excessive noise** from parties, machinery, animals, or commercial activities
- **Odors** from trash, animals, chemicals, or business operations
- **Light pollution** from security lights or commercial lighting
- **Unsightly conditions** like excessive junk, abandoned vehicles, or

unmaintained properties

- **Encroaching vegetation**, such as tree roots damaging foundations or branches hanging over property lines
- **Smoke, dust, or other air quality issues**

Nuisance law balances property rights. You have the right to use your property, but not in ways that unreasonably interfere with others' rights to use theirs. What counts as "unreasonable" depends on the location, the severity and frequency of the interference, and community standards.

In residential areas, running a loud business or housing many animals might be a nuisance. In rural or industrial areas, the same activities might be acceptable. Courts consider whether the complaining neighbor is unusually sensitive or whether most reasonable people would be bothered.

Many nuisance disputes can be resolved through conversation, mediation, or local code enforcement before they become lawsuits. However, if the interference is severe and ongoing, legal remedies may include court orders to stop the behavior (injunctions) or monetary damages.

Tree Disputes

Trees are a surprisingly common source of property conflicts. Issues include:

Branches or roots extending onto neighboring property. Generally, you can trim branches or roots that cross the property line, but you cannot enter your neighbor's property to do so, and you cannot harm the tree's health.

Trees on the property line. These are usually considered jointly owned, and neither neighbor can remove or significantly alter the tree without the other's permission.

Falling trees or limbs. If a healthy tree falls due to a storm, the property owner where it lands typically bears the cost. But if the tree was diseased or dead, and the owner knew or should have known, they may be liable for damage.

View obstruction. Generally, property owners have no right to a view, and neighbors can allow trees to grow even if they block your view. However, some communities have view ordinance laws that create limited protections.

Protected trees. Many cities have laws protecting certain trees based on size, species, or historic significance. Removing protected trees without permission can result in substantial fines.

Trees near property lines should be addressed carefully. Removing a neighbor's tree without permission, even if branches hang over your property, can lead to significant legal liability. In some states, damages for wrongfully cutting down trees can be tripled.

Fences and Property Lines

Fence disputes are extremely common. Issues include:

Who pays for the fence? In many areas, fences on the property line are considered shared, and costs should be split. However, if one neighbor wants a fence and the other does not, the neighbor who wants it typically pays.

Fence location. Fences should be built on or just inside the property line. Building on a neighbor's property without permission can lead to removal requirements or adverse possession claims.

Fence height and appearance. Local ordinances often regulate fence height, materials, and placement. Homeowners associations may have additional restrictions.

Spite fences. Fences built purely to annoy a neighbor, with no legitimate purpose, may be illegal in some jurisdictions.

Before building a fence, check property lines, local regulations, and HOA rules. If the fence will sit on the property line, discussing plans with your neighbor can prevent future disputes. Even if you are not legally required to consult them, doing so builds goodwill and may avoid litigation.

Homeowners' Association (HOA) Conflicts

Many properties are subject to homeowners' association rules. HOAs are private organizations that enforce community standards through covenants, conditions, and restrictions (CC&Rs) that are legally binding on all property owners in the community.

When you buy property in an HOA community, you automatically agree to follow its rules, pay its fees, and submit to its authority. Common HOA powers include:

- **Regulating exterior appearance**, such as paint colors, landscaping, fences, and architectural changes

- **Restricting certain uses**, such as running businesses, parking commercial vehicles, or renting properties
- **Requiring maintenance standards** for lawns, driveways, and building exteriors
- **Collecting fees and assessments** for common area maintenance, amenities, and reserves
- **Imposing fines** for rule violations
- **Placing liens on properties** for unpaid fees, which can even lead to foreclosure

HOA disputes often arise when:

- **Rules are enforced inconsistently**, with some violations ignored while others are strictly punished
- **Owners disagree about whether a rule is reasonable** or whether they violated it
- **Owners fall behind on fees** due to financial hardship
- **The HOA changes rules** in ways that negatively affect property use or value
- **Architectural requests are denied** or take too long to process

While HOAs provide benefits like maintaining property values and common amenities, they also limit individual freedom. Before buying in an HOA community, review the CC&Rs, bylaws, meeting minutes, and financial statements carefully. Understand what you are agreeing to and whether you can live with those restrictions.

If you are already in an HOA dispute, check whether the HOA followed its own procedures. Many disputes can be resolved if the HOA failed to provide proper notice, hold required hearings, or follow governing documents. Some states also require mediation or arbitration before HOA disputes can go to court.

Foreclosure, Liens, and Mortgage Disputes

Foreclosure is the legal process where a lender takes ownership of property when the borrower fails to make mortgage payments. Foreclosure can also occur when homeowners associations foreclose for unpaid fees, or when contractors or governments foreclose for unpaid bills or taxes.

Judicial foreclosure requires the lender to sue the borrower and obtain a court order before selling the property.

Non-judicial foreclosure allows the lender to sell the property without court involvement, following procedures specified in the mortgage or deed of trust.

Which type applies depends on state law and the loan documents. Non-judicial foreclosure is faster and cheaper for lenders but provides fewer protections for borrowers.

If you fall behind on mortgage payments, the worst thing you can do is ignore the problem. Lenders would often prefer to work out a payment plan, loan modification, or other alternative than to foreclose. Once foreclosure proceedings begin, your options become more limited and expensive.

Other types of liens can also threaten property ownership:

- **Tax liens** arise from unpaid property taxes and usually take priority over all other claims, including mortgages.
- **Mechanic's liens** can be filed by contractors, subcontractors, or suppliers who were not paid for work on your property.
- **HOA liens** result from unpaid association fees or fines.
- **Judgment liens** arise when someone sues you, wins, and records the judgment against your property.

These liens attach to the property, not just to you personally. When the property is sold, liens must typically be paid from the proceeds before you receive any money. In extreme cases, lien holders can force the sale of your property to satisfy the debt.

Preventing liens requires staying current on all payments and obligations. If you hire contractors, ensure they are paid and obtain lien waivers (documents confirming they have been paid and will not file liens). If a lien is filed improperly, you can challenge it, but this requires prompt legal action.

Eminent Domain and Government Takings

Governments have the power to take private property for public use through a process called eminent domain. This power is limited by the Constitution, which requires:

- **Public use.** The taking must be for a public purpose, such as roads, schools, parks, or utilities. In recent decades, courts have interpreted "public use" broadly to include economic development.

- **Just compensation.** The government must pay fair market value for the property taken.

Eminent domain can involve taking the entire property or just a portion (a partial taking). Even without a formal taking, government actions that severely restrict property use may constitute a "regulatory taking" that requires compensation.

If the government initiates eminent domain proceedings against your property, you have the right to challenge both whether the taking is valid and whether the offered compensation is adequate. Property owners often need expert appraisers and attorneys to ensure they receive fair value.

Homeowner Responsibilities

Unlike renters, homeowners bear full responsibility for the condition and legal compliance of their property. These responsibilities exist whether or not the owner lives in the home full-time.

Maintaining Safe Conditions

Property owners have a legal duty to maintain their property in a reasonably safe condition. This duty extends to:

- **Invited guests**, such as friends, family, and service providers, for whom you have the highest duty of care

- **Licensees**, such as salespeople or social visitors, for whom you must warn about known dangers

- **Trespassers**, for whom your duty is generally limited, though you cannot set traps or intentionally harm them

The exact scope of these duties varies by state and by the circumstances. However, common safety obligations include:

- **Repairing hazards** like broken steps, loose railings, or slippery surfaces

- **Warning about non-obvious dangers** that you know about but visitors might not
- **Maintaining walkways, driveways, and common areas** in safe condition
- **Securing swimming pools** with fences or covers to prevent child drowning
- **Addressing dangerous animals** that might harm visitors
- **Removing snow and ice** from walkways (in some jurisdictions)

Homeowners who fail to maintain safe conditions can be held liable for injuries that result. These lawsuits (called premises liability claims) can seek compensation for medical bills, lost wages, pain and suffering, and other damages.

Building Codes and Zoning Compliance

Local governments regulate property use through building codes and zoning ordinances. Building codes establish minimum standards for construction, electrical work, plumbing, and structural safety. Zoning laws control how property can be used (residential, commercial, industrial) and what can be built (size, height, setbacks from property lines).

Before making significant changes to your property, such as additions, renovations, or new structures, you typically need:

- **Building permits**, which require you to submit plans, pay fees, and allow inspections
- **Zoning compliance**, which may limit what you can build based on your property's zoning designation
- **HOA approval** (if applicable), which may impose stricter requirements than government regulations

Many homeowners make improvements without permits, hoping to save time and money. This creates several risks:

- **Difficulty selling the property**, since unpermitted work must be disclosed and can scare off buyers or lenders

- **Orders to remove improvements** or bring them up to code at your expense
- **Fines and penalties** from local governments
- **Inability to obtain insurance coverage** for unpermitted work
- **Liability if unpermitted work causes injury** or damage

Even work done by previous owners can create problems for you. If you discover unpermitted work when you try to sell, you may need to obtain after-the-fact permits, hire contractors to bring work up to code, or reduce your asking price.

Some jurisdictions are more aggressive about code enforcement than others, but the risk always exists. Obtaining proper permits protects your investment and ensures work is done safely.

Property Taxes and Assessments

Property owners must pay property taxes based on the assessed value of their land and improvements. Tax rates and assessment methods vary widely by location.

Key points about property taxes:

Taxes are typically due annually or semi-annually, and failing to pay can result in penalties, interest, and eventually tax liens or foreclosure.

Assessed value may not match market value. Some jurisdictions assess property well below what it would sell for, while others assess closer to market rates.

You can usually challenge assessments if you believe your property is overvalued compared to similar properties. This requires evidence and often a formal appeal process.

Tax exemptions may be available for seniors, veterans, disabled persons, or primary residences.

Special assessments can be charged for infrastructure improvements, such as new sewer lines or street paving, that benefit your property.

Unpaid property taxes create a lien that takes priority over your mortgage and most other debts. If taxes remain unpaid long enough, the government can sell your property at a tax sale, and you can lose ownership entirely. Unlike mortgage foreclosure, where you might negotiate with the lender, tax foreclosures are generally less flexible.

Homeowners Association Fees

If your property is part of an HOA, you must pay regular fees (often monthly or quarterly) and possibly special assessments for major repairs or improvements to common areas.

These fees are not optional. The HOA can:

- **Charge late fees and interest** on unpaid amounts
- **Suspend privileges** such as use of pools, gyms, or other amenities
- **File a lien** against your property
- **Foreclose** to collect unpaid fees, even if your mortgage is current

HOA foreclosures are less common than mortgage foreclosures but do occur, particularly when fees go unpaid for extended periods. Before buying in an HOA community, review the fee structure, payment history of the community, and the HOA's reserve fund to ensure it is financially stable.

Insurance Requirements

Most mortgage lenders require homeowners insurance as a condition of the loan. Even if you own your home outright, insurance is a critical protection against financial loss.

Standard homeowners insurance typically covers:

- **Dwelling coverage** for the structure itself
- **Personal property coverage** for belongings inside the home
- **Liability coverage** if someone is injured on your property
- **Additional living expenses** if the home becomes uninhabitable due to a covered event

However, standard policies contain important exclusions. Common events **not covered** by basic homeowners insurance include:

- **Floods**, which require separate flood insurance
- **Earthquakes**, which require separate earthquake coverage in most states
- **Maintenance-related damage**, such as gradual deterioration or neglect
- **Intentional damage** caused by the homeowner
- **Certain types of water damage**, such as sewer backups or groundwater seepage
- **Business activities** conducted from the home (which may require business insurance)

Reading your policy carefully and understanding what is and is not covered can prevent devastating financial losses. Many people discover coverage gaps only when filing a claim after a major loss.

Maintaining adequate insurance is not just about protecting yourself. If you have a mortgage, your lender's interest in the property must be protected. If you allow insurance to lapse, the lender can force-place insurance (at your expense) or even declare the loan in default.

Landlord Responsibilities

If you rent out your property, you take on additional legal responsibilities as a landlord. These include:

- **Maintaining habitable conditions**, such as working heat, plumbing, and structural soundness
- **Making necessary repairs** within a reasonable time
- **Complying with fair housing laws** in tenant selection and management
- **Following eviction procedures** if tenant problems arise
- **Providing required notices** about lead paint, security deposits, and other matters
- **Returning security deposits** according to legal requirements
- **Maintaining liability insurance** to cover tenant injuries or property

damage

Landlord-tenant law is complex and varies significantly by state and even by city. Many jurisdictions heavily regulate rental housing, and violations can result in fines, lawsuits, or inability to collect rent. If you plan to rent your property, understanding your legal obligations is essential.

Protecting Your Property Investment

Title and Deed Issues

After you buy property, keep your deed and title insurance policy in a safe place. These documents prove your ownership and protect against title defects.

If you refinance, make improvements, or discover encumbrances on your property, ensure any new documents are properly recorded. Recording provides public notice and protects your interests against competing claims.

Property Records and Documentation

Maintain thorough records of:

- **All improvements and repairs**, including permits, invoices, and contractor information
- **Communications with neighbors** about boundaries, easements, or shared responsibilities
- **HOA correspondence**, including rule changes, violation notices, and fee assessments
- **Insurance claims and property damage**
- **Tax assessments and payments**
- **Surveys, appraisals, and inspections**

These records can be invaluable if disputes arise or when you sell the property. They document your compliance with laws, support your position in conflicts, and help buyers understand the property's history.

When to Seek Legal Help

Many property issues can be resolved without attorneys through direct communication, mediation, or HOA processes. However, legal advice is important when:

- **Buying or selling property**, especially in complex transactions
- **Facing foreclosure or serious financial difficulty**
- **Involved in boundary disputes** or adverse possession claims
- **Dealing with significant code violations** or government enforcement actions
- **Sued by a neighbor, contractor, or other party**
- **Considering major improvements** that may affect property rights or require permits
- **Inheriting property** or dealing with estates
- **Starting eviction proceedings** against tenants

Early legal consultation is often less expensive than waiting until a problem escalates. Many attorneys offer initial consultations at reduced rates or will answer basic questions briefly to help you determine whether you need further assistance.

Why This Chapter Matters

Property ownership offers stability and long-term value, but it also exposes individuals to legal and financial risks that are often underestimated. Disputes with neighbors, regulatory violations, and liability claims can threaten even homes that have been owned for decades.

Understanding the legal aspects of buying, selling, and maintaining property helps owners protect their investment, avoid unnecessary conflicts, and make informed decisions. Property law touches nearly every aspect of ownership, from the purchase process through daily use and eventual sale.

When owners know their rights and responsibilities, they are better equipped to prevent problems or address them before they spiral out of control. Small issues, like a boundary disagreement or a minor code violation, can be resolved through communication and compromise if caught early. The same issues, if ignored, can lead to costly litigation, damaged relationships, and threats to your ownership.

The legal framework surrounding property exists to balance competing interests: your right to use your property as you wish against your neighbors' rights to enjoy theirs, government interests in public safety and welfare, and lenders' interests in protecting their investment. Understanding how these interests interact helps you navigate property ownership successfully.

Property law also connects to many other legal areas. Your property can be affected by contract law (purchase agreements), tort law (liability for injuries), family law (divorce and inheritance), tax law (property taxes and capital gains), and more. The more you understand about how property law works, the better prepared you are to make sound decisions throughout your life as a property owner.

Whether you are buying your first home, managing a property you have owned for years, or planning to sell, knowing the legal landscape empowers you to protect your rights, meet your obligations, and avoid the costly mistakes that catch many property owners by surprise.

The next chapter turns to accidents, injuries, and lawsuits, areas where property ownership and legal liability often intersect in unexpected ways.

PART VI: Money, Accidents, and Lawsuits

12

Car Accidents and Personal Injury

Car accidents are one of the most common ways people unexpectedly encounter the legal system. They happen in seconds, often without warning, and can leave lasting physical, financial, and emotional consequences. In the moments and days that follow, people are forced to make important decisions (sometimes while injured, shaken, or overwhelmed) without fully understanding how those decisions may affect their legal rights.

What many people do not realize is that a car accident is not just a medical event or an inconvenience. It is also a legal event. Insurance coverage, fault, documentation, and deadlines all begin to matter almost immediately. Choices made early on (what is said at the scene, when medical care is sought, and how insurance claims are handled) can shape the outcome long after the accident itself.

This chapter explains what to do after an accident, how insurance claims work, when legal action may be appropriate, and how to protect yourself throughout the process.

What to Do Immediately After an Accident

The minutes following a car accident can be confusing and stressful, but they are critically important. Actions taken, or not taken, during this time can affect safety, insurance coverage, and potential legal claims.

Prioritize Safety First

If you are able to do so safely, move vehicles out of traffic to prevent further collisions. Turn on hazard lights to alert other drivers. Check yourself and others for injuries. If anyone is hurt, if vehicles are severely damaged, or if traffic is blocked, call emergency services immediately.

Police and medical responders create official records that may later become important. A police report documents what happened, who was involved, and the officer's observations about the scene. Medical records establish when injuries occurred and how serious they were. Both types of records carry weight with insurance companies and, if necessary, in court.

Even if the accident seems minor, calling the police is often wise. Some injuries do not appear right away, and what seems like minor vehicle damage may hide more serious problems underneath. A police report provides an independent account of the accident.

Document Everything

Documentation can protect you later, even if the accident seems minor at the time. The more information you gather, the stronger your position will be if disputes arise.

Important steps include:

Exchange information with other drivers. Get names, phone numbers, addresses, driver's license numbers, license plate numbers, and insurance details (company name, policy number, and contact information). If there are passengers in any vehicle, get their names and contact information as well.

Take photographs. Use your phone to capture as much as possible. Photograph all vehicles involved from multiple angles, showing the full vehicle and close-ups of damage. Photograph license plates, the overall scene (including street signs, traffic signals, and road markings), skid marks or debris, weather conditions, and anything else that might be relevant. If you are injured, photograph visible injuries as well.

Record details about the scene. Write down or type into your phone the date, time, and exact location of the accident. Note weather conditions (rain, fog, ice, clear skies), road conditions (wet, dry, icy, construction zones), lighting (daylight, dusk, nighttime, streetlights), traffic conditions, and the posted speed limit. These details fade from memory quickly but can become important later.

Identify witnesses. If anyone saw the accident, ask for their name and contact information. Independent witnesses can be valuable if the facts are later disputed. Do not assume the other driver will tell the truth or that insurance companies will automatically believe your version of events.

Avoid discussing the accident on social media. Insurance companies and opposing lawyers sometimes search social media for posts that contradict injury claims. A photo of you at a party or on vacation after an accident may be taken out of context and used to suggest your injuries are not serious.

Photos and notes taken at the scene often carry more weight than memories recalled days or weeks later. Memory fades. Details get confused. Written records and images do not change.

Be Careful With Statements

It is natural to want to apologize or explain what happened. You may feel embarrassed, upset, or responsible. But statements made at the scene can later be used against you, even if they were not accurate or were made in the heat of the moment.

Avoid admitting fault, speculating about causes, or offering opinions about who was responsible. Saying "I'm sorry" or "I didn't see you" can later be presented as an admission of liability. Provide basic information to law enforcement (your name, insurance information, what you observed), but keep conversations with others brief and factual.

Do not agree to settle the matter privately without involving insurance. The other driver may seem reasonable at the scene but later claim more serious injuries or damage. Once you leave the scene, you lose the ability to document what really happened.

If the other driver is aggressive, threatening, or appears intoxicated, stay in your vehicle with the doors locked and wait for police to arrive. Your safety is more important than exchanging information.

Seek Medical Attention Promptly

Not all injuries are immediately obvious. Adrenaline can mask pain, and some conditions (such as concussions, whiplash, soft tissue injuries, or internal injuries) may not appear for hours or days.

Go to the emergency room, an urgent care center, or your doctor as soon as possible after the accident. Explain that you were in a car accident and describe all symptoms, even if they seem minor. Headaches, dizziness, neck pain, back pain, numbness, tingling, or confusion should all be reported.

Delaying treatment can worsen health outcomes and make it harder to link injuries to the accident in insurance or legal claims. Insurance companies often argue that delayed medical care means injuries were not serious or were caused by something else. Gaps in treatment can be used to reduce or deny claims.

Follow all treatment recommendations. Attend all appointments. If you are prescribed physical therapy, go to every session. If you are told to follow up with a specialist, do so. Failing to follow medical advice gives insurance companies a reason to question the severity of your injuries.

Keep copies of all medical records, bills, prescriptions, and receipts. Track mileage to medical appointments. Document how your injuries affect daily life, such as difficulty sleeping, inability to work, or needing help with household tasks.

Understanding Insurance Claims

For most people, insurance is the first legal system they encounter after an accident. The claims process can be confusing, and insurance companies have strategies designed to minimize what they pay.

Types of Coverage

Car insurance policies typically include several types of coverage:

Liability coverage pays for injuries and property damage you cause to others. Most states require drivers to carry minimum liability coverage, but those minimums are often too low to cover serious accidents.

Collision coverage pays to repair or replace your vehicle after an accident, regardless of fault.

Comprehensive coverage pays for damage to your vehicle from non-collision events, such as theft, vandalism, hail, or hitting an animal.

Uninsured/underinsured motorist coverage protects you if you are hit by a driver with no insurance or not enough insurance to cover your losses.

Medical payments coverage (MedPay) or **personal injury protection (PIP)** pays for medical expenses for you and your passengers, regardless of fault.

Understanding what coverage you have (and what coverage the other driver has) is critical to knowing where compensation will come from.

Fault-Based vs. No-Fault Systems

Insurance rules vary by state. Some states follow a fault-based system, where the driver who caused the accident is responsible for damages through their liability insurance. In fault-based states, the injured person can file a claim against the at-fault driver's insurance or file a lawsuit if insurance does not cover all losses.

Other states use no-fault insurance, which requires each driver to rely on their own insurance (usually PIP coverage) for medical expenses and lost wages, regardless of who caused the accident. In no-fault states, lawsuits are only allowed if injuries meet certain thresholds (such as permanent injury, disfigurement, or medical expenses above a certain amount).

A few states use hybrid systems or allow drivers to choose between fault and no-fault options. Understanding which system applies in your state affects who pays, how quickly claims move, and whether lawsuits are allowed.

Filing a Claim

After an accident, you will likely need to file a claim with your own insurance company, the other driver's insurance company, or both.

When you contact an insurance company, provide basic facts: the date, time, and location of the accident, the other driver's information, and a brief description of what happened. Avoid giving a detailed recorded statement until you understand the full extent of your injuries and have reviewed your policy.

Insurance companies investigate claims by reviewing police reports, interviewing drivers and witnesses, examining vehicle damage, and reviewing medical records. Adjusters evaluate claims based on liability (who was at fault), damages (how much the injuries or property damage cost), and policy limits (how much coverage is available).

How Insurance Companies Operate

Insurance companies are businesses. Their goal is to resolve claims for as little money as possible. While adjusters may seem friendly or helpful, they work for the insurance company, not for the injured person.

Common tactics used by insurance companies include:

Requesting recorded statements early. You may be asked to give a recorded statement shortly after the accident, often before you know the full extent of your injuries. Statements made early can be used later to minimize claims. You are generally required to cooperate with your own insurance company, but you are not required to give a recorded statement to the other driver's insurer.

Offering quick settlement offers. Insurance companies sometimes make fast, lowball settlement offers before medical treatment is complete. These offers may seem attractive, especially if you are facing bills and missed work, but they often do not account for future medical expenses, ongoing pain, or long-term limitations. Once a settlement is accepted, the right to seek additional compensation is usually lost, even if injuries worsen later.

Delaying claims. Some insurers drag out the process, hoping the injured person will accept less money out of frustration or financial desperation.

Disputing liability. Even in clear-cut cases, insurers may argue that the injured person was partly at fault in order to reduce the payout.

Minimizing injuries. Adjusters may claim that injuries are not as serious as reported, that they were pre-existing, or that they were caused by something other than the accident.

Surveillance. In cases involving significant claims, insurance companies sometimes hire investigators to watch claimants, follow them, or review their social media to find evidence that contradicts their injury claims.

Common Mistakes to Avoid

People recovering from accidents often make mistakes that hurt their claims:

Giving recorded statements before understanding injuries. Wait until you have seen a doctor and understand the severity of your injuries before providing detailed statements.

Accepting quick settlement offers. Do not settle until medical treatment is complete and you know the full extent of your injuries and financial losses.

Failing to document symptoms, treatment, or time missed from work. Keep detailed records of all medical appointments, prescriptions, therapy sessions, and how injuries affect your daily life and ability to work.

Assuming insurance will automatically take care of everything. Insurance companies do not work for you. They work to protect their bottom line.

Posting on social media. Avoid discussing the accident, your injuries, or your activities online. Assume anything you post can be found and used against you.

Signing medical authorizations without review. Insurance companies may ask you to sign broad authorizations allowing them to access all of your medical records, including unrelated conditions. Limit authorizations to records directly related to the accident.

When Lawsuits Make Sense

Most car accident claims are resolved through insurance settlements. Lawsuits become more likely when:

- Injuries are serious, permanent, or life-altering
- Fault is disputed between drivers
- Insurance coverage is insufficient to cover losses
- An insurer refuses to offer fair compensation
- The accident involved drunk driving, reckless conduct, or intentional harm

What a Personal Injury Lawsuit Involves

A personal injury lawsuit seeks compensation for harm caused by another party's negligence. Negligence means failing to act with reasonable care.

To succeed in a car accident lawsuit, the injured person (the plaintiff) generally must prove:

The other party owed a duty of care. All drivers have a legal duty to operate their vehicles safely and follow traffic laws.

That duty was breached. The other driver violated that duty by speeding, running a red light, driving while distracted, or otherwise acting carelessly.

The breach caused the injury. The plaintiff must show that the other driver's conduct directly caused the accident and the resulting injuries.

Actual damages resulted. The plaintiff must have suffered real harm, such as medical expenses, lost wages, pain and suffering, or property damage.

Damages You Can Recover

Compensation in a personal injury lawsuit can include:

Economic damages: Medical bills (past and future), rehabilitation costs, lost wages, lost earning capacity, property damage, and other out-of-pocket expenses.

Non-economic damages: Pain and suffering, emotional distress, loss of enjoyment of life, disfigurement, and disability.

Punitive damages: In rare cases involving especially reckless or intentional conduct (such as drunk driving), courts may award punitive damages to punish the wrongdoer and deter others.

The value of a claim depends on the severity of injuries, the strength of evidence, the credibility of witnesses, the skill of attorneys, and the jurisdiction where the case is filed.

The Litigation Process

Lawsuits involve formal procedures, evidence gathering, and legal deadlines known as statutes of limitations. Missing these deadlines can permanently bar a claim, regardless of its merits.

The litigation process generally includes:

Investigation and filing. Before filing a lawsuit, an attorney investigates the accident, gathers evidence, reviews medical records, and evaluates the strength of the claim. If the case is strong, a complaint is filed in court, formally starting the lawsuit.

Discovery. Both sides exchange information through written questions (interrogatories), document requests, and depositions (recorded interviews under oath). Discovery allows each side to learn the other's evidence and arguments.

Motions. Either side may file motions asking the court to make decisions on legal issues, dismiss parts of the case, or rule in their favor without a trial.

Settlement negotiations. Most cases settle before trial. Attorneys negotiate on behalf of their clients, often with the help of mediators or through formal settlement conferences.

Trial. If no settlement is reached, the case goes to trial. A judge or jury hears evidence, listens to arguments, and decides who is responsible and how much compensation is owed.

Appeals. The losing party may appeal the decision, arguing that the court made legal errors.

Litigation takes time, often months or years, and involves uncertainty. Outcomes depend on evidence, witness credibility, legal arguments, and sometimes the unpredictability of juries. But litigation may be necessary when injuries are severe or financial losses are substantial.

When to Hire an Attorney

Not every car accident requires an attorney. Minor accidents with no injuries and clear liability can often be handled directly with insurance companies.

Consider consulting an attorney if:

- You were seriously injured or required hospitalization
- You face long-term disability or permanent impairment
- Fault is disputed or unclear
- The insurance company denies your claim or offers an unreasonably low settlement
- The other driver was uninsured or underinsured
- Your medical bills exceed available insurance coverage
- You are being blamed for an accident you did not cause
- The accident involved a commercial vehicle, government entity, or multiple parties

Most personal injury attorneys work on a contingency fee basis, meaning they are paid a percentage of the settlement or verdict (typically 33 to 40 percent) and only if you recover compensation. This arrangement allows people to pursue claims without paying attorney fees upfront.

An experienced attorney can evaluate the strength of a claim, handle negotiations with insurers, gather evidence, retain experts (such as accident reconstruction specialists or medical experts), and determine whether filing a lawsuit is the best option. Attorneys understand insurance tactics and know how to counter lowball offers and bad-faith practices.

Statutes of Limitations: Deadlines Matter

Every state has statutes of limitations that set deadlines for filing lawsuits. These deadlines vary by state and by the type of claim.

For car accident personal injury claims, statutes of limitations typically range from one to six years from the date of the accident. For property damage claims, deadlines may differ.

Missing the deadline usually means losing the right to sue, regardless of how strong the case is. There are limited exceptions, such as when the injured person is a minor or when injuries are not immediately discovered, but these exceptions are narrow.

If you are considering legal action, do not wait. Evidence disappears, witnesses move or forget details, and documents get lost. The sooner you act, the stronger your case will be.

Dealing With Insurance After the Accident: Practical Steps

Notify Your Insurance Company Promptly

Most insurance policies require you to report accidents within a certain timeframe, often within 24 to 72 hours. Failing to report an accident can result in denial of coverage.

When you call your insurer, provide basic information but avoid speculating about fault or the extent of injuries. Your insurer will assign a claims adjuster to investigate.

Understand Your Policy

Review your insurance policy to understand what coverage you have, what your deductibles are, and what your policy limits are. Knowing your coverage helps you understand what expenses will be covered and whether you need to pursue compensation from the other driver's insurance.

Keep Detailed Records

Create a file (physical or digital) to organize everything related to the accident:

- Police report
- Photos and videos from the scene
- Contact information for all drivers, passengers, and witnesses
- Insurance information for all parties
- Medical records and bills
- Repair estimates and receipts
- Records of lost wages or missed work
- Notes about phone calls with insurance adjusters (date, time, who you spoke with, what was discussed)
- Correspondence with insurance companies

Good record-keeping makes it easier to support your claim and harder for insurers to dispute facts.

Do Not Sign Anything Without Understanding It

Insurance companies may ask you to sign releases, authorizations, or settlement agreements. Read everything carefully. If you do not understand something, ask questions or consult an attorney before signing.

Once you sign a settlement release, you usually give up the right to pursue additional compensation, even if your injuries turn out to be worse than expected.

Be Honest, But Cautious

Always tell the truth, but be mindful of how much detail you provide to the other driver's insurance company. You are required to cooperate with your own insurer, but you have no obligation to make their job easier by providing information that could be used against you.

Stick to facts. Avoid speculation. Do not downplay injuries, but do not exaggerate them either. Inconsistencies can be used to discredit your claim.

Special Situations

Hit-and-Run Accidents

If the other driver flees the scene, call the police immediately. Try to note the vehicle's make, model, color, license plate number, and direction of travel.

If the driver is not found, you may still be able to recover compensation through your own uninsured motorist coverage. Review your policy and contact your insurer.

Accidents Involving Uninsured or Underinsured Drivers

If the at-fault driver has no insurance or insufficient insurance, your uninsured/underinsured motorist coverage may cover your losses. This coverage is optional in some states and mandatory in others.

You may also have the option to sue the at-fault driver personally, but uninsured drivers often lack assets to pay a judgment.

Accidents With Commercial Vehicles

Accidents involving trucks, delivery vans, buses, or other commercial vehicles can be more complex. Commercial drivers and their employers may have higher insurance coverage, but they also have legal teams working to minimize liability.

Multiple parties may be responsible, including the driver, the trucking company, the vehicle owner, or a maintenance company. Claims may involve federal regulations, logbooks, and specialized evidence.

These cases often require experienced legal representation.

Accidents on Government Property or Involving Government Vehicles

Claims against government entities (such as accidents involving city buses, police vehicles, or poorly maintained roads) are subject to special rules and shorter deadlines.

You may need to file a notice of claim within 30 to 180 days of the accident, depending on the jurisdiction. Missing this deadline can bar your claim entirely.

Consult an attorney promptly if a government entity may be involved.

Protecting Your Rights Throughout the Process

Stay Organized

Keep everything related to the accident in one place. Use a notebook or app to track symptoms, medical appointments, phone calls, and expenses.

Follow Medical Advice

Attend all appointments, follow treatment plans, and do not minimize your symptoms. If you stop treating, insurance companies will argue you must not have been seriously hurt.

Be Patient but Persistent

Insurance claims and lawsuits take time. Do not let frustration lead you to accept an unfair settlement.

Know When to Get Help

If you feel overwhelmed, if the insurance company is not treating you fairly, or if your injuries are serious, consult an attorney. Most offer free consultations and can explain your options without obligation.

Why This Chapter Matters

Car accidents are chaotic, but the legal consequences unfold slowly over months or even years. Early missteps, such as delaying medical care, failing to document injuries, or accepting rushed settlements, can limit recovery long after the crash itself.

Understanding how accidents intersect with insurance and personal injury law allows individuals to protect both their health and their legal rights. Being informed does not mean preparing for a lawsuit. It means knowing how to respond wisely when an accident happens, understanding how insurance companies operate, and recognizing when professional help is needed.

The next chapter explores lawsuits more broadly, explaining how civil cases work and what to expect when disputes move into court.

13

Suing and Being Sued

Most people never expect to see their name on a court document. For many, the idea of a lawsuit feels overwhelming, intimidating, or even embarrassing. Yet civil lawsuits are a routine part of American life. They grow out of ordinary situations: broken contracts, car accidents, property disputes, unpaid debts, workplace conflicts, and disagreements between individuals or businesses.

You do not need to be wealthy, reckless, or dishonest to end up involved in a lawsuit. Often, lawsuits arise simply because two sides see the same situation differently and cannot resolve it on their own. Whether you are considering filing a lawsuit to protect your rights or have just been served with legal papers, understanding how the civil system works can reduce fear, prevent costly mistakes, and help you respond effectively.

This chapter explains the basics of civil lawsuits, how small claims court differs from other courts, why most cases never reach trial, and what you need to know to protect your interests.

Understanding Small Claims Court

Small claims court exists to provide a faster, simpler way to resolve disputes involving relatively small amounts of money. These courts are designed for everyday people, not legal experts, and they intentionally limit formality and expense.

Common Small Claims Cases

The types of disputes heard in small claims court reflect the everyday conflicts that arise between consumers, landlords, tenants, and small businesses. Common cases include:

- Disputes over security deposits when a tenant moves out
- Unpaid personal loans or bills between individuals
- Minor property damage, such as a neighbor's tree falling on a fence
- Simple contract disagreements over services or goods
- Repair work done poorly or left incomplete
- Unpaid rent or utility bills
- Damage to rental property
- Return of borrowed items or money

Dollar Limits and Filing Fees

Each state sets a maximum dollar amount that can be claimed in small claims court. These limits vary widely across the country. Some states cap claims at $2,500 or $3,000, while others allow claims up to $10,000 or even $15,000. A few states have different limits depending on whether the plaintiff is an individual or a business.

Before filing in small claims court, verify your state's current limit. If your claim exceeds that amount, you will need to either reduce your claim to fit within the limit or file in a higher court, which involves more complex procedures and usually requires an attorney.

Filing fees in small claims court are intentionally kept low, typically ranging from $30 to $100, though they vary by jurisdiction and sometimes by the amount being claimed. Some courts waive fees for parties who cannot afford them.

The Small Claims Process

Procedures are simplified compared to other courts. Hearings are often scheduled quickly, sometimes within weeks of filing. The parties present their cases directly to a judge or hearing officer without extensive procedural formalities.

In many states, lawyers are not allowed to represent parties in small claims court, or their role is limited. This rule is intended to level the playing field and keep costs down. However, it also means you must prepare your own evidence, organize your arguments, and present your case clearly and persuasively.

Preparing Your Small Claims Case

Success in small claims court depends heavily on preparation and documentation. The judge will have limited time to hear your case, often just 10 to 20 minutes, so clarity and organization matter.

Gather every relevant document before your hearing:

- Written contracts or agreements
- Receipts, invoices, and billing statements
- Photographs of damage or property conditions
- Emails, text messages, or letters between the parties
- Estimates or repair bills
- Cancelled checks or payment records
- Witness statements or contact information

Organize your documents chronologically or by topic. Make copies for the judge and the other party. Prepare a brief, clear summary of what happened, focusing on facts rather than emotions. Practice explaining your case in plain language, as if talking to a friend who knows nothing about the situation.

Bring any witnesses who have direct knowledge of the dispute. A witness who saw the damage occur or heard the agreement being made can strengthen your case significantly.

What Happens at the Hearing

Small claims hearings are less formal than trials in other courts, but they still follow basic rules. Arrive early, dress appropriately, and bring all your documents and any witnesses.

The judge will typically ask each side to explain their version of events. You will have a chance to present your evidence and call any witnesses. The other party will do the same. The judge may ask questions to clarify facts or understand the dispute better.

Speak clearly and directly. Address the judge respectfully. Stick to the facts of your case and avoid personal attacks or emotional arguments. If the other party says something incorrect, wait for your turn to respond rather than interrupting.

After hearing both sides, the judge will make a decision. In some courts, the decision is announced immediately. In others, it arrives by mail days or weeks later.

Collecting Your Judgment

Winning a case in small claims court does not automatically mean getting paid. The court issues a judgment stating that one party owes money to the other, but collecting on that judgment is your responsibility.

If the losing party does not pay voluntarily, you may need to take additional legal steps. These can include:

- Garnishing wages if the person is employed
- Placing a lien on property or real estate
- Seizing money from bank accounts through a levy
- Requesting that the debtor appear in court to disclose assets

Each of these collection methods involves additional paperwork, fees, and court procedures. Some are more practical than others depending on the debtor's financial situation. If someone has no job, no property, and no money in the bank, even a valid judgment may be difficult or impossible to collect.

Before filing a lawsuit, consider whether the other party has the means to pay if you win. A judgment against someone with no assets is called a "paper judgment" and may not be worth the time and expense of pursuing.

Civil Lawsuits Beyond Small Claims

Civil lawsuits outside of small claims court follow a more formal and structured process. These cases can involve higher dollar amounts, more complex legal issues, and longer timelines. They also typically require the assistance of an attorney.

When to Consider a Civil Lawsuit

A civil lawsuit may be appropriate when:

- The amount of money at stake exceeds small claims limits
- The legal issues are complex or involve multiple parties
- You need court orders beyond just money damages, such as an injunction
- The dispute involves significant personal injury or property damage
- A business relationship or contract has broken down
- Your rights under a law or regulation have been violated

Civil lawsuits are expensive and time-consuming. Before filing, consider whether negotiation, mediation, or other dispute resolution methods might work. Many conflicts can be resolved through direct communication or with the help of a neutral third party.

How a Civil Lawsuit Begins

A lawsuit begins when the plaintiff files a complaint with the court. This document explains what happened, why the defendant is legally responsible, and what relief or damages are being requested. The complaint must comply with specific legal and formatting requirements.

The defendant must be formally notified through a process known as service of process. This usually means that a professional process server or sheriff's deputy personally delivers the court papers to the defendant. Proper service is critical. If done incorrectly, the case can be delayed or even dismissed.

Once served, the defendant has a limited time to respond, typically 20 to 30 days depending on the jurisdiction. The response, called an answer, addresses each allegation in the complaint and may raise defenses or counterclaims.

Ignoring a lawsuit or failing to respond on time can result in a default judgment. This means the plaintiff automatically wins, even if the defendant has valid defenses. Default judgments can be difficult and sometimes impossible to undo.

The Discovery Phase

After the initial filings, the case typically enters discovery. This phase allows both sides to gather information, request documents, and take sworn testimony. Discovery is where most cases are won or lost.

Common discovery tools include:

Interrogatories: Written questions that must be answered under oath. These might ask about witnesses, documents, facts, or the opposing party's version of events.

Requests for Production: Formal demands for documents, emails, photographs, contracts, financial records, or other physical evidence relevant to the case.

Depositions: In-person questioning under oath, recorded by a court reporter. Lawyers ask detailed questions, and the answers can be used later at trial. Depositions can last hours or even days.

Requests for Admission: Statements that one party asks the other to admit or deny. If admitted, those facts are established and cannot be disputed later.

Discovery can be time-consuming and expensive. Attorneys spend hours reviewing documents, preparing questions, and attending depositions. In complex cases, discovery can stretch on for months or even years.

The information exchanged during discovery often determines whether a case settles or proceeds to trial. Strong evidence uncovered during discovery can push one side to settle. Weak evidence may lead a party to reconsider their position.

Motions and Court Procedures

As the case moves forward, parties may file motions asking the court to make decisions on specific issues. Common motions include:

Motion to Dismiss: Argues that even if everything the plaintiff alleges is true, there is no legal basis for the lawsuit. Courts grant these motions when the complaint fails to state a valid legal claim.

Motion for Summary Judgment: Argues that there are no factual disputes requiring a trial and that one party should win as a matter of law. These motions are supported by evidence from discovery and are decided by the judge, not a jury.

Motion to Compel: Asks the court to force the other party to respond to discovery requests they have ignored or inadequately answered.

Motion in Limine: Requests that certain evidence be excluded from trial because it is irrelevant, prejudicial, or inadmissible under the rules of evidence.

At every stage, strict procedural rules apply. Courts impose deadlines for filings, require specific formats for documents, and enforce rules about how evidence can be presented. Missing deadlines, filing incorrect paperwork, or failing to follow court orders can seriously damage a case or end it entirely.

This is one reason why most people hire attorneys for civil cases outside small claims court. The procedural requirements are complex, and mistakes can be costly.

Settlements vs. Trials

Despite popular portrayals in movies and television, trials are the exception rather than the rule. Studies show that more than 90 percent of civil cases end in settlement, where the parties agree to resolve the dispute without a judge or jury deciding the outcome.

Why Cases Settle

Settlements happen for practical reasons. Both sides face uncertainty, expense, and delay if they go to trial. Even a party with a strong case must consider the risks.

Trials are unpredictable. Witnesses may perform poorly. Evidence may be excluded. Judges or juries may interpret facts differently than expected. A case that seems winnable can result in a devastating loss.

Trials are also expensive. Attorney fees, expert witness costs, court reporter fees, and other expenses add up quickly. A trial that lasts several days can cost tens of thousands of dollars or more in legal fees alone.

Trials take time. It is not unusual for a case to take two or three years from filing to trial, sometimes longer in busy court systems. For individuals and businesses, this delay creates uncertainty and stress.

Settlement negotiations can occur at any point in a lawsuit. Some cases settle quickly, before discovery even begins. Others settle on the eve of trial, after both sides have invested significant time and money.

Advantages of Settlement

Settlements offer several advantages over trials:

Predictability and Control: The parties decide the outcome rather than leaving it to a judge or jury. They can craft creative solutions that a court might not be able to order.

Lower Legal Costs: Settling before trial avoids the enormous expense of trial preparation and courtroom time.

Faster Resolution: Settlement ends the case immediately, while trials can be delayed for months or years.

Privacy: Settlement agreements are often confidential. The terms do not become public record, and the parties can agree not to discuss the case.

Finality: Settlement agreements usually include a release, meaning neither party can sue the other again over the same dispute. This provides closure and allows both sides to move forward.

Preservation of Relationships: In disputes between business partners, neighbors, or family members, settlement may preserve relationships that a trial would destroy.

Advantages of Going to Trial

Trials also offer benefits that settlements cannot provide:

Public Decision and Vindication: A trial results in a formal determination of fault and responsibility. For some parties, public vindication matters more than money.

Possibility of Higher Awards: Juries sometimes award larger damages than a defendant would agree to pay in settlement, particularly in personal injury or wrongful death cases.

Clear Legal Precedent: Trial decisions can establish legal principles and protect rights beyond the immediate case.

Enforcement Through Court Orders: A judgment from a trial can be enforced through the power of the court, including contempt sanctions for noncompliance.

Deterrence: A trial and public judgment may deter the defendant or others from similar conduct in the future.

Making the Choice

Choosing between settlement and trial depends on multiple factors:

- The strength of the evidence and legal arguments
- The costs of continuing the case versus settling
- The importance of the issues at stake
- Each party's tolerance for risk and uncertainty
- Time pressures and the need for resolution
- The likelihood of collecting on a judgment
- The parties' personal or business goals

Both options involve trade-offs. Settlements require compromise, and neither side typically gets everything they want. Trials involve uncertainty, expense, emotional stress, and delay. Even a strong case carries risk when placed in the hands of a judge or jury.

Experienced attorneys help clients weigh these factors realistically. They assess the strength of the case, estimate costs, and provide guidance on whether settlement offers are reasonable given the circumstances.

Understanding the Stakes

Civil lawsuits have real consequences. Money damages awarded in a lawsuit must be paid. Court orders must be followed. Judgments can affect credit ratings, result in wage garnishment, or lead to liens on property.

For defendants, losing a lawsuit can mean financial hardship, especially if the judgment is large and insurance does not cover it. For plaintiffs, winning a lawsuit does not always result in recovery if the defendant lacks assets.

Understanding these realities helps parties make better decisions about whether to file, how to respond, and when to settle.

Common Mistakes to Avoid

Many people lose civil cases not because they are wrong, but because they misunderstand the process or fail to act in time. Common mistakes include:

Ignoring Court Papers: Failing to respond to a lawsuit results in default judgment. Always respond, even if you think the lawsuit has no merit.

Missing Deadlines: Courts strictly enforce filing deadlines. Missing one can mean losing important rights or defenses.

Destroying Evidence: Throwing away documents, deleting emails, or discarding physical evidence can lead to severe penalties, including automatic loss of the case.

Talking About the Case: Discussing your case on social media or with third parties can create evidence that hurts your position. Assume anything you say or post can be used against you.

Representing Yourself in Complex Cases: While self-representation works in small claims court, it rarely succeeds in higher courts with complex procedures and rules.

Failing to Preserve Evidence: Document everything as soon as a dispute arises. Take photographs, save emails, keep receipts, and gather witness information before memories fade.

Making Unrealistic Demands: Refusing reasonable settlement offers based on emotion rather than legal reality can backfire badly.

The Role of Attorneys

Most civil lawsuits outside small claims court require professional legal help. Attorneys understand court procedures, know how to gather and present evidence, and can negotiate effectively on your behalf.

Finding the right attorney matters. Look for someone with experience in your type of case. Ask about their track record, fee structure, and communication style. Many attorneys offer free initial consultations.

Legal fees vary widely. Some attorneys charge hourly rates ranging from $150 to $500 or more per hour. Others work on contingency, meaning they take a percentage of any recovery but charge nothing if you lose. Still others charge flat fees for specific services.

Discuss fees clearly from the beginning. Understand what is included, what costs are additional, and how billing works. Get fee agreements in writing.

When Legal Help Is Not Affordable

Not everyone can afford an attorney, but options exist:

Legal Aid Organizations: Provide free legal services to low-income individuals in civil matters. Eligibility requirements vary.

Pro Bono Programs: Some attorneys volunteer their time to help those who cannot afford legal fees.

Law School Clinics: Many law schools operate clinics where supervised students provide free or low-cost legal assistance.

Limited Scope Representation: Some attorneys will handle specific tasks, such as reviewing documents or coaching you on procedures, for a reduced fee rather than taking on the entire case.

Self-Help Resources: Courts often provide forms, instructions, and informational materials for common types of cases.

None of these options guarantees success, but they can provide valuable guidance when full legal representation is not possible.

Why This Chapter Matters

Civil lawsuits are governed by rules that reward preparation, organization, and attention to detail and penalize delay and inaction. Understanding how small claims court works, how civil lawsuits progress, and why settlements are so common allows individuals to approach legal disputes strategically rather than emotionally.

Knowledge reduces fear and empowers people to make informed decisions when the stakes are high. Whether you are considering filing a lawsuit to enforce your rights or have been served with papers requiring a response, understanding the process helps you protect your interests and avoid costly mistakes.

The legal system exists to resolve disputes and protect rights, but it works best for those who understand how to navigate it. This chapter provides that foundation.

PART VII: Immigration Law Basics

14

Immigration Status: Visas, Green Cards, and Citizenship

Immigration law affects millions of people living and working in the United States, yet it is one of the most complex and unforgiving areas of the legal system. Small mistakes, missed deadlines, or misunderstandings can have consequences that last a lifetime. Unlike many other legal issues, immigration problems often cannot be easily fixed after the fact.

For people who are not immigration lawyers, the system can feel deliberately confusing. Terms like "visa," "green card," and "permanent residence" are used interchangeably in casual conversation, but they have very different legal meanings. A misstep based on confusion between these terms can derail years of careful planning, separate families, or end careers.

Whether you are living in the U.S. on a visa, considering applying for permanent residence, or helping a family member navigate the process, understanding the differences between immigration statuses is essential. This chapter explains the basic categories of immigration status: visas, permanent residence, and citizenship. It also clarifies why these distinctions matter in daily life and what can go wrong when people misunderstand the rules.

What Is a Visa?

A visa is permission to enter or remain in the United States for a specific purpose and time period. Visas come in many forms, each with strict conditions attached. Think of a visa as a temporary pass with detailed instructions: you can come in, but only for this reason, only for this long, and only under these rules.

Common Types of Visas

Work visas allow foreign nationals to work for specific employers or in certain fields. Examples include H-1B visas for specialty occupations, L-1 visas for intracompany transfers, and O-1 visas for individuals with extraordinary ability. These visas typically tie the worker to a specific employer. If you lose your job or change employers, you may need to leave the country or apply for a new visa. The process can take months, and there is no guarantee of approval.

Student visas permit foreign nationals to study at approved institutions. F-1 visas are for academic students, while M-1 visas are for vocational programs. Students must maintain full-time enrollment and make satisfactory academic progress. Dropping below the required course load, even for one semester, can result in loss of status. Working without authorization, even a few hours per week, can have serious consequences.

Family-based visas allow relatives of U.S. citizens or permanent residents to visit or live in the United States temporarily or as a step toward permanent residence. Some family visas are intended as temporary visits. Others are part of the process toward obtaining a green card. Understanding which type you have is critical, as the rules and limitations differ significantly.

Visitor visas cover tourists, people visiting family, or individuals attending business meetings. B-1/B-2 visas are the most common in this category. These visas prohibit any form of employment or enrollment in academic programs. Even unpaid work or volunteering can be considered a violation. Business visitors can attend meetings and conferences but cannot perform productive work or receive payment from a U.S. source.

The Temporary Nature of Visas

Visas are temporary by nature. They often restrict employment, length of stay, and travel. For example, a student on an F-1 visa generally cannot work off-campus without specific authorization from U.S. Citizenship and Immigration Services (USCIS). A visitor on a B-2 visa cannot accept employment at all. Violating visa terms, even unintentionally or due to an employer's mistake, can result in loss of status, deportation, or future ineligibility to return.

Many people mistakenly believe that a visa guarantees long-term stay or leads automatically to permanent residence. In reality, each visa has specific rules, and transitions between categories are highly regulated. Overstaying a visa by even one day can trigger bars to reentry that last years or even permanently. Changes in personal circumstances, such as marriage, job loss, or dropping out of school, can affect visa validity and require immediate action.

Understanding Dual Intent

Some visas allow "dual intent," meaning the holder can pursue permanent residence while maintaining temporary status. The H-1B visa and L-1 visa are examples of dual intent visas. Holders of these visas can apply for green cards without jeopardizing their current status.

Other visas do not allow dual intent. For example, F-1 student visas and B-1/B-2 visitor visas are considered non-immigrant visas with no dual intent. Applying for a green card while on certain visas can result in a visa denial or accusation of fraud. Immigration officers may conclude that you misrepresented your intentions when you applied for the visa, which can have serious long-term consequences. Understanding which category applies to you is critical.

What Happens When You Violate Visa Terms

Even minor violations can have major consequences. Common violations include working without authorization, staying beyond the authorized period, or failing to maintain the conditions of your visa category. For example, an F-1 student who drops to part-time status without approval has violated their visa terms, even if they plan to return to full-time enrollment the following semester.

When you violate visa terms, you typically lose your legal status. This can happen immediately or after USCIS formally determines that a violation occurred. Once you are out of status, you may be subject to removal proceedings. You may also become ineligible for future visas or immigration benefits. Some violations trigger three-year or ten-year bars to reentry, even if you leave voluntarily.

Common Visa Mistakes

One common mistake is assuming that having a valid visa stamp in your passport means you have valid status. The visa stamp allows you to enter the United States, but your status inside the country is controlled by the terms of your admission and your I-94 arrival/departure record. You can have a valid visa but be out of status if you violated the terms of your admission.

Another mistake is failing to track expiration dates carefully. Many people focus on the expiration date of their visa stamp and forget about the expiration date on their I-94 or the expiration of their authorized stay. Missing these deadlines, even by a day or two, can trigger serious consequences.

People also underestimate how quickly their circumstances can change. A job offer, a marriage proposal, or a family emergency can all create immigration complications. What seems like a simple decision (accepting a new job, getting married, taking a semester off) can have immigration consequences that are not immediately obvious.

What Is a Green Card?

A green card grants lawful permanent residence. Green card holders may live and work in the United States indefinitely without needing to renew permission every few years. However, they are not citizens and do not have all the rights and protections that citizenship provides.

Responsibilities of Green Card Holders

Permanent residents must meet several ongoing requirements to maintain their status.

Maintain continuous residence. This means making the U.S. your primary home. Taking extended trips abroad, especially for six months or longer, can raise questions about whether you have abandoned your residency. Immigration officers look at factors like where you work, where your family lives, where you pay taxes, and where you maintain a home. Even if you return within six months, a pattern of spending more time abroad than in the United States can lead to questions about your intent to maintain permanent residence.

If you need to travel abroad for extended periods, you can apply for a reentry permit before you leave. A reentry permit allows you to remain outside the United States for up to two years without abandoning your residence. However, the permit does not guarantee that you will be admitted when you return. Immigration officers can still question whether you truly maintained your residence.

Avoid certain criminal convictions. Even minor offenses can trigger removal proceedings for permanent residents. Crimes involving moral turpitude, drug offenses, domestic violence, and many other convictions can put a green card at risk. The immigration consequences of a criminal conviction are often far more serious than the criminal penalties themselves.

A conviction that results in probation or a small fine in criminal court can result in deportation in immigration court. This is true even for offenses that occurred years ago. Green card holders are sometimes arrested and placed in removal proceedings based on convictions from decades earlier.

Some crimes make you deportable. Others make you inadmissible, which can affect your ability to travel and return to the United States. Still others can affect your eligibility to naturalize. It is critical to understand the immigration consequences of any criminal charge before you plead guilty or go to trial. An immigration attorney should be consulted in addition to a criminal defense attorney.

Comply with tax and reporting obligations. Green card holders are considered U.S. tax residents and must report worldwide income to the IRS, even if they live or work abroad temporarily. Failing to file tax returns or pay required taxes can affect your ability to naturalize. It can also result in civil and criminal penalties.

Green card holders must also carry proof of their status at all times. The physical green card is proof of your lawful permanent resident status. If you lose your card, you must apply for a replacement. Failing to carry evidence of your status is a misdemeanor, though it is rarely prosecuted on its own.

How to Obtain a Green Card

Green cards can be obtained through several pathways.

Family relationships are the most common way people obtain green cards. U.S. citizens can sponsor spouses, children, parents, and siblings. Lawful permanent residents can sponsor spouses and unmarried children. The process and wait times vary significantly depending on the relationship and the country of origin.

Immediate relatives of U.S. citizens (spouses, unmarried children under 21, and parents) are not subject to numerical limits, so green cards are generally available without long waits. Other family categories are subject to annual limits, and wait times can range from a few years to more than a decade, depending on the category and country.

Employment is another common pathway. Employers can sponsor foreign workers for permanent residence if they can demonstrate that no qualified U.S. workers are available for the position. The process is complex and expensive, often requiring labor certification from the Department of Labor before the green card application can proceed. Certain categories of workers, such as those with extraordinary ability or advanced degrees in certain fields, may qualify for green cards without employer sponsorship.

Humanitarian programs provide green cards to refugees, asylees, victims of certain crimes, victims of trafficking, and other vulnerable populations. These programs have specific eligibility requirements and application procedures.

The diversity visa lottery allocates a limited number of green cards each year to individuals from countries with low rates of immigration to the United States. Winners are selected randomly, but they must still meet all eligibility requirements and pass background checks.

Other pathways include investment-based green cards (EB-5 visas), special immigrant categories for religious workers and certain other groups, and special programs like the registry provision for long-term residents.

Conditional Green Cards

Some green cards are conditional, meaning they are valid for only two years and require additional steps to remove conditions. For example, green cards obtained through marriage to a U.S. citizen within two years of the marriage are conditional. The couple must jointly petition to remove those conditions before the card expires. If they fail to file the petition on time, the green card becomes invalid and the foreign spouse can be placed in removal proceedings.

The requirement to file jointly creates problems when marriages end in divorce or when there is abuse in the relationship. There are waivers available for people who can demonstrate that the marriage was entered in good faith but ended, or that removal of conditions should be granted due to extreme hardship or abuse. These waivers require substantial evidence and are often difficult to obtain.

Conditional green cards are also issued to some investors and entrepreneurs. The conditions must be removed by demonstrating that the required investment was made and maintained, and that the required jobs were created.

How Permanent Residence Can Be Lost

Permanent residence can be lost in several ways. Extended travel abroad, certain crimes, immigration violations, or even failing to file the paperwork to remove conditions on a conditional green card can place status at risk. Unlike a visa, which simply expires, losing a green card often involves formal removal proceedings and can result in being barred from reentering the U.S. for years.

Green card holders who are placed in removal proceedings have the right to a hearing before an immigration judge. They may be eligible for relief from removal, such as cancellation of removal or asylum, but eligibility requirements are strict and the burden of proof is high.

Some permanent residents voluntarily relinquish their green cards. This might happen if they decide to live permanently in another country and no longer wish to maintain U.S. tax obligations and other responsibilities. Relinquishing a green card is a formal process that involves filing specific paperwork. Simply staying abroad for extended periods does not formally terminate your status, but it can result in a determination that you abandoned your residence.

Limitations of Permanent Residence

Green card holders cannot vote in federal elections. They cannot serve on juries in most jurisdictions. They cannot hold certain government jobs, particularly those requiring security clearances or involving sensitive national security functions. They can be deported for conduct that would not result in consequences for a U.S. citizen.

Permanent residents are also subject to the public charge ground of inadmissibility if they leave the United States and seek to return. This means that if immigration officers determine that you are likely to become primarily dependent on the government for support, you can be denied reentry. This is less common for established permanent residents, but it can be an issue for those who have been outside the United States for extended periods or who have significant changes in their circumstances.

While permanent residence offers far more stability than a visa, it is not as secure as citizenship. Green card holders live with the knowledge that their status can be taken away under certain circumstances. For many, naturalization is the next logical step.

What Is U.S. Citizenship?

U.S. citizenship is the most secure immigration status. Citizens have the right to vote, hold certain public offices, serve on juries, and receive full constitutional protections. They cannot be deported, and their status cannot be easily revoked.

How Citizenship Is Obtained

Citizenship is typically obtained in three ways.

Birth in the United States. Any person born on U.S. soil is automatically a U.S. citizen, with very limited exceptions. This is guaranteed by the Fourteenth Amendment to the Constitution. It does not matter whether the parents are citizens, permanent residents, visa holders, or undocumented immigrants. The child is a U.S. citizen from birth.

The only exceptions involve children born to foreign diplomats and children born to members of invading armies during wartime. These exceptions are extremely rare.

Birth abroad to U.S. citizen parents. Children born outside the United States may acquire citizenship at birth if one or both parents are U.S. citizens and meet certain residency requirements. The rules are complex and depend on whether one or both parents are citizens, whether the parents are married, and how long the citizen parent lived in the United States before the child's birth.

Naturalization after meeting residency and eligibility requirements. Foreign nationals who have been lawful permanent residents for a certain period can apply to become citizens through naturalization. This is the most common way immigrants become U.S. citizens.

The Naturalization Process

Naturalization typically requires that you have been a lawful permanent resident for at least five years. If you are married to a U.S. citizen, the requirement is reduced to three years, provided you have been living in marital union with your citizen spouse for the entire three-year period.

You must demonstrate continuous residence in the United States. This means you must not have taken trips abroad that break the continuity of your residence. Generally, any single trip of six months or longer is presumed to break continuous residence, though you can overcome this presumption with evidence. Any trip of one year or longer will definitively break continuous residence unless you obtained permission in advance.

You must also demonstrate physical presence in the United States for at least half of the required residency period. This means you must have been physically present for at least 30 months out of the five years preceding your application (or 18 months out of three years if applying based on marriage to a U.S. citizen).

You must demonstrate good moral character. This is a broad and somewhat subjective requirement. USCIS looks at your criminal history, tax compliance, financial responsibility, and whether you have been truthful in your dealings with the government. Certain crimes will automatically bar a finding of good moral character. Others will require you to demonstrate rehabilitation and the passage of time.

You must demonstrate knowledge of U.S. history and government. Applicants must pass a civics test covering American history, government structure, and constitutional principles. The test is administered orally, and you must answer six out of ten questions correctly. Study materials are available from USCIS.

You must demonstrate an ability to read, write, and speak basic English. There are exceptions based on age and length of residence. If you are over 50 years old and have been a permanent resident for at least 20 years, or if you are over 55 and have been a permanent resident for at least 15 years, you may take the civics test in your native language. If you are over 65 and have been a permanent resident for at least 20 years, you may take a simplified version of the civics test in your native language.

You must demonstrate attachment to the principles of the U.S. Constitution and be willing to take an oath of allegiance to the United States. During the naturalization interview, you will be asked whether you are willing to bear arms on behalf of the United States or perform noncombatant service. There are exceptions for those with religious or conscientious objections.

The Documentation and Review Process

The naturalization process is detailed and documentation-heavy. You must submit tax returns, travel records, employment history, addresses for the past five years, and extensive information about your background. Background checks are thorough, and even old issues like unpaid taxes, minor criminal convictions, or previous immigration violations can delay or derail an application.

USCIS conducts FBI fingerprint checks, name checks, and reviews of immigration and criminal records. If anything concerning appears, your application may be delayed for months or even years while USCIS investigates. You have a right to request information about the status of your background check if your case has been pending for an unreasonable length of time.

During the naturalization interview, an immigration officer will review your application, test your knowledge of English and civics, and ask questions about your background and eligibility. The officer has broad discretion to ask follow-up questions about anything in your application or anything that comes up during the interview.

If your application is approved, you will be scheduled for a naturalization ceremony where you will take the oath of allegiance and receive your certificate of naturalization. You are not a U.S. citizen until you take the oath. The ceremony may take place on the same day as your interview or may be scheduled for a later date.

The Security of Citizenship

Once obtained, citizenship is difficult to revoke, making it the strongest form of legal status. Denaturalization can occur in rare cases involving fraud in the application process or concealment of disqualifying facts, but the government must meet a high burden of proof. For most naturalized citizens, citizenship is permanent and offers complete protection from immigration enforcement.

Denaturalization cases typically involve situations where the applicant lied about criminal history, concealed participation in human rights violations or war crimes, obtained citizenship through a fraudulent marriage, or was not actually eligible at the time of naturalization. The government must prove its case by clear and convincing evidence, and in some cases involving very serious conduct, the standard is beyond a reasonable doubt.

Even if the government succeeds in denaturalizing someone, that person typically returns to the status of lawful permanent resident rather than being immediately deported, unless the green card itself was also fraudulently obtained.

Benefits of Citizenship

Citizens can sponsor family members for immigration benefits more easily than permanent residents. U.S. citizens can sponsor spouses, children, parents, and siblings, while permanent residents can only sponsor spouses and unmarried children. Immediate relatives of U.S. citizens are not subject to numerical limits or long wait times.

Citizens can live abroad indefinitely without risking their status. Unlike permanent residents, who must maintain continuous residence in the United States, citizens can live and work anywhere in the world without losing their citizenship.

Citizens can pass citizenship to their children born abroad under certain conditions. The rules are complex and depend on the parent's residency history, but many children born to U.S. citizens abroad acquire citizenship automatically at birth.

Citizens have full voting rights in all elections, federal, state, and local. They can run for public office (except for the presidency and vice presidency, which require natural-born citizenship). They can obtain U.S. passports and receive protection from U.S. embassies and consulates abroad.

Citizens are eligible for federal jobs and security clearances that are not available to non-citizens. They can serve on juries, which is both a right and a civic duty. They cannot be denied entry to the United States or deported under any circumstances, short of denaturalization for fraud.

Why This Chapter Matters

Immigration status affects employment, family unity, education, travel, and access to benefits. The wrong status, or a misunderstanding of the limits of your current status, can prevent you from accepting a job, enrolling in school, traveling to see family, or accessing public services.

The Employment Consequences of Immigration Status

Your immigration status determines whether you can work and for whom. Visa holders are often restricted to specific employers or types of work.

Accepting a job outside the scope of your visa, even if the new employer is willing to sponsor you, can result in loss of status. Permanent residents can work for any employer, but certain government jobs and positions requiring security clearances may be unavailable. Only citizens have completely unrestricted employment rights.

The Family Consequences of Immigration Status

Immigration status affects your ability to live with family members. If you are on a temporary visa and your status changes, your spouse and children may lose their derivative status. If you lose your job, your entire family may need to leave the country. If you are a permanent resident and want to sponsor a family member, you may face long wait times. Only citizens can sponsor the full range of family members with the shortest wait times.

The Education Consequences of Immigration Status

Students must maintain valid status to continue their studies. Dropping below full-time enrollment, changing schools without authorization, or working without permission can all result in loss of status. Children of visa holders may face challenges accessing in-state tuition or financial aid. Permanent residents and citizens have far more flexibility and access to educational benefits.

The Travel Consequences of Immigration Status

Your ability to travel in and out of the United States depends on your immigration status. Visa holders may have restrictions on travel and may risk denial of reentry if they travel for too long or to certain countries. Permanent residents who travel for extended periods may be questioned about whether they abandoned their residence. Only citizens can travel freely without any risk to their status.

The Consequences of Immigration Mistakes

Mistakes can lead to denial of applications, removal from the United States, or permanent bars to reentry. Some immigration violations trigger automatic bars that prevent individuals from returning for three years, ten years, or even permanently, with very limited exceptions.

For example, if you overstay a visa by more than 180 days but less than one year, and then leave the United States, you are subject to a three-year bar. If you overstay by one year or more, the bar is ten years. These bars apply even if you leave voluntarily and even if you have a family member who wants to sponsor you.

Other violations can make someone ineligible for future benefits, even if they leave voluntarily. Fraud or misrepresentation in an immigration application can result in a permanent bar. Certain criminal convictions can make someone permanently inadmissible.

Some mistakes can be waived under certain circumstances, but waivers are difficult to obtain and require a showing of extreme hardship to a qualifying relative. The level of hardship must be well above what would normally be expected from separation. Economic hardship alone is typically not enough.

The Importance of Accurate Information

Understanding visas, green cards, and citizenship helps individuals make informed decisions, avoid unnecessary risks, and recognize when professional legal help is essential. Immigration law does not reward good intentions or honest mistakes. It rewards careful planning, attention to detail, and timely action.

Many people navigate the immigration system with the help of family members, friends, or online resources. While these can be helpful starting points, immigration law is dense, constantly changing, and full of exceptions. What worked for one person may not apply to another. A relative who successfully obtained a green card ten years ago may not know that the rules have changed. An online forum may provide general information but cannot account for your specific circumstances.

Professional legal guidance is often the difference between success and a life-altering mistake. Immigration attorneys are trained to spot issues that non-lawyers might miss. They understand how different parts of the immigration system interact and can help you plan a path forward that accounts for your long-term goals.

When to Seek Legal Help

You should consider seeking legal help if you are facing removal proceedings, if you have any criminal history, if you have overstayed a visa or violated immigration law in the past, if your application has been denied, or if you are attempting a complex immigration process like adjustment of status or naturalization.

You should also seek legal help if you are unsure whether you are eligible for a particular benefit, if you have been asked to attend an interview at a USCIS office or immigration court, or if you have received any official correspondence from immigration authorities that you do not fully understand.

Immigration attorneys can review your situation, identify potential problems, and develop a strategy to address them. They can help you gather evidence, prepare applications, and represent you in interviews or court proceedings. While hiring an attorney involves expense, the cost of a mistake can be far higher.

Looking Ahead

This chapter has provided an overview of the three main categories of immigration status: visas, permanent residence, and citizenship. Each category has different rights, responsibilities, and limitations. Understanding these distinctions is essential for anyone navigating the U.S. immigration system.

The next chapter examines common immigration problems and enforcement issues, where legal guidance can be especially critical. It will cover topics like removal proceedings, detention, immigration court, and the consequences of immigration violations. Understanding what can go wrong and how the enforcement system works is an important part of protecting yourself and your family.

15

Common Immigration Problems

Immigration problems often arise quietly, through a missed deadline, an unexpected job change, or a misunderstanding about status. By the time a person realizes something is wrong, the consequences may already be serious. Unlike many areas of law, immigration violations can have permanent effects, even when there was no intent to break the rules.

The immigration system does not distinguish between honest mistakes and deliberate violations. It does not care if you misread a date on your visa, if your employer gave you bad advice, or if you were following instructions from a well-meaning friend. The system operates on strict timelines, rigid requirements, and harsh penalties. A single day can be the difference between maintaining legal status and triggering a multi-year ban from the United States.

For many people, immigration problems start small. A student works a few hours off-campus without realizing they need special authorization. A worker stays a week past their visa expiration because they thought the departure date on their plane ticket was what mattered. A parent brings their child to a scheduled immigration appointment but accidentally misses a separate notice to appear in court. Each of these situations can spiral into serious consequences that affect employment, family unity, and the ability to remain in or return to the United States.

This chapter addresses some of the most common immigration problems, explains how they happen, and why early action is critical. Recognizing a problem early, before it becomes unsolvable, can make all the difference.

Overstays

An overstay occurs when a person remains in the United States beyond the authorized period of their visa or admission. This can happen unintentionally, especially when entry dates, extensions, or status changes are misunderstood.

Understanding the Dates That Matter

Many people assume their visa expiration date is the same as the date they must leave the country. This is not always true. The date stamped on the visa itself may differ from the "admit until" date marked in the passport or on the electronic I-94 arrival/departure record. Confusing these dates is one of the most common reasons for accidental overstays.

The visa in your passport shows when the visa expires, meaning the last date you can use that visa to request entry into the United States. But once you are admitted, what matters is the date on your I-94 form, which shows how long you are authorized to stay. You can check your I-94 online at the official government website. Failing to do this before your stay expires is a mistake that catches many people off guard.

For example, imagine you have a tourist visa valid for ten years. You arrive in the United States in January, and your visa itself does not expire until 2034. However, when you enter, the border officer stamps your passport or creates an electronic I-94 record that says you are admitted until July of the same year. If you stay past July, you have overstayed, even though your visa itself is still valid. The visa allows you to apply for entry, but the I-94 controls how long you can remain.

Overstays During Pending Applications

Other overstays happen because of processing delays. A person files for an extension or change of status before their current authorization expires, but the application takes months to process. In some cases, the person is allowed to remain while the application is pending. In other cases, they are not. The rules depend on the specific visa type and timing, and many people do not realize they have overstayed until they check their status or try to travel.

For certain visa categories, filing an extension before your status expires creates what is called a "period of authorized stay" while the application is reviewed. For other categories, there is no such protection, and remaining in the United States while the application is pending may constitute unlawful presence. Knowing which rule applies to your visa category is essential, but many people make assumptions based on what worked for a friend or what they read online without verifying it applies to their specific situation.

What Happens When You Overstay

Overstays can trigger a range of severe consequences, depending on how long you remain unlawfully present in the United States.

Loss of lawful status: Once you overstay, you are unlawfully present in the United States. This means you are vulnerable to removal proceedings and cannot legally work or travel internationally without risking being unable to return. Your status is no longer valid, and you lose the protections that came with your visa.

Bars on future reentry: The most serious consequence of overstaying is the reentry bar that applies once you leave the United States. If you overstay by more than 180 days but less than one year and then leave the U.S., you face a three-year bar on returning. If you overstay by one year or more, the bar is ten years. These bars apply even if you leave voluntarily, and they prevent you from obtaining a visa or green card during the ban period. There is no way to simply pay a fine and make the problem go away. The bar is automatic, and it begins the moment you depart the United States.

Ineligibility for certain benefits or adjustments: Overstays make it much harder to adjust status to permanent residence, extend your visa, or change to a different visa category. Some immigration benefits become completely unavailable after an overstay. For example, if you overstay and then try to adjust your status to a green card based on a family petition or employment offer, your overstay may disqualify you from adjusting status while remaining in the United States. You may be forced to leave the country to process your application abroad, which then triggers the three-year or ten-year bar.

Even short overstays can complicate future immigration applications. A visa officer reviewing a new application years later may ask why you overstayed previously. Even a brief overstay can be interpreted as a lack of respect for immigration law, which can influence decisions on future applications. Visa officers have wide discretion, and any negative mark in your immigration history can become a reason to deny a future petition.

The 180-Day Rule and Unlawful Presence

It is important to understand that not all time spent in the United States beyond your authorized period counts as "unlawful presence" for purposes of the reentry bars. Unlawful presence generally begins the day after your I-94 expires or the day USCIS formally denies your application to extend or change status, whichever comes first.

For individuals under the age of 18, time spent unlawfully present does not count toward the three-year or ten-year bars. Similarly, individuals who had bona fide asylum applications pending were previously exempt from accruing unlawful presence, though recent policy changes have limited this protection.

These exceptions are narrow, and most people who overstay begin accruing unlawful presence immediately. Once you hit 180 days of unlawful presence, leaving the United States triggers the three-year bar. Once you hit one year, the ten-year bar applies. There is no prorating or reduction for partial years.

Waivers and Exceptions

Certain waivers exist for the three-year and ten-year bars, but they require proving extreme hardship to a U.S. citizen or lawful permanent resident spouse or parent. This is a high legal standard that is difficult to meet. Extreme hardship means more than the normal hardship that any family would experience from separation. It requires showing that your qualifying relative would suffer consequences that go far beyond what is typical.

Financial hardship alone is usually not enough. Medical conditions, the inability to relocate to your home country, psychological harm, or country conditions that would place your family member in danger may support a hardship claim, but these claims require substantial documentation, including medical records, psychological evaluations, country condition reports, and affidavits.

The waiver process itself can take many months or even years, and approval is not guaranteed. Filing for a waiver does not stop the clock on your reentry bar. If your waiver is denied, you remain barred from the United States for the remainder of the three-year or ten-year period.

What to Do If You Realize You Have Overstayed

Because overstay consequences depend on timing, intent, and specific visa categories, addressing the issue early can sometimes limit damage. If you realize you have overstayed, or if your authorized stay is about to expire and you need more time, consulting an immigration attorney immediately may preserve options that disappear once you become unlawfully present.

Do not assume that because you overstayed by only a few days or weeks, the problem will not matter. Do not wait to see what happens. Do not book international travel hoping the issue will not be noticed. Overstays are tracked electronically, and immigration officers will see the overstay on your record.

If you are still in the United States and have not yet accrued 180 days of unlawful presence, leaving immediately may prevent the three-year or ten-year bar from applying. If you have already accrued significant unlawful presence, leaving may trigger the bar, but staying longer only makes the problem worse. An attorney can help you evaluate your options, determine whether you qualify for any relief, and advise you on the least damaging course of action.

Work Authorization

Many immigration statuses restrict employment. Work authorization determines whether, where, and how someone may legally work in the United States. This is not an automatic right for most non-citizens, and the rules are strict and inflexible.

Understanding whether you are authorized to work, what type of work you can do, and how long your authorization lasts is essential to maintaining lawful status. Violating work authorization rules can have consequences that extend far beyond losing a job.

Common Work Authorization Problems

Working without authorization: Some visas, like tourist visas (B-1/B-2), do not permit any employment. Working while on one of these visas, even for a family member or for cash, is a violation that can result in removal and permanent ineligibility for future visas. It does not matter if the work was temporary, part-time, or unpaid. It does not matter if you were helping out a relative or doing a favor for a friend. If the activity would normally be compensated, it counts as unauthorized employment.

Continuing to work after authorization expires: Many people have work authorization tied to a specific document, such as an Employment Authorization Document (EAD), that expires on a set date. Continuing to work even one day past expiration is unauthorized employment, even if a renewal application is pending. Unlike some visa categories that allow you to remain in the United States while an extension is pending, work authorization does not automatically extend. Once your EAD expires, you must stop working immediately unless you have received a new EAD or qualify for an automatic extension under very specific circumstances.

Assuming a visa automatically permits employment: Some people assume that because they are legally in the United States on a valid visa, they can accept any job. This is not true. Student visa holders (F-1), for example, can only work on-campus or with specific off-campus authorization such as Curricular Practical Training (CPT) or Optional Practical Training (OPT). Working off-campus without authorization, even for a few hours per week, violates the terms of the student visa and can result in termination of status and removal from the United States.

Dependent spouses on certain visas cannot work at all unless they obtain separate work authorization. For example, spouses of H-1B visa holders must apply for an H-4 EAD if they want to work, and not all H-4 spouses are eligible. Spouses of F-1 students on F-2 visas cannot work at all, even with an EAD. Taking a job without understanding these restrictions can destroy your immigration status.

The Myth of Cash Work and "Under the Table" Jobs

Some people believe that working "under the table" or for cash avoids detection. This is incorrect. Employment history can be uncovered through tax records, background checks, social media, or statements made in immigration interviews. Immigration officers are trained to ask detailed questions about how you supported yourself during your time in the United States. If your bank records show deposits that cannot be explained, or if your tax returns do not match your claimed source of income, this will raise red flags.

Even unpaid internships or volunteer work in certain fields may count as unauthorized employment if they would normally be paid positions. If you are performing work that displaces a paid employee, or if you are in a position that would typically result in compensation, immigration authorities may consider it unauthorized employment regardless of whether you actually received money.

Employer Obligations and Consequences

Employers also face penalties for hiring unauthorized workers, which is why documentation and compliance are closely scrutinized. Employers must verify work authorization for all new hires using Form I-9 and the E-Verify system. Employers who knowingly hire or continue to employ unauthorized workers can face fines, criminal charges, and loss of business licenses. This means that even if you are willing to risk your own immigration status, most employers will not take that risk.

Many employers now use E-Verify, an online system that checks employment eligibility against government databases. If your work authorization has expired, E-Verify will flag the discrepancy, and the employer will be required to terminate your employment. Attempting to use false documents or someone else's work authorization is immigration fraud, which can result in criminal prosecution and permanent bars from immigration benefits.

Consequences of Unauthorized Employment

Unauthorized employment can jeopardize current status and future applications, even if the work was short-term, unpaid, or arranged informally. Immigration officers view unauthorized employment as a serious violation of the terms of admission, and it can be used as evidence of bad moral character in future applications, including applications for permanent residence or citizenship.

If you work without authorization and later apply for a green card, the immigration officer reviewing your application will ask about your employment history. Lying about unauthorized employment is fraud, which carries even more severe penalties. Admitting to unauthorized employment may disqualify you from certain forms of relief or adjustment of status.

For individuals in removal proceedings, unauthorized employment can be used as evidence that you violated the terms of your visa and should be removed from the United States. It can also undermine claims that you deserve discretionary relief, such as cancellation of removal, because it shows a disregard for immigration law.

What Counts as Work Authorization

Not all visas come with work authorization, and not all work authorization is the same. Some common categories include:

Employment Authorization Documents (EADs): These are cards issued by USCIS that grant permission to work for any employer in the United States. EADs are issued to certain categories of immigrants, including asylum seekers, DACA recipients, adjustment of status applicants, and spouses of certain visa holders. EADs have expiration dates, and you must renew them before they expire to maintain continuous work authorization.

Visa-specific work authorization: Certain visas, such as H-1B, L-1, O-1, and TN visas, allow the holder to work, but only for the specific employer who petitioned for the visa. Changing employers requires filing a new petition. Working for anyone other than the petitioning employer is unauthorized employment.

Student work authorization: F-1 students can work on-campus up to 20 hours per week during the school year and full-time during breaks. Off-campus work requires specific authorization, such as CPT (Curricular Practical Training) or OPT (Optional Practical Training). CPT must be related to the student's major and authorized by the school. OPT is available after completing a degree program and allows up to 12 months of work authorization, with extensions available for STEM degree holders.

Self-employment: In most cases, work authorization allows you to be self-employed or work as an independent contractor. However, certain visa categories, such as H-1B, do not permit self-employment. If you hold an H-1B visa, you can only work for the employer listed on your petition, and you cannot freelance or start your own business without obtaining separate authorization.

What to Do If Your Work Authorization Is Expiring

If you are unsure whether your current status allows you to work, or if your work authorization is about to expire, do not wait. Acting before your authorization lapses can prevent violations that close doors permanently.

If your EAD is expiring, file for a renewal at least 180 days before the expiration date if possible. USCIS processing times can be unpredictable, and waiting until the last minute may result in a gap in work authorization. Some categories of EAD holders qualify for automatic extensions of up to 180 days if they file a timely renewal, but not all categories qualify, and you must meet specific requirements.

If you are on a visa that ties your work authorization to a specific employer and you want to change jobs, consult an immigration attorney before accepting a new offer. Depending on your visa type, changing employers may require filing a new petition, and you may not be able to start working for the new employer until the petition is approved.

If you have lost your job and your work authorization was tied to that employer, understand that your status may be in jeopardy. For example, if you are on an H-1B visa and you are laid off, you typically have a 60-day grace period to find a new employer and file a new petition, or to change to another status. If you do not take action within that window, you may fall out of status and begin accruing unlawful presence.

Deportation Concerns

Deportation, formally known as removal, is the process by which the government orders a non-citizen to leave the United States. Deportation proceedings can be triggered by immigration violations, criminal charges, or denied applications. Once removal proceedings begin, the person is in immigration court and must defend their right to remain in the United States.

Removal proceedings are among the most serious immigration matters a person can face. The consequences extend beyond being forced to leave the country. A removal order can result in bars from reentering the United States for years or even permanently. It can separate families, end careers, and uproot lives built over decades.

Common Triggers for Removal Proceedings

Visa overstays: As discussed earlier, overstaying a visa can result in removal proceedings, especially if the overstay is discovered during a routine immigration check, airport screening, or application process. Immigration and Customs Enforcement (ICE) prioritizes certain overstays for removal, particularly those involving individuals with criminal records, prior immigration violations, or overstays of significant duration.

Criminal convictions: Even minor criminal offenses can trigger removal proceedings for non-citizens, including lawful permanent residents. Crimes involving moral turpitude, drug offenses (including simple possession of marijuana in some cases), domestic violence, firearms offenses, theft, fraud, and many others can result in deportation. In some cases, a conviction that results in no jail time, a suspended sentence, or a plea deal can still lead to removal.

The immigration consequences of a criminal conviction are often far more severe than the criminal penalty itself. A conviction that results in probation or community service in criminal court can result in mandatory deportation in immigration court. Many non-citizens, including green card holders who have lived in the United States for decades, do not realize that accepting a plea deal can trigger automatic removal with no possibility of relief.

Fraud or misrepresentation: Lying on an immigration application, providing false documents, or concealing material facts can result in removal and a permanent bar from obtaining future immigration benefits. Even small lies, such as claiming to be single when married, or stating that a prior visa overstay never happened, can have devastating consequences years later. Immigration fraud is taken extremely seriously, and there is often no waiver available for fraud-based removal grounds.

Failure to comply with immigration orders: Missing a court hearing, failing to report an address change, or not appearing for a required interview can result in an automatic removal order. Once an in absentia removal order is issued, it is very difficult to reopen the case. You must show that you did not receive notice of the hearing, or that your failure to appear was due to exceptional circumstances beyond your control, such as a medical emergency or a natural disaster.

Many people miss immigration court hearings because they moved and did not update their address with the court, or because they did not understand the importance of the hearing. Immigration court notices are mailed to the address on file, and if you do not receive the notice because you moved, the court will not know. You are responsible for updating your address within ten days of any move, and failure to do so can result in an in absentia removal order even if you never knew about the hearing.

What Happens in Removal Proceedings

Removal proceedings are complex and adversarial. They take place in immigration court before an immigration judge, with a government attorney arguing that you should be removed. Deadlines are strict, and options for relief may be limited. Unlike criminal cases, there is no right to a free attorney in immigration court. If you cannot afford a lawyer, you must represent yourself.

The government attorney, known as the Assistant Chief Counsel for ICE, will present evidence that you are removable from the United States. This may include evidence of visa overstays, criminal convictions, fraud, or other immigration violations. You will have the opportunity to present evidence and argue that you should be allowed to remain, but the burden of proof is on you to show that you qualify for relief from removal.

Immigration judges have broad discretion, but they are also bound by strict legal standards. Even if a judge is sympathetic to your situation, they cannot grant relief unless you meet the specific legal requirements. Relief from removal is not guaranteed, and many people who go through removal proceedings are ultimately ordered to leave the United States.

Forms of Relief from Removal

Some people facing removal may be eligible for relief, such as cancellation of removal, asylum, adjustment of status, or waivers of inadmissibility. However, these forms of relief have strict eligibility requirements, and proving eligibility often requires extensive documentation, witness testimony, and legal arguments.

Cancellation of removal for permanent residents: Lawful permanent residents who have been convicted of certain crimes may be eligible for cancellation of removal if they have held a green card for at least five years, have resided in the United States continuously for at least seven years, and have not been convicted of an aggravated felony. Even if these requirements are met, the judge has discretion to deny relief based on the severity of the criminal offense or other negative factors.

Cancellation of removal for non-permanent residents: Non-permanent residents who have been physically present in the United States for at least ten years, have good moral character, and can show that their removal would cause exceptional and extremely unusual hardship to a U.S. citizen or permanent resident spouse, parent, or child may qualify for cancellation of removal. This is an extremely high standard, and most applicants are denied.

Asylum: Individuals facing persecution in their home country based on race, religion, nationality, political opinion, or membership in a particular social group may apply for asylum, even if they are in removal proceedings. Asylum applications require proving a well-founded fear of persecution, and the process can take years.

Adjustment of status: In some cases, individuals in removal proceedings may be eligible to adjust their status to permanent residence based on a family petition or employment petition. However, many grounds of inadmissibility and deportability cannot be waived, and adjustment of status is not available to everyone in removal proceedings.

The Notice to Appear

Many people do not realize they are in removal proceedings until they receive a Notice to Appear (NTA), a legal document ordering them to appear in immigration court. The NTA includes the charges against you, the reasons the government believes you are removable, and the date and time of your initial hearing.

Receiving an NTA is a serious matter. It means that the government has decided to begin the process of removing you from the United States, and you now have the burden of proving that you should be allowed to stay. Ignoring an NTA or failing to appear at your hearing will result in an automatic removal order.

Others find out they are in removal proceedings when they try to travel internationally and are stopped at the airport or border. If you have an outstanding removal order, you will not be allowed to leave the United States voluntarily. You will be detained and removed by immigration authorities.

The Impact of Deportation on Families

Deportation affects not only the person facing removal but also their family members, especially U.S. citizen children and spouses. It can separate families, end careers, and uproot lives built over decades. The emotional and financial costs are immense.

U.S. citizen children whose parents are deported face impossible choices. They can remain in the United States without their parents, often in the care of relatives or foster care, or they can leave with their parents to a country they may never have lived in and where they may not speak the language.

Spouses face similar hardships. Even if one spouse is a U.S. citizen, they may not be able to petition for their non-citizen spouse to return to the United States if the deportation was based on certain grounds, such as immigration fraud or aggravated felonies.

The financial impact of deportation can be devastating. Families lose income, homes, and stability. The cost of legal representation, court fees, and travel can drain savings. Many families go into debt trying to fight removal, only to lose the case and face removal anyway.

Leaving Voluntarily vs. Contesting Removal

Once removal proceedings begin, some people consider leaving the United States voluntarily to avoid a formal removal order. Voluntary departure can sometimes preserve future immigration options, because it does not carry the same stigma as a removal order. However, leaving voluntarily can also trigger reentry bars, and it means giving up the chance to fight your case in court.

If you leave the United States while removal proceedings are pending, the court will issue a removal order in absentia. This removal order can carry severe consequences, including bars from returning to the United States for ten years, twenty years, or permanently, depending on the grounds of removal.

Staying to fight the case without legal help can also result in an order of removal that makes it nearly impossible to return. Immigration court is not the place to represent yourself. The law is complex, the procedures are strict, and the stakes are too high. If you are in removal proceedings, you need an attorney.

What to Do If You Are Facing Removal

If you receive a Notice to Appear, or if you believe you may be placed in removal proceedings, do not wait to seek legal help. Immigration law changes frequently, and the options available to you today may not be available tomorrow.

Do not rely on advice from friends, family, or online forums. Immigration law is too complex, and the consequences of making a mistake are too severe. An immigration attorney can evaluate your case, explain your options, and help you build the strongest possible defense.

Do not assume that because you have lived in the United States for a long time, or because you have U.S. citizen family members, you will automatically be allowed to stay. Immigration judges are required to follow the law, and in many cases, the law requires removal even when the result seems unjust.

Do not miss your court hearings. If you cannot attend a hearing because of a medical emergency or another serious reason, contact the court immediately to request a continuance. Missing a hearing will result in an automatic removal order, and reopening the case later is extremely difficult.

How Immigration Problems Intersect with Other Areas of Law

Immigration problems often intersect with criminal law, employment law, and family law, multiplying their impact. What seems like a minor issue can quickly escalate into a life-altering crisis.

Immigration and Criminal Law

The intersection of immigration and criminal law is one of the most dangerous areas for non-citizens. A criminal arrest or conviction can trigger removal proceedings, bars from future immigration benefits, and denial of applications for citizenship.

Many criminal defense attorneys do not fully understand immigration law, and they may not warn their non-citizen clients about the immigration consequences of a guilty plea or conviction. A plea deal that seems favorable in criminal court can be a disaster in immigration court.

For example, a conviction for possession of drug paraphernalia, even if it results in no jail time and is later expunged, can make you deportable and permanently ineligible for a green card or citizenship. A domestic violence conviction, even a misdemeanor, can result in mandatory deportation with no possibility of relief.

Before accepting any plea deal or going to trial on criminal charges, non-citizens should consult with an immigration attorney to understand the potential immigration consequences. In some cases, it may be better to go to trial and risk a harsher criminal sentence than to accept a plea deal that will result in deportation.

Immigration and Employment Law

Employment law and immigration law intersect in complex ways, particularly around work authorization, employer compliance, and discrimination.

Employers are required to verify work authorization for all employees, but they are also prohibited from discriminating against employees based on citizenship status or national origin. Employers cannot refuse to hire someone because they are not a U.S. citizen, as long as the person is authorized to work. Employers also cannot require more documentation from non-citizens than from U.S. citizens.

If you lose your job and your work authorization was tied to that employer, understanding your rights and options under both employment law and immigration law is critical. You may have a limited window to find new employment or change status, and missing that window can result in accruing unlawful presence.

Immigration and Family Law

Family law issues such as divorce, child custody, and domestic violence can have profound immigration consequences.

For individuals whose immigration status is based on marriage to a U.S. citizen or permanent resident, divorce before obtaining permanent residence can jeopardize their status. If you are on a conditional green card and you divorce before the two-year period ends, you may need to file a waiver to have the conditions removed. This waiver requires proving that the marriage was entered into in good faith, or that you were the victim of domestic violence.

Child custody disputes can complicate immigration cases, particularly if one parent is facing removal. Courts may issue orders preventing a parent from taking a child out of the country, which can conflict with removal orders or voluntary departure agreements.

Domestic violence can have both immigration benefits and consequences. Victims of domestic violence may be eligible for immigration relief under the Violence Against Women Act (VAWA) or the U visa program. However, a conviction for domestic violence, even in cases where both parties were arrested or where the charges are later dropped, can result in deportation.

The Importance of Early Action

A single mistake can lead to a chain reaction. An overstay can lead to loss of work authorization, which can lead to financial hardship, which can lead to missed immigration appointments, which can lead to removal proceedings. A minor criminal charge can result in deportation, even for someone who has lived in the United States legally for years.

Understanding common problems such as overstays, work authorization violations, and deportation risks helps individuals recognize danger signs early and seek help before options disappear. Immigration law does not offer second chances easily. Many relief options have time limits or eligibility windows that close once a violation becomes too severe.

Why You Cannot Afford to Wait

Immigration problems do not improve with time. They get worse. Unlawful presence accumulates daily. Work authorization violations become part of your permanent record. Removal orders are enforced.

If you are facing an immigration problem, or if you think you might be, do not ignore it. Do not assume it will go away. Do not rely solely on advice from friends, family, or online forums. Immigration law is too complex, too unforgiving, and too important to navigate without professional help.

The sooner you address an immigration problem, the more options you have. Waiting until you are in removal proceedings, or until you have accrued years of unlawful presence, or until you have been convicted of a crime, limits your options dramatically. In many cases, early intervention can prevent a problem from becoming unsolvable.

Finding the Right Help

Not all immigration help is created equal. In the United States, the term "notario" or "notario público" is often misused to deceive immigrants. While this term refers to licensed legal professionals in many Latin American countries, in the United States a notary public is only authorized to witness signatures and has no legal training. Some dishonest individuals exploit this confusion by advertising as "notarios" to trick people into believing they can provide legal services.

Immigration consultants and document preparers are also not attorneys and cannot provide legal advice or represent you in immigration matters. Many people have lost money, and lost their cases, by trusting unlicensed individuals who promised easy solutions.

If you need immigration help, seek out a licensed attorney who specializes in immigration law. Many attorneys offer consultations, and some work on a sliding scale or offer payment plans. Non-profit legal aid organizations also provide free or low-cost immigration assistance to qualifying individuals.

Check credentials carefully. An attorney should be licensed to practice law and should be a member in good standing of the state bar. You can verify an attorney's credentials online through the state bar website.

Be wary of anyone who guarantees results, promises a quick fix, or asks you to lie on an application. Immigration cases are fact-specific, and no attorney can guarantee an outcome. Any attorney who asks you to provide false information or to misrepresent facts is putting your case, and your future, at risk.

Conclusion

Immigration law is unforgiving. It does not account for good intentions, honest mistakes, or difficult circumstances. It operates on strict deadlines, rigid requirements, and harsh penalties. A single day can mean the difference between maintaining status and facing a multi-year ban. A single conviction can mean the difference between remaining with your family and being deported to a country you barely remember.

But immigration law also offers opportunities for relief, for protection, and for building a life in the United States. Understanding the rules, recognizing problems early, and seeking professional help can make all the difference.

The next chapter shifts to an area of law where federal and state rules often conflict: drugs and marijuana.

PART VIII: Drugs, Marijuana, and State Law Confusion

16

Marijuana Laws in America

Few areas of law cause as much confusion as marijuana. Many people assume that legalization in their state means marijuana is fully legal and risk-free. Others believe it remains illegal everywhere. Both assumptions are wrong. Marijuana law in the United States exists in a state of contradiction, where federal and state rules often point in different directions.

This creates real problems for ordinary people. A person who legally purchases marijuana from a licensed dispensary in one state can be arrested and charged with a federal crime for driving across state lines with that same product. An employee who uses medical marijuana as prescribed by a doctor can be fired for failing a workplace drug test, even in a state where medical marijuana is legal. A college student who smokes marijuana recreationally in a state where it is legal can lose federal financial aid. An immigrant with a green card can be deported for a marijuana-related offense that would result in no jail time for a U.S. citizen.

The confusion is not accidental. It results from a fundamental conflict between federal law, which still prohibits marijuana entirely, and state laws, which increasingly permit it. Neither side has fully given in, and the result is a patchwork system where what is legal depends on who is enforcing the law, where you are, what you are doing, and who you are.

This chapter explains how marijuana laws actually work, what legalization does and does not protect, and where legal risks still exist. It is written for people who want to understand the law as it actually functions, not as they wish it would.

Federal vs. State Legality

Under federal law, marijuana remains illegal. It is classified as a Schedule I controlled substance under the Controlled Substances Act, the same category as heroin and LSD. This classification means the federal government considers marijuana to have a high potential for abuse, no accepted medical use, and a lack of accepted safety for use under medical supervision. Possession, distribution, cultivation, and trafficking are all federal crimes. This federal status has not changed, even as many states have legalized marijuana in various forms.

States, however, have the authority to decide how they enforce their own criminal laws. The Constitution does not require states to criminalize marijuana simply because federal law does. Many states have legalized marijuana for medical or recreational use, or have reduced penalties for possession to fines or civil infractions rather than criminal charges.

This creates a legal conflict:

- State law may permit marijuana use
- Federal law still prohibits it

In practice, federal enforcement against individual users in legal states is rare, but it is not impossible. Federal agencies like the Drug Enforcement Administration (DEA), the Federal Bureau of Investigation (FBI), and U.S. Attorneys have the authority to prosecute marijuana offenses anywhere in the United States, regardless of state law. While federal policy under recent administrations has generally deprioritized prosecuting individual users and small-scale possession in states where marijuana is legal, these policies are not laws. They are enforcement priorities that can change with a new administration, a new attorney general, or a shift in political climate.

Federal law also affects banking, interstate travel, and certain professions in ways that many people do not expect:

Banking: Because marijuana remains illegal under federal law, banks and credit unions (which are federally regulated or insured) are often unwilling to provide services to marijuana businesses. This forces many dispensaries and growers to operate on a cash-only basis, creating safety and logistical challenges.

Interstate travel: Crossing state lines with marijuana, even between two states where it is legal, is a federal crime. Airports, even those in legal states, are under federal jurisdiction, and possessing marijuana in an airport or on an airplane is a federal offense. Many people have been arrested after legally purchasing marijuana in one state and attempting to bring it home to another legal state.

Federal employment and housing: Federal employees, contractors, and anyone working in positions requiring federal security clearances can be denied employment or lose their jobs for marijuana use, even if it occurs legally under state law. Residents of federally subsidized housing can be evicted for marijuana use, even medical use, because federal housing programs must comply with federal drug laws.

The result is a system where people can follow state law perfectly and still face serious federal consequences under the wrong circumstances.

Medical vs. Recreational Use

States that legalize marijuana often distinguish between medical and recreational use. These are not the same thing, and the protections and restrictions differ significantly.

Medical marijuana programs typically require:

A qualifying medical condition: States that allow medical marijuana provide a list of conditions that qualify, such as chronic pain, cancer, epilepsy, PTSD, multiple sclerosis, Crohn's disease, glaucoma, or HIV/AIDS. The specific conditions vary by state, and not all conditions qualify everywhere.

Physician certification: A licensed physician must evaluate the patient, confirm they have a qualifying condition, and certify that marijuana may be beneficial. This is not the same as a prescription, because federal law prohibits doctors from prescribing Schedule I substances. Instead, doctors provide a written certification or recommendation.

Registration with a state program: Most states require medical marijuana users to register with a state health department or similar agency and obtain a medical marijuana card. This card proves the person is legally authorized to possess and use marijuana under state law.

Medical users may receive stronger legal protections than recreational users, such as higher possession limits, the ability to grow more plants at home, or limited employment protections in some states. Some states also allow medical marijuana users to designate a caregiver who can purchase and possess marijuana on their behalf, which is especially important for patients who are too ill to visit a dispensary themselves.

Recreational legalization usually allows adults over a certain age (typically 21) to possess limited amounts of marijuana without a doctor's recommendation. These laws often include restrictions on where marijuana can be used (usually private property only, not in public spaces or vehicles), how much can be possessed (often one ounce or less), and whether it can be grown at home (some states allow a small number of plants per household, others do not).

Violating these rules, even in a legal state, can still result in criminal penalties. Possessing more than the legal limit, selling marijuana without a license, using marijuana in public, or providing it to minors are all crimes that can result in arrest, fines, and jail time. In some states, penalties for these violations are more severe than they were before legalization because the law expects people to comply with the new regulatory framework.

The distinction between medical and recreational use also matters for taxes. Many states impose high excise taxes on recreational marijuana sales but tax medical marijuana at lower rates or exempt it entirely. This makes medical marijuana significantly cheaper in some states, which incentivizes people to seek medical cards even when recreational use is legal.

Employment and Criminal Risks

Legal marijuana use does not guarantee workplace protection. This is one of the most misunderstood aspects of marijuana legalization, and it catches many people by surprise.

Employers may:

Prohibit marijuana use entirely: Even in states where marijuana is legal, employers can adopt drug-free workplace policies that prohibit employees from using marijuana, whether on or off duty. Private employers have broad authority to set workplace rules, and in most states, marijuana use is not a protected activity like religion or political affiliation.

Conduct drug testing: Employers can require pre-employment drug tests, random drug tests, or post-accident drug tests. A positive test for marijuana can result in a job offer being rescinded, disciplinary action, or termination, even if the marijuana use was legal and occurred off duty weeks earlier.

Discipline or terminate employees for positive tests: In most states, employment is "at will," meaning employers can fire employees for almost any reason that is not explicitly illegal discrimination. Using marijuana, even legally, is not protected, so firing someone for a positive drug test is usually lawful.

Some states provide limited protections for medical marijuana users, but these protections are narrow and often exclude safety-sensitive jobs. For example, a state might prohibit employers from discriminating against medical marijuana cardholders in hiring or firing decisions, but still allow employers to discipline or terminate employees who test positive if the job involves operating heavy machinery, driving commercial vehicles, working in healthcare, or other roles where impairment could pose a safety risk. Federal contractors and employers in certain regulated industries (like transportation, aviation, or nuclear energy) must comply with federal drug-free workplace requirements, which prohibit marijuana use entirely.

Even when state law provides some employment protections for medical marijuana users, those protections rarely extend to using marijuana at work, being impaired on the job, or possessing marijuana on company property. Employers can still enforce workplace conduct rules that prohibit these activities.

Criminal risks also remain, even in states where marijuana is legal. Marijuana-related charges can arise from:

Possession over legal limits: If recreational users can legally possess one ounce but you are caught with two ounces, you can be charged with illegal possession. The penalties may not be as severe as they were before legalization, but they are still criminal charges.

Driving under the influence: Driving while impaired by marijuana is illegal in every state, just like driving under the influence of alcohol. Some states have set legal limits for THC in the bloodstream, similar to blood alcohol limits, while others rely on officer observations of impairment. A DUI conviction can result in fines, license suspension, jail time, and a permanent criminal record.

Distribution without authorization: Selling marijuana without a license is illegal in every state, even where marijuana is legal. Giving marijuana to friends, especially in exchange for money, can be prosecuted as distribution. Even sharing marijuana socially can violate the law in some states.

Crossing state lines: As discussed earlier, transporting marijuana across state lines is a federal crime, even between two states where it is legal.

Federal consequences may arise in contexts such as immigration, federal employment, or housing programs. For non-citizens, including green card holders, any marijuana-related offense can trigger deportation proceedings, denial of citizenship applications, or bars to reentry. Federal law does not recognize state legalization, so even a minor marijuana possession charge in a legal state can be treated as a drug offense for immigration purposes. This applies even to lawful permanent residents who have lived in the U.S. for decades.

Why This Chapter Matters

Marijuana legalization has reduced criminal penalties in many states, but it has not eliminated legal risk. Confusion about the law leads many people to assume they are protected when they are not.

People make decisions based on incomplete information. They assume that because marijuana is sold in stores and advertised on billboards, it must be safe and legal in all contexts. They assume that a medical marijuana card protects them at work. They assume that what they do in private cannot affect their immigration status or federal benefits. These assumptions are often wrong, and the consequences can be severe.

Understanding the difference between federal and state law, medical and recreational use, and employment and criminal exposure helps individuals make informed choices in a legally inconsistent landscape. Marijuana law is not settled. It is evolving, state by state, administration by administration, and the rules today may not be the rules tomorrow.

If you use marijuana, or are considering it, take time to understand the law where you live and where you work. Know your employer's policies. Understand how it could affect your immigration status, your professional licenses, your custody arrangements, or your eligibility for federal programs. Legal marijuana does not mean risk-free marijuana.

The next chapter turns to contracts and business relationships, where assumptions can be just as costly, but the risks are often less obvious.

PART IX: Business, Contracts, and Intellectual Property

17

Contracts in Everyday Life

Contracts are not limited to boardrooms and courtrooms. They shape daily life: employment agreements, apartment leases, phone plans, service subscriptions, credit card terms, gym memberships, car purchases, home repairs, freelance work arrangements, and even informal arrangements between friends. Many people enter contracts without realizing it, misunderstand what they have agreed to, or assume a contract is unenforceable because it seems unfair or informal.

The word "contract" feels formal and intimidating to many people. It suggests lawyers, lengthy documents, and complicated legal language. In reality, most contracts people encounter are simple, everyday agreements. When you click "I agree" on a website, sign a lease, accept a job offer, hire someone to fix your roof, or promise to pay a friend back for concert tickets, you are entering into a contract.

The problem is that most people do not treat these agreements as seriously as they should. They skim terms of service without reading them. They sign leases without understanding the penalty clauses. They make verbal promises without realizing those promises might be legally binding. They assume they can back out of agreements if circumstances change or if the deal no longer seems fair.

These misunderstandings lead to disputes, lawsuits, and financial losses that could often be avoided with a better understanding of how contracts work. A person who signs a gym membership without reading the cancellation policy may find themselves locked into payments for years. A freelancer who agrees to complete a project without a written contract may never get paid. A tenant who breaks a lease early without understanding the penalties may owe thousands of dollars they did not anticipate.

This chapter explains how contracts actually work, what makes them legally binding, and how common mistakes can turn simple agreements into serious legal problems. It is written for people who want to protect themselves in everyday transactions, not legal experts.

What Makes a Contract Binding

At its core, a contract is a legally enforceable agreement. It is a promise, or set of promises, that the law will back up. If you break a contract, the other party can take you to court and ask a judge to force you to honor your promise or pay compensation for the harm caused by breaking it.

Most contracts require four basic elements:

Offer: One party proposes specific terms. This could be a job offer, a price quote, a proposed lease, or any clear proposal that indicates willingness to enter into an agreement. The offer must be definite enough that the other party knows exactly what is being proposed. "I'll sell you my car" is not a complete offer because it does not include a price. "I'll sell you my car for $5,000" is a complete offer.

Acceptance: The other party agrees to those terms. Acceptance must be clear and unambiguous. Saying "yes," signing a document, or performing the action requested (like paying money or starting work) can all be forms of acceptance. However, a counteroffer is not acceptance. If someone offers to sell you a car for $5,000 and you respond "I'll pay $4,500," you have not accepted the offer. You have made a counteroffer, which the other party can accept or reject.

Consideration: Each side gives or promises something of value. Consideration is what makes a contract different from a gift. If you promise to give someone $100 for no reason, that is a gift, not a contract. If you promise to give someone $100 in exchange for mowing your lawn, that is a contract. Consideration does not have to be money. It can be a service, a product, a promise to do something, or even a promise not to do something (like a non-compete agreement). The law does not generally care if the consideration is equal or fair, only that something of value is exchanged.

Capacity and legality: The parties must have legal capacity, and the agreement must involve lawful activity. Capacity means the parties are legally able to enter into contracts. Minors (people under 18 in most states), people who are severely intoxicated, and people with certain mental impairments may lack capacity. Contracts with people who lack capacity are often voidable, meaning the person without capacity can choose to cancel the contract. Legality means the contract must not require anyone to do something illegal. A contract to sell stolen goods or commit a crime is unenforceable.

Contracts do not always have to be written. Many verbal agreements are legally binding, though they are much harder to prove in court. If you and a friend verbally agree that you will pay them $50 to help you move, and they show up and do the work, you are legally obligated to pay them. The challenge is proving what was agreed to if there is a dispute later.

Some contracts, however, are required by law to be in writing. This requirement is known as the Statute of Frauds, and it applies to certain types of agreements, such as:

- Contracts for the sale of real estate
- Contracts that cannot be completed within one year
- Contracts for the sale of goods over a certain dollar amount (usually $500)
- Agreements to pay someone else's debt
- Prenuptial agreements

If a contract falls into one of these categories and is not in writing, it generally cannot be enforced, no matter how clear the verbal agreement was.

Signing a contract generally means you are bound by its terms, even if you did not read or fully understand them. This is one of the most important and least understood principles in contract law. Courts rarely excuse obligations based on regret or surprise. The reasoning is simple: if people could escape contracts by claiming they did not read them, no one would honor their agreements. The law places the burden on individuals to read and understand what they are signing before they sign it.

There are exceptions. If someone tricks you into signing a contract by lying about its terms, if the contract contains language that is deliberately hidden or deceptive, or if you signed under duress (threats or coercion), you may be able to void the contract. But these exceptions are narrow. Generally, "I didn't read it" or "I didn't understand it" is not a defense.

Breaking a Contract

A contract is broken when one party fails to perform as promised. This is known as a breach of contract. Breaches can be minor or material, depending on how significant the failure is.

A **minor breach** (sometimes called a partial breach) occurs when a party fails to perform a small part of the contract but still substantially completes their obligations. For example, if you hire a contractor to paint your house by Friday and they finish on Saturday, that is a minor breach. You still got what you paid for, just a day late. You might be entitled to compensation for any harm caused by the delay, but you generally cannot cancel the entire contract.

A **material breach** is a significant failure that defeats the purpose of the contract. If you hire a contractor to paint your house and they never show up, or they show up and paint it the wrong color despite clear instructions, that is a material breach. Material breaches often give the non-breaching party the right to cancel the contract and refuse further performance.

When a breach occurs, the non-breaching party may have remedies such as:

Monetary damages: The most common remedy is money. The goal is to put the non-breaching party in the position they would have been in if the contract had been performed. This can include direct losses, lost profits, and sometimes additional costs incurred because of the breach.

Cancellation of the contract: If the breach is material, the non-breaching party can often cancel the contract and walk away. They may also be entitled to damages for harm already suffered.

Court orders requiring performance: In some cases, money is not enough. If the contract involves something unique, like the sale of a specific piece of real estate or a rare item, the court can order the breaching party to perform as promised. This is called specific performance, and it is relatively rare.

Not every broken promise is a breach. Contracts often include conditions, deadlines, and exceptions that determine when and how obligations must be performed. Understanding these details is essential before assuming legal fault. For example, many contracts include force majeure clauses, which excuse performance if something extraordinary and unforeseeable happens, like a natural disaster or war. Others include notice requirements, meaning you must formally notify the other party of a breach before you can take legal action.

Sometimes contracts are broken for legitimate reasons, such as impossibility, fraud, or mutual agreement to terminate:

Impossibility: If performance becomes truly impossible, not just difficult or expensive, the contract may be excused. For example, if you hire someone to perform at your event and they die before the event, the contract is discharged due to impossibility.

Fraud: If one party was tricked into signing the contract through lies or misrepresentations, the contract may be voidable.

Mutual agreement: If both parties agree to cancel the contract or modify its terms, that is perfectly legal and enforceable.

Determining whether a breach is excusable, material, or minor often requires careful legal analysis. What seems like an obvious breach to one party may not be a breach at all if the contract includes language that allows the conduct in question.

Common Contract Mistakes

Many contract disputes stem from avoidable errors. Understanding these mistakes can help you protect yourself before problems arise.

Common mistakes include:

Relying on informal promises not included in the contract: Many people make verbal agreements or assumptions outside the written contract and then are surprised when those promises are not honored. If something is important to you, get it in writing. Courts generally enforce what is written in the contract, not what was discussed beforehand. Many contracts include "integration clauses" or "merger clauses" that explicitly state the written document is the entire agreement and supersedes any prior discussions.

Failing to read or understand key terms: People routinely sign contracts without reading them, especially long, dense agreements like terms of service, employment contracts, or loan documents. They assume the terms are standard or non-negotiable. Later, they discover clauses they did not expect, like mandatory arbitration provisions, automatic renewal terms, or penalty fees.

Assuming standard forms are non-negotiable: Many people believe that printed contracts, like leases or service agreements, cannot be changed. This is often untrue. Standard forms are starting points. You can ask to modify terms, cross out sections, or add clauses. The other party may say no, but it does not hurt to ask, especially in significant agreements like apartment leases or employment contracts.

Ignoring deadlines or notice requirements: Contracts often require parties to take action by certain dates or provide written notice before doing something. Missing these deadlines can forfeit your rights. For example, if your lease requires 60 days' notice before moving out and you only give 30 days, you may owe rent for the extra month even if you have already moved.

Believing a contract is invalid simply because it seems unfair: Courts generally enforce contracts as written unless there is fraud, coercion, or illegality. The fact that you got a bad deal, or that the terms now seem unreasonable, is usually not enough to escape the contract. There are exceptions for contracts that are so one-sided that they are "unconscionable," but this is a high bar to meet. Generally, the law assumes adults are capable of making their own decisions and living with the consequences.

Underestimating the importance of documentation: Emails, texts, and written confirmations often become critical evidence in contract disputes. If you make a verbal agreement, follow up with an email summarizing what was agreed to. If someone promises to do something, ask them to confirm it in writing. Documentation creates a paper trail that can prove what was said and when. In disputes, memories fade and stories change, but written records remain.

Why This Chapter Matters

Contracts quietly govern much of modern life. A misunderstanding can lead to financial loss, damaged relationships, or litigation that could have been avoided.

People lose contract disputes not because they were wrong about what was promised, but because they cannot prove it. They trusted informal assurances, signed without reading, or assumed the other party would be reasonable if problems arose. When disputes develop, what matters is not what you thought was agreed to, but what you can prove was agreed to.

Understanding what makes a contract binding, how breaches are handled, and which mistakes to avoid allows individuals to protect themselves before problems arise, not after. It means reading before you sign. It means getting important promises in writing. It means understanding what you are agreeing to and recognizing when a deal is not in your interest.

Contracts are tools. Used wisely, they protect you, clarify expectations, and provide a clear path forward if things go wrong. Used carelessly, they lock you into obligations you did not anticipate and limit your options when you need flexibility most.

The next chapter focuses on starting a business, where contracts, liability, and legal structure play an even more central role.

18

Starting a Business

Starting a business is often driven by creativity, ambition, or necessity, but it is also a legal act. The choices made at the beginning of a business can determine who is liable for debts, how taxes are paid, and how disputes are resolved. Many small businesses fail not because the idea was bad, but because legal foundations were ignored or misunderstood.

For many people, starting a business feels like a leap into the unknown. There is excitement about being your own boss, pursuing a passion, or building something from the ground up. There is also fear: fear of failure, fear of financial loss, and fear of the unfamiliar legal and regulatory landscape that comes with business ownership.

The legal side of starting a business intimidates people because it feels complex, expensive, and full of traps. It involves words like "entity formation," "registered agent," "operating agreement," and "employer identification number." It requires decisions that feel permanent and high-stakes. Many new business owners respond by avoiding these decisions entirely, operating informally and hoping they can figure it out later.

This approach is understandable but dangerous. Operating a business without proper legal structure, licenses, or contracts is like driving without insurance. Most of the time, nothing goes wrong. But when something does go wrong, whether it is a lawsuit, a tax audit, an employee dispute, or a contract breach, the consequences can be devastating. Business owners can lose not only their business but also their homes, savings, and personal assets.

The good news is that most of these problems are avoidable. The legal steps required to start a business properly are not as complicated or expensive as many people fear. More importantly, getting them right from the beginning saves time, money, and stress down the road.

This chapter explains the basic legal structures for new businesses, the regulatory requirements that often apply, and the risks entrepreneurs commonly face in the early stages. It is written for people who are starting their first business and want to understand what they need to do, why it matters, and what happens if they skip these steps.

LLCs, Corporations, and Sole Proprietorships

One of the first legal decisions a business owner must make is how the business will be structured. This choice affects liability, taxes, paperwork, and how the business can raise money and distribute profits. Unfortunately, many entrepreneurs do not fully understand the differences between structures, and they choose based on what their friends did or what seems easiest rather than what fits their situation.

Sole Proprietorship

A sole proprietorship is the simplest form. The business and the owner are legally the same entity. If you start selling products or offering services without formally creating a business entity, you are automatically operating as a sole proprietor.

This structure requires minimal paperwork and has no formal filing requirements in most states. You report business income and expenses on your personal tax return using Schedule C. If you operate under your own name (for example, "Jane Smith Consulting"), you usually do not need to register a business name. If you use a different name (for example, "Summit Consulting"), you may need to file a "doing business as" (DBA) name with your county or state.

However, a sole proprietorship offers no protection from personal liability. Business debts and legal claims can reach the owner's personal assets. If your business is sued or cannot pay its debts, creditors can go after your house, car, savings, and other personal property. If a customer is injured by your product or service, they can sue you personally.

This unlimited personal liability is the biggest drawback of sole proprietorships. It makes this structure appropriate only for very low-risk businesses or for people just starting out who plan to transition to a different structure as the business grows.

LLC (Limited Liability Company)

An LLC (limited liability company) is a popular choice for small businesses. It creates a legal entity separate from the owner, which can limit personal liability while allowing flexible management and tax options.

The main advantage of an LLC is liability protection. If the LLC is sued or goes into debt, creditors generally cannot reach the personal assets of the LLC's owners (called members). The LLC itself is liable, but the owners are shielded, as long as they have maintained the LLC properly.

LLCs also offer tax flexibility. By default, a single-member LLC is taxed like a sole proprietorship, and a multi-member LLC is taxed like a partnership. However, LLCs can elect to be taxed as corporations if that is more advantageous. This flexibility allows business owners to choose the tax treatment that works best for their situation.

Forming an LLC requires filing articles of organization with the state, paying a filing fee (usually a few hundred dollars), and appointing a registered agent to receive legal documents on behalf of the business. Most states also require LLCs to file annual reports and pay annual fees to remain in good standing.

However, liability protection depends on proper formation and ongoing compliance. If you fail to keep business and personal finances separate, if you fail to maintain required records, or if you use the LLC to commit fraud, a court can "pierce the corporate veil" and hold you personally liable. This means the LLC structure offers no protection if you treat it casually or ignore the rules.

Common mistakes that can destroy LLC protection include:

- Mixing personal and business funds in the same bank account
- Failing to sign contracts in the name of the LLC
- Not holding required meetings or keeping minutes (for multi-member LLCs)

- Undercapitalizing the LLC (starting it with so little money that it cannot realistically operate)
- Using the LLC to shield fraudulent or illegal activity

Corporation

A corporation is a more formal structure, often used for larger or growth-focused businesses. Like an LLC, a corporation is a separate legal entity that can own property, enter contracts, and be sued. Shareholders own the corporation, a board of directors oversees major decisions, and officers (like a president or CEO) handle day-to-day operations.

Corporations offer strong liability protection. Shareholders are generally not personally liable for corporate debts or lawsuits. This makes corporations attractive for businesses that carry significant risk or need to raise money from investors.

However, corporations involve stricter governance, reporting requirements, and tax considerations. Corporations must hold annual shareholder meetings, maintain detailed records, file annual reports, and follow specific procedures for major decisions. They are also subject to "double taxation" in many cases: the corporation pays taxes on its profits, and then shareholders pay taxes again on dividends they receive. (S corporations, a special type of corporation, can avoid double taxation, but they have strict eligibility requirements.)

Because of the complexity and costs, corporations are typically used by businesses that plan to grow large, raise money from outside investors, or eventually go public. For most small businesses, an LLC provides similar liability protection with less administrative burden.

Choosing the Wrong Structure

Choosing the wrong structure, or failing to maintain it properly, can eliminate liability protections entirely. Many business owners form an LLC or corporation and then never follow through with the ongoing requirements. They file the initial paperwork and assume they are protected, but they continue operating informally, mixing personal and business expenses, and ignoring compliance obligations.

When a lawsuit or debt collection happens, they discover too late that their liability protection is worthless because they failed to treat the business as a separate entity.

Licenses and Permits

Most businesses require licenses or permits to operate legally. These requirements vary by industry, location, and business activity. The specific licenses you need depend on what you do, where you do it, and how you do it.

Common examples include:

Business licenses: Many cities and counties require a general business license for any business operating within their jurisdiction. This is often a basic registration that generates tax revenue and allows the city to track businesses.

Professional or occupational licenses: Certain professions require state licenses, such as contractors, real estate agents, cosmetologists, accountants, lawyers, doctors, and many others. Operating without the required professional license is illegal and can result in fines, criminal charges, and lawsuits.

Health and safety permits: Businesses that handle food, provide healthcare, or involve public safety often require health department permits or inspections. Restaurants, food trucks, daycares, tattoo parlors, and salons typically fall into this category.

Zoning or home occupation permits: If you operate a business from your home, local zoning laws may require a permit. Some residential zones prohibit business activity entirely, while others allow it with restrictions (for example, no employees, no customer visits, no signage).

Seller's permits: If you sell tangible goods, most states require a seller's permit (also called a resale permit or sales tax license). This allows you to collect sales tax from customers and remit it to the state.

Employer-related permits: If you hire employees, you must register with federal and state agencies, obtain an Employer Identification Number (EIN) from the IRS, register for unemployment insurance and workers' compensation, and comply with wage and hour laws.

Operating without required licenses can lead to fines, shutdowns, or loss of contracts. Many entrepreneurs assume compliance will be handled later, only to discover that violations have already occurred. Some assume they are too small to need licenses or that the rules do not apply to informal or part-time businesses. These assumptions are often wrong.

Regulators do not care if you intended to comply eventually. They care whether you are complying now. Violations can result in immediate cease-and-desist orders, daily fines, and in some cases, criminal charges. Even if penalties are not imposed immediately, operating without licenses can cause problems later when you try to open a bank account, secure financing, bid on contracts, or sell the business.

Understanding regulatory obligations early prevents interruptions and builds credibility with customers, partners, and investors. It also protects you from liability. If something goes wrong and you were operating without the required licenses, you may face not only regulatory penalties but also personal liability for damages.

Finding out which licenses you need can be confusing because requirements are scattered across federal, state, and local levels. The Small Business Administration (SBA) website provides tools to help identify requirements by state and industry. Local chambers of commerce, small business development centers, and attorneys who specialize in business formation can also help.

Legal Risks New Businesses Face

New businesses face a range of legal risks, often before they realize they exist. These risks can derail a business quickly, especially when the owner is focused on getting customers and generating revenue rather than on legal compliance.

Common legal risks include:

Contract disputes: New businesses often operate on informal agreements, handshake deals, or poorly drafted contracts. When a customer refuses to pay, a supplier fails to deliver, or a partner walks away, these informal arrangements offer little protection. Without a clear written contract specifying obligations, deadlines, payment terms, and remedies, disputes become expensive and difficult to resolve.

Employment law violations: Hiring employees triggers a host of legal obligations, including minimum wage and overtime rules, anti-discrimination laws, workplace safety requirements, tax withholding, and unemployment insurance. Many new business owners misclassify employees as independent contractors to avoid these obligations, not realizing that misclassification can result in back taxes, penalties, and lawsuits. Others violate wage and hour laws by failing to track hours, pay overtime, or provide required breaks.

Intellectual property conflicts: Using a business name, logo, or slogan without checking whether it is already trademarked can result in costly infringement lawsuits. Copying content, images, or designs from competitors or the internet without permission can lead to copyright claims. Failing to protect your own intellectual property can allow competitors to copy your ideas, branding, or products without consequence.

Tax compliance issues: New businesses often struggle with estimated tax payments, sales tax collection, payroll taxes, and tax deductions. Missing tax deadlines or failing to pay taxes can result in penalties, interest, liens, and even criminal charges in severe cases. The IRS and state tax agencies are aggressive about collecting business taxes, and they have broad powers to seize assets and shut down businesses.

Personal liability exposure: Even when a business is structured as an LLC or corporation, personal liability can arise if the business owner personally guarantees a loan, signs a contract in their personal name rather than the business's name, or engages in fraudulent or illegal conduct. Many landlords, lenders, and suppliers require personal guarantees from new business owners, which eliminates the liability protection the business structure was supposed to provide.

Informal arrangements, handshake deals, and copied templates can create significant problems. Without clear contracts, disputes become harder to resolve and more expensive to defend. A $5,000 contract dispute can easily cost $10,000 or more in legal fees to litigate, making it a losing proposition even if you win.

Insurance, proper documentation, and early legal advice can reduce exposure dramatically, but many entrepreneurs delay these steps until problems arise. Business liability insurance, professional liability insurance (also called errors and omissions insurance), and workers' compensation insurance can protect against many common risks. Written contracts with clear terms, signed by all parties, prevent misunderstandings. Legal advice during the formation stage, while not free, is far cheaper than legal help after a lawsuit has been filed.

The cost of compliance and proper planning is almost always lower than the cost of fixing problems after they occur.

Why This Chapter Matters

Starting a business is more than an idea. It is a legal commitment with real consequences. Understanding business structures, licensing requirements, and common risks helps entrepreneurs protect their livelihoods and build sustainable ventures.

Every business decision you make early on has legal implications. The structure you choose affects how much you pay in taxes, whether your personal assets are at risk, and how easily you can bring in partners or investors. The contracts you sign (or fail to sign) determine what happens when disputes arise. The licenses you obtain (or neglect to obtain) determine whether you can operate legally or face fines and shutdowns.

Many people start businesses without thinking about these issues because they are focused on the exciting parts: the product, the brand, the customers. Legal compliance feels like boring paperwork that can wait. But ignoring the legal side of business is like building a house without a foundation. Everything may look fine on the surface, but the first storm reveals how unstable the structure really is.

The next chapter addresses intellectual property: how ideas, brands, and creative work are legally protected, and why failing to protect them early can be costly.

19

Intellectual Property

In a modern economy, ideas have value. Names, logos, designs, inventions, and creative works can be a business's most valuable assets, or a source of costly disputes if they are not protected. Many people assume that simply creating something gives them full legal ownership. In reality, intellectual property law is precise, technical, and often misunderstood.

For most people, intellectual property feels abstract and complicated. It involves words like "trademark," "copyright," "patent," and "trade secret," each with different rules, requirements, and protections. It requires understanding not just what you created, but how you created it, when you created it, whether anyone else created something similar, and what steps you took to protect it.

The confusion leads to costly mistakes. Entrepreneurs launch businesses using names that are already trademarked, forcing them to rebrand after investing thousands of dollars in marketing. Photographers discover their images being used without permission but cannot sue because they never registered their copyrights. Inventors publicly demonstrate their products before filing for patents, unknowingly destroying their ability to obtain patent protection. Freelancers create work for clients without clear contracts, only to find the client claims ownership of everything they produced.

These problems are almost always avoidable. Intellectual property law provides clear tools for protecting ideas, brands, and creative work, but only if you understand what each tool does and use it correctly. Waiting until a dispute arises to worry about intellectual property is often too late. By then, your rights may be lost, your brand may be compromised, and your options may be limited to expensive litigation with uncertain outcomes.

This chapter explains the main types of intellectual property, what each one protects, and how individuals and businesses can safeguard their ideas and brands. It is written for creators, entrepreneurs, freelancers, and anyone who wants to understand how to protect the value they create.

Trademarks

A trademark protects words, names, symbols, logos, and slogans that identify the source of goods or services. Trademarks exist to prevent consumer confusion and to protect brand identity. When you see a swoosh logo or hear the phrase "Just Do It," you immediately know the source. That instant recognition is what trademark law protects.

Trademark rights can arise from actual use in commerce, not just registration. This is called "common law" trademark protection. If you start using a unique business name or logo in connection with your products or services, you automatically gain some trademark rights in the geographic areas where you use it. However, these common law rights are limited, difficult to enforce, and easy to lose.

Registration provides stronger protection and clearer enforcement rights. Federal trademark registration through the United States Patent and Trademark Office (USPTO) gives you nationwide protection, even in areas where you have not yet done business. It creates a legal presumption that you own the mark and have the exclusive right to use it. It also allows you to use the ® symbol, file lawsuits in federal court, and recover damages and attorney's fees from infringers.

Common misconceptions include:

Thinking a business name registration automatically creates a trademark: Registering your business with the state to form an LLC or corporation does not give you trademark rights. State business registrations and federal trademarks are separate systems. You can register "ABC Consulting LLC" with your state, but if another company is already using "ABC Consulting" as a trademark, they can force you to stop using the name, even though your state registration is valid.

Assuming trademarks protect ideas rather than brand identifiers: Trademarks do not protect business concepts, product features, or general ideas. They only protect names, logos, slogans, and other identifiers that distinguish your goods or services from others. You cannot trademark "fast food restaurant" or "affordable clothing," but you can trademark "McDonald's" or "Old Navy."

Believing registration guarantees absolute protection: Trademark rights are not absolute. They are limited to the specific goods or services you use the mark with. "Delta" is a trademark for airlines, faucets, and dental insurance, because these are different industries and there is no likelihood of confusion. Registration also does not prevent others from using similar (but not confusingly similar) marks, or from using your trademark in non-trademark ways, like in news articles or product reviews.

Trademark disputes often arise when businesses grow, expand into new markets, or move online. A small local business that never worried about trademarks suddenly discovers a national competitor with the same name when they try to launch a website. A company that used a name informally for years finds out another business registered the trademark first and is demanding they stop using it.

Early searches and proper registration can prevent expensive conflicts later. Before choosing a business name, product name, or logo, search the USPTO database, state trademark databases, and the internet to make sure no one else is already using it. If the name is available, register it as soon as possible. Trademark applications cost a few hundred dollars, far less than the cost of rebranding or defending a trademark lawsuit.

Trademark rights also require active use and enforcement. If you stop using a trademark for several years, you can lose your rights through "abandonment." If you allow others to use your trademark without permission and do not take action to stop them, you can lose your rights through "genericide" (when a trademark becomes a generic term, like "escalator" or "thermos").

Copyrights

Copyright protects original creative works, such as books, music, art, photographs, videos, software, architectural designs, and even choreography. Copyright arises automatically when an original work is created and fixed in a tangible form. As soon as you write a sentence, take a photograph, or record a song, you own the copyright, even if you never register it or put a copyright notice on it.

Copyright protects expression, not ideas. This is one of the most important and most misunderstood principles of copyright law. Two people can independently write books on the same topic, and both books are protected by copyright. What copyright prevents is copying the specific way someone expressed an idea, not the underlying idea itself. You cannot copyright the idea of a boy wizard attending magic school, but J.K. Rowling owns the copyright to the specific characters, plot, dialogue, and descriptions in the Harry Potter books.

This distinction matters because people often believe copyright protects more than it does. You cannot copyright facts, titles, names, short phrases, or ideas. You can only copyright your original expression of those things. This means you cannot stop someone from writing about the same topic you wrote about, or from taking inspiration from your work. You can only stop them from copying your actual words, images, or other creative expression.

Registration is not required for copyright to exist, but it is often necessary to enforce rights in court and to recover certain damages. If you want to sue someone for copyright infringement, you must register your copyright with the U.S. Copyright Office first. Registration also allows you to recover statutory damages (preset amounts) and attorney's fees, which can make litigation economically feasible. Without registration, you can only recover your actual damages, which are often difficult to prove and may be less than the cost of litigation.

Copyright registration is inexpensive (usually under $100) and straightforward. For creators who make a living from their work, registration is essential protection. For hobbyists or people creating work primarily for personal use, it may be less critical, but it is still valuable if the work has commercial potential.

Digital content sharing has increased copyright disputes, particularly around online posting, licensing, and reuse. Many people believe that anything posted online is free to use, or that giving credit is enough to avoid infringement. Both beliefs are wrong. Copyright protection applies to digital content just as it does to physical content. Taking someone's photograph from their website and using it in your marketing materials is copyright infringement, even if you credit them. Sharing a copyrighted video on social media can be infringement, even though social media platforms are designed for sharing.

There are exceptions, most notably "fair use," which allows limited use of copyrighted material for purposes like criticism, commentary, news reporting, teaching, and parody. However, fair use is a complex legal doctrine with no clear rules. Whether a use is fair depends on factors like the purpose of the use, the nature of the copyrighted work, how much was used, and the effect on the market for the original. Fair use is not a guaranteed defense, and many people who believe they are protected by fair use are not.

Creators also need to be careful about work-for-hire situations. If you create something as an employee, your employer owns the copyright, not you. If you create something as a freelancer or independent contractor, you usually own the copyright unless your contract says otherwise. This means freelancers should use written contracts that specify who owns the work, especially if they want to retain rights to use the work in their portfolio or for other clients.

Patents

A patent protects inventions and technological processes. Patents grant exclusive rights to make, use, or sell an invention for a limited time, typically 20 years from the filing date. During that time, no one else can make, use, sell, or import the patented invention without permission. This gives inventors a temporary monopoly to recoup their investment in developing the invention.

Patents are complex and expensive. They require:

Novelty: The invention must be new. If it has been publicly disclosed, sold, or used before, it cannot be patented. This includes your own public disclosures. If you demonstrate your invention at a trade show, post a video of it online, or sell it before filing a patent application, you may lose your ability to obtain a patent. (The U.S. has a one-year grace period for your own disclosures, but most other countries do not, so international patent rights can be lost immediately.)

Usefulness: The invention must have a practical application. It cannot be purely theoretical or abstract.

Non-obviousness: The invention must not be an obvious improvement to someone skilled in the field. This is a subjective and often disputed requirement. Just because something is new does not mean it is non-obvious.

If an engineer in your field would think "of course, that's the logical next step," the invention may not be patentable.

Unlike trademarks and copyrights, patent rights do not exist without formal application and approval. You do not automatically get a patent just by inventing something. You must file a detailed application with the USPTO, which includes written descriptions, drawings, and claims that define exactly what the invention is and how it works. The application is reviewed by a patent examiner who searches existing patents and publications to determine if your invention meets the requirements.

Public disclosure before filing can destroy patent eligibility. This is one of the most common and most devastating mistakes inventors make. They are excited about their invention and want to show it to potential investors, customers, or the media. They demonstrate it publicly, post about it on social media, or offer it for sale. Later, when they try to file a patent application, they discover they have forfeited their patent rights in most countries, and their U.S. patent rights are at risk if more than a year has passed.

The lesson is clear: file first, disclose later. If you have an invention you think is patentable, consult a patent attorney before making any public disclosures. You can file a provisional patent application, which is less expensive and less formal than a full patent application, to establish a filing date and buy yourself a year to develop the invention further before filing a full application.

Because of their complexity, patents often require professional assistance, and mistakes can permanently eliminate protection. Patent attorneys are expensive, often charging $10,000 to $15,000 or more to prepare and file a utility patent application. For many small inventors, this cost is prohibitive. However, for inventions with real commercial potential, patent protection can be worth far more than the cost. Without a patent, competitors can freely copy your invention, making it difficult to profit from your innovation.

Patent protection also varies by type. **Utility patents** protect how an invention works. **Design patents** protect how an invention looks (the ornamental design). **Plant patents** protect new plant varieties. Each type has different requirements and protections.

Protecting Ideas and Brands

Not all ideas are protectable, but how ideas are expressed, branded, or implemented often is. A business concept alone cannot be protected, but the name, logo, marketing materials, software, product designs, and processes used to implement that concept can be.

Protecting intellectual property requires proactive steps, including:

Conducting searches before using names or designs: Before you commit to a business name, logo, or product name, search trademark databases and the internet to make sure you are not infringing someone else's rights. A quick search can save you from having to rebrand later, which can cost tens of thousands of dollars in lost marketing investment, new signage, website changes, and legal fees.

Registering trademarks and copyrights when appropriate: Do not assume your rights are protected just because you created something. Register your most important trademarks and copyrights to strengthen your rights and improve your ability to enforce them. Prioritize the assets that are most central to your business or creative work.

Using contracts to control ownership and licensing: Whenever you work with freelancers, contractors, employees, or collaborators, use written contracts that specify who owns the intellectual property created during the relationship. If you hire a graphic designer to create your logo, make sure the contract says you own the copyright. If you license your content to someone else, make sure the contract specifies what they can and cannot do with it.

Monitoring and enforcing rights: Intellectual property rights are not self-enforcing. If you discover someone infringing your trademark, copyright, or patent, you must take action. Send a cease-and-desist letter, file a takedown notice, or pursue litigation if necessary. If you ignore infringement, you signal that you do not care about your rights, which can weaken your ability to enforce them in the future.

Failure to protect intellectual property early can result in loss of rights, forced rebranding, or inability to stop infringement. Many businesses learn this lesson the hard way. They build a brand, invest in marketing, and gain customer recognition, only to receive a cease-and-desist letter from another company that owns the trademark. They are forced to change their name, lose all their branding investment, and start over. Or they create valuable content that goes viral, only to watch others profit from it because they never registered their copyright or enforced their rights.

Intellectual property protection is not just for large corporations. Small businesses, freelancers, artists, inventors, and content creators all benefit from understanding and using intellectual property law. The key is to act early, before problems arise, and to be strategic about what you protect and how.

Why This Chapter Matters

Intellectual property disputes are often preventable. Understanding what each type of protection covers, and what it does not, allows creators and entrepreneurs to secure value rather than lose it.

Ideas alone have limited value. Value comes from execution, and execution requires protecting the names, designs, content, and innovations that make your work distinct. Without intellectual property protection, competitors can copy what makes you successful, customers can confuse your brand with others, and you have no legal recourse to stop them.

The time to protect intellectual property is before you need the protection, not after. Once you discover infringement, your options are limited and expensive. Once you lose rights through abandonment, public disclosure, or failure to register, those rights may be gone forever.

The next chapter turns to wills, probate, and inheritance, where planning ahead determines how assets and responsibilities are handled after death.

PART X: Death, Wills, and Inheritance

20

Wills, Probate, and Estates

Few legal topics are avoided as consistently as death. Yet failing to plan for it does not avoid legal consequences. It guarantees them. Wills, probate, and estate laws determine who receives property, who makes decisions, and how disputes are resolved after someone dies. When plans are unclear or absent, families often face delays, expenses, and conflict during an already difficult time.

Most people know they should have a will. They know it is important. They intend to do it eventually. But death feels distant, estate planning feels complicated and expensive, and there always seems to be something more urgent to deal with. So they postpone it, year after year, until it is too late.

The result is that most Americans die without a will. When that happens, the state makes the decisions for them. The state decides who inherits their property, who raises their children, and who manages their affairs. Those decisions may align with what the person would have wanted, or they may not. Either way, the family has no control over the outcome and no voice in the process.

Even when people do have wills, they often make mistakes that cause problems later. They use outdated wills that do not reflect their current family situation. They fail to update beneficiary designations on retirement accounts and life insurance policies. They do not coordinate their will with other estate planning tools, like trusts or joint ownership arrangements. They assume their family will figure it out or that their wishes are obvious, not realizing that without proper documentation, their assumptions may be legally meaningless.

Estate planning is uncomfortable because it requires confronting mortality, making difficult decisions, and sometimes having hard conversations with family members. But avoiding it does not make those issues go away. It just shifts the burden to the people left behind, who must navigate the legal system while grieving, often without clear guidance about what their loved one wanted.

This chapter explains how estate law works, what happens without a will, and why inheritance disputes are so common. It is written for people who want to protect their families from unnecessary hardship and ensure their wishes are honored after they are gone.

What Happens If You Die Without a Will

Dying without a will is known as dying "intestate." When this happens, state law, not personal preference, determines how property is distributed. Every state has intestate succession laws that specify exactly who inherits and in what order. These laws are rigid, impersonal, and may produce results that contradict what the deceased person would have wanted.

Intestate laws typically prioritize:

A surviving spouse: In most states, a surviving spouse inherits a significant portion of the estate, but rarely everything. The exact share depends on whether there are children, how long the couple was married, and whether the property was acquired before or during the marriage. Some states give the spouse one-half, others give one-third, and the formula can become extremely complicated.

Biological or legally adopted children: If there is no surviving spouse, children typically inherit everything, divided equally among them. If there is a surviving spouse, children usually share the estate with the spouse. This can create tension, especially in blended families where the surviving spouse is not the biological parent of all the children.

Other close relatives: If there is no spouse or children, the estate goes to parents, then siblings, then more distant relatives. The exact order of priority varies by state. If no relatives can be found, the estate eventually goes to the state, a process called "escheat."

Unmarried partners, stepchildren (unless legally adopted), friends, and charities often receive nothing unless specifically provided for in a valid will or estate plan. Intestate laws do not recognize long-term relationships that are not formalized through marriage or adoption. A person who has lived with a partner for 20 years, raised stepchildren, or built close relationships with friends may intend for those people to inherit, but without a will, they have no legal claim.

This can be devastating. A surviving partner may lose the home they shared with the deceased, forced out by biological children or other relatives. Stepchildren who were raised by the deceased may be cut out entirely while estranged biological children inherit everything. Causes and organizations the deceased cared about receive nothing.

Intestate succession may also require court-appointed administrators and additional oversight. Without a will naming an executor, the court must appoint someone to manage the estate. This person may not be who the deceased would have chosen. Family members may fight over who should serve. The court may appoint a professional administrator who charges fees, reducing what the heirs ultimately receive.

The process of settling an intestate estate is also typically slower and more expensive than settling an estate with a clear will. The administrator must post a bond, file additional paperwork, and obtain court approval for many routine actions. Each step adds time and legal costs.

Many people assume their family "will know what to do." Legally, they may not have the authority to do it. A spouse may not be able to access jointly owned bank accounts without jumping through legal hoops. Adult children may not be able to sell the family home without court approval. Family members may disagree about what the deceased would have wanted, leading to conflict and litigation.

A simple will, which costs a few hundred dollars to prepare or can even be done through an online service with proper care, would avoid most of these problems. Yet millions of people die without one every year, leaving their families to deal with the consequences.

Probate Explained Simply

Probate is the court-supervised process of settling a deceased person's estate. It involves validating a will (if one exists), identifying and valuing assets, paying debts and taxes, and distributing remaining assets to heirs or beneficiaries. Probate gives the court authority to ensure the estate is handled properly and provides a legal framework for resolving disputes and paying creditors.

Probate is not inherently bad, but it can be:

Time-consuming: Probate typically takes several months to over a year, depending on the complexity of the estate and whether any disputes arise. During this time, assets are generally frozen. Heirs cannot access them, sell them, or distribute them. This can create financial hardship for family members who were depending on an inheritance to pay bills, especially if the deceased was the primary breadwinner.

Public: Probate is a court proceeding, which means it is part of the public record. The will, a list of assets, the names of heirs, and any disputes become public information that anyone can access. For people who value privacy, this can be uncomfortable. It can also attract unwanted attention from creditors, scammers, or estranged family members.

Expensive: Probate involves court fees, legal fees, appraiser fees, and executor fees. These costs are paid from the estate before heirs receive anything. In some states, probate costs can consume 3% to 7% or more of the estate's value. For a $500,000 estate, that could mean $15,000 to $35,000 in costs before a single dollar is distributed to heirs.

Some assets bypass probate entirely, such as:

Jointly owned property with right of survivorship: Property owned jointly by spouses or others automatically passes to the surviving owner without going through probate. This is common for family homes and bank accounts.

Accounts with named beneficiaries: Life insurance policies, retirement accounts (401(k)s, IRAs), and payable-on-death (POD) or transfer-on-death (TOD) bank accounts pass directly to the named beneficiaries without probate. This is one of the simplest ways to avoid probate for specific assets.

Assets held in trust: Property transferred to a living trust during the owner's lifetime bypasses probate because the trust, not the deceased person, technically owns the property.

Other assets pass through probate regardless of intent. Any property owned solely by the deceased, with no beneficiary designation or co-owner, must go through probate. This includes real estate, vehicles, bank accounts, personal belongings, and business interests.

The complexity of probate depends on the size of the estate, the clarity of documents, and whether disputes arise. A simple estate with a clear will, no disputes, and minimal assets may move through probate relatively quickly and inexpensively. A complex estate with unclear documents, fighting heirs, or complicated assets (like business ownership or foreign property) can take years and cost tens of thousands of dollars in legal fees.

Many states offer simplified probate procedures for small estates, often defined as estates worth less than $50,000 to $150,000, depending on the state. These procedures involve less court supervision, lower fees, and faster timelines. However, simplified probate is only available if the estate qualifies, and many estates exceed the threshold.

People often ask whether they should avoid probate. The answer depends on their situation. For small estates or estates with assets that already bypass probate (like beneficiary-designated accounts), the cost and effort of avoiding probate may not be worth it. For larger estates, or for people who value privacy and want to minimize costs and delays, probate avoidance strategies like living trusts can make sense.

Inheritance Disputes

Inheritance disputes often arise from unclear wills, unequal distributions, blended families, or allegations of undue influence. These disputes can tear families apart, cost tens of thousands of dollars in legal fees, and delay distributions for years. Many could be avoided with clearer estate planning and better communication.

Common disputes include:

Challenges to will validity: Heirs who are unhappy with a will may challenge it by claiming the deceased lacked mental capacity when the will was signed, was unduly influenced by someone, or that the will was forged or improperly executed. These challenges rarely succeed, but they can tie up an estate in litigation for years. Even unsuccessful challenges cost money, which comes out of the estate and reduces what everyone receives.

Conflicts between heirs and executors: The executor is responsible for managing the estate, paying debts, and distributing assets. Sometimes heirs believe the executor is mismanaging the estate, taking too long, or acting in their own interest. They may accuse the executor of stealing, hiding assets, or favoring certain heirs. These conflicts often require court intervention and legal representation.

Disagreements over asset valuation: Heirs may disagree about what an asset is worth, especially for items with sentimental or subjective value, like family businesses, real estate, or personal property. One heir may want to sell an asset quickly, while another wants to keep it. One may believe an appraisal is too low, while another thinks it is fair. These disagreements can escalate into full litigation.

Blended family conflicts: Estates involving blended families (where one or both spouses have children from prior relationships) are particularly prone to disputes. Biological children may resent a stepparent inheriting assets they believe should go to them. A surviving spouse may change the deceased spouse's will after death, cutting out stepchildren. These situations are emotionally charged and legally complicated.

Unequal distributions: When parents leave unequal inheritances to their children, even with good reasons (for example, one child received financial help during the parent's lifetime, or one child served as primary caregiver), the unequal treatment often breeds resentment and legal challenges. Children who receive less may feel unloved or disrespected, leading them to contest the will even if they have little legal basis for doing so.

Allegations of undue influence: When an elderly or ill person changes their will shortly before death, especially to benefit a caregiver, new spouse, or one child over others, heirs may claim the person was manipulated. Proving undue influence is difficult, but the allegation alone can delay probate and create lasting family rifts.

Courts generally aim to honor valid wills, but litigation can delay distributions and reduce estate value through legal costs. Even when a will is clear and legally valid, disputes can arise over interpretation, asset valuation, or executor actions. Once litigation starts, legal fees accumulate quickly, often consuming 10% to 30% or more of the estate's value.

Clear planning, proper documentation, and regular updates reduce the likelihood of disputes. Specific strategies include:

Updating your will regularly: Review and update your will after major life events like marriage, divorce, birth of children, death of beneficiaries, or significant changes in assets. Outdated wills create confusion and opportunities for disputes.

Explaining your decisions: If you plan to make unequal distributions or disinherit someone, consider explaining your reasoning in a separate letter or document. While this is not legally binding, it can reduce hurt feelings and discourage challenges.

Using clear, unambiguous language: Vague terms like "most of my assets" or "fairly divided" invite disputes. Be specific about who gets what.

Discussing your plans with family: While not always possible or appropriate, talking with family members about your estate plan can prevent surprises and give people a chance to voice concerns while you are still alive and able to address them.

Choosing the right executor: Select someone who is organized, honest, impartial, and able to handle potential conflicts. Consider naming a professional executor (like a bank or attorney) for complicated or contentious estates.

Why This Chapter Matters

Estate planning is not just about wealth. It is about control, clarity, and minimizing conflict. Even modest estates benefit from clear instructions. A will is not just a legal document; it is a final act of care for the people you leave behind.

Without a will, you lose control over who gets your property, who raises your children, and who manages your affairs. The state makes those decisions for you according to formulas that may not reflect your wishes or values. With a will, you retain that control and can ensure your wishes are honored.

Estate planning also protects your family from unnecessary stress, expense, and conflict during an already difficult time. Losing a loved one is hard enough without adding legal battles, court proceedings, and financial uncertainty. A clear estate plan is a gift to the people you care about most.

Understanding wills, probate, and inheritance law allows individuals to protect loved ones from unnecessary legal complications and ensure their wishes are carried out. It takes a few hours and a few hundred dollars to create a basic estate plan. It can take months or years and tens of thousands of dollars to fix the problems that arise without one.

The next chapter focuses on knowing when legal issues require professional help and how to find it.

PART XI: Knowing When to Get a Lawyer

21

When To Seek Professional Legal Help

The internet has made legal information more accessible than ever. With a few searches, anyone can find explanations, templates, and advice on almost any legal issue. Online forums are filled with people sharing their experiences. Legal websites offer free guides, downloadable forms, and step-by-step instructions. Apps and services promise to help you draft contracts, file documents, and represent yourself in court, all without hiring a lawyer.

But accessibility does not equal accuracy, and information does not equal strategy. There are moments when searching online stops being helpful and starts becoming risky.

The problem is that legal information online is often incomplete, outdated, or wrong. It may apply to a different state or a different situation. It may overlook critical details that change everything. A template contract you download may be missing clauses that protect you, or include clauses that harm you. Advice from a forum poster who "went through the same thing" may be based on a misunderstanding of what actually happened in their case.

More importantly, even accurate legal information does not tell you how to apply it to your specific situation. Knowing what the law says is different from knowing what to do about it. A person facing criminal charges might read online that they have the right to a jury trial, but that information does not tell them whether requesting a jury trial is strategically wise in their particular case. A business owner might learn that certain contract clauses are enforceable, but not know how to negotiate those clauses or what alternatives exist.

Legal problems are also high-stakes. Unlike other areas where trial and error is acceptable, legal mistakes often cannot be undone. Miss a court deadline, and you lose by default. Say the wrong thing to police, and it can be used against you. Sign the wrong contract, and you may be locked in for years. File the wrong immigration form, and you could trigger deportation. Use a template will incorrectly, and your estate plan may be invalid.

This chapter explains how to recognize when professional legal help is necessary, how to choose the right lawyer, and what options exist when cost is a concern. It is written for people who want to be informed consumers of legal services and who want to understand when self-help ends and professional help begins.

Red Flags That Require Professional Help

Some legal situations are too serious, complex, or time-sensitive to handle alone. These are the situations where the cost of getting it wrong far exceeds the cost of hiring help. While this list is not exhaustive, these are common red flags that should prompt you to seek professional legal advice immediately.

Common red flags include:

Criminal charges or arrest: If you are arrested, charged with a crime, or under criminal investigation, you need a lawyer immediately. Do not talk to police without a lawyer present, even if you think you can explain your innocence. Anything you say can and will be used against you, and even truthful statements can be twisted or misunderstood in ways that harm your defense. Public defenders are available if you cannot afford a private attorney, and you should request one as soon as possible. Criminal convictions can result in jail time, fines, probation, loss of professional licenses, immigration consequences, and a permanent record that affects employment and housing for the rest of your life.

Court papers with strict deadlines: If you are served with a lawsuit, eviction notice, restraining order, or any other legal document that requires a response by a specific date, take it seriously. These deadlines are not suggestions. Missing a deadline can result in a default judgment against you, meaning you automatically lose even if you have a strong defense. If you receive court papers, read them carefully, note all deadlines, and consult a lawyer immediately. Even if you ultimately decide to represent yourself, an initial consultation can help you understand what you are facing and what your options are.

Immigration issues involving status or removal: Immigration law is extremely complex, constantly changing, and unforgiving. If you are facing deportation proceedings, visa denial, status issues, or any problem that could affect your ability to remain in or return to the United States, you need an immigration attorney. Immigration mistakes can separate families, end careers, and result in permanent bars to reentry. Even people with strong cases can lose due to procedural errors or missed deadlines. Immigration judges and officers cannot give you legal advice, and the government will have an attorney arguing against you.

Serious injury or significant financial loss: If you have been seriously injured due to someone else's negligence, or if you have suffered significant financial harm due to fraud, breach of contract, or professional malpractice, you may have a claim worth pursuing. Personal injury lawyers and civil litigation attorneys typically work on contingency (they get paid a percentage of any recovery, usually 30% to 40%), so you may not need to pay upfront. However, these cases often have short statutes of limitations (deadlines to file), and evidence can disappear quickly. The sooner you consult a lawyer, the better your chances of recovery.

Business or contract disputes with large stakes: If a business relationship has broken down, a contract dispute has escalated, or you are facing a lawsuit involving significant money or business assets, you need legal representation. Business litigation is expensive, but losing can be far more expensive. A lawyer can help you evaluate your options (settlement, litigation, arbitration), develop strategy, and protect your interests.

Family law cases involving children or property: Custody disputes, divorce proceedings involving significant assets or debt, adoption, guardianship, and domestic violence matters are emotionally charged and legally complex. The outcomes of these cases affect families for years or even decades. Courts have broad discretion in family law matters, and judges make decisions based on evidence, credibility, and legal arguments. Self-represented parties are at a significant disadvantage, especially if the other side has an attorney. If children or substantial property are involved, professional representation is critical.

Another warning sign is uncertainty about consequences. If a decision could affect your freedom, immigration status, housing, or long-term finances, professional guidance is often worth the cost. When you do not know what you do not know, you are most vulnerable to making mistakes that cannot be fixed.

Waiting too long can eliminate options. Many rights are lost through inaction rather than bad decisions. A claim that could have been filed if you acted within the statute of limitations becomes worthless a day after the deadline. A lease you could have negotiated before signing becomes binding the moment you sign it. Evidence that could have supported your case disappears if you wait too long to preserve it. The cost of professional help early in a legal problem is almost always lower than the cost of fixing mistakes later.

How to Find the Right Lawyer

Not all lawyers handle all legal problems. Law is specialized, and finding the right fit matters. Hiring a real estate lawyer to handle your criminal case, or a divorce lawyer to help with your immigration problem, is like going to a foot doctor for heart surgery. They may be excellent at what they do, but they are not trained or experienced in the area you need.

Key steps include:

Identifying the relevant practice area: Lawyers specialize in specific areas such as criminal defense, personal injury, family law, immigration, estate planning, business law, employment law, real estate, bankruptcy, and many others. Within those broad categories, there are often subspecialties. For example, within criminal defense, some lawyers focus on white-collar crimes, others on drug offenses, others on DUI. Start by identifying what type of lawyer you need, and then narrow down to someone who handles cases like yours regularly.

Checking credentials and experience: Once you identify lawyers who practice in the right area, research their background. How long have they been practicing? What percentage of their practice is devoted to this area? Have they handled cases similar to yours? What are their results? Most lawyers have websites that describe their experience, and many states have online directories where you can check whether a lawyer is licensed, in good standing, and has any disciplinary history. Do not hire a lawyer based solely on advertising or a flashy website. Look for substance.

Asking about strategy, communication, and fees: During an initial consultation, ask the lawyer how they would approach your case. What are the possible outcomes? What are the risks? What is their strategy? Also ask about communication. Will you work directly with the lawyer, or will most of your contact be with paralegals or assistants? How quickly do they respond to calls and emails? What is their fee structure? Get everything in writing. A good lawyer will be transparent about costs, realistic about outcomes, and clear about what they can and cannot do for you.

Understanding who will actually handle the case: In some law firms, especially larger ones, the lawyer you meet during the initial consultation may not be the one who actually works on your case. Ask directly: will you be handling my case personally, or will it be assigned to an associate or paralegal? If others will be involved, meet them and understand their role. You want to know who you will be working with and what their qualifications are.

Referrals from trusted sources and local bar associations can help narrow choices. If someone you trust (a friend, family member, accountant, or financial advisor) had a good experience with a lawyer, that referral is valuable. State and local bar associations often have referral services that match you with lawyers in your area who handle your type of case. Many bar associations also offer free or reduced-fee initial consultations.

Initial consultations are often free or low-cost and provide an opportunity to assess fit. Use this time to evaluate whether the lawyer listens to you, understands your problem, explains things clearly, and seems genuinely interested in helping you. Trust your instincts. If a lawyer makes you uncomfortable, talks down to you, rushes you, or pressures you to hire them immediately, look elsewhere. The lawyer-client relationship is built on trust and communication, and you need to feel confident in the person representing you.

Red flags when choosing a lawyer include:

- Guaranteeing a specific outcome (no lawyer can guarantee results)
- Pressuring you to sign a retainer agreement immediately
- Being vague or evasive about fees

- Having a disciplinary history or complaints
- Promising results that sound too good to be true
- Failing to return calls or emails during the consultation process

Legal Costs and Alternatives

Legal services can be expensive, but cost should not be the only consideration. Poor advice or missed deadlines often cost more in the long run. A lawyer who charges $300 per hour but resolves your problem efficiently may be cheaper in the long run than a lawyer who charges $150 per hour but drags the case out or misses critical opportunities.

That said, legal costs are a real barrier for many people. Understanding fee structures and alternatives can help make legal services more accessible.

Common fee structures include:

Hourly fees: The lawyer charges for each hour (or fraction of an hour) they work on your case. Hourly rates vary widely based on location, experience, and practice area, typically ranging from $150 to $500+ per hour. You will usually be required to pay a retainer (an upfront deposit) that the lawyer draws from as they work. You receive regular billing statements showing how your retainer is being used. Hourly fees are common for business law, family law, and most litigation.

Flat fees: The lawyer charges a single fixed price for the entire matter. This is common for routine services like drafting a will, forming an LLC, handling an uncontested divorce, or representing you on a simple criminal charge. Flat fees provide cost certainty, but make sure you understand exactly what is and is not included. If complications arise, the lawyer may charge additional fees.

Contingency fees: The lawyer takes a percentage of any money recovered on your behalf, typically 30% to 40%. If you do not win or recover money, you do not pay attorney fees (though you may still be responsible for court costs and expenses). Contingency fees are common in personal injury cases, employment discrimination cases, and some other civil matters where money damages are sought. This structure allows people to pursue claims without paying upfront, but it also means the lawyer only takes cases they believe have a good chance of success.

Hybrid fees: Some lawyers use a combination, such as a reduced hourly rate plus a smaller contingency percentage, or a flat fee for certain tasks with hourly billing for additional work.

Alternatives to full representation may include:

Limited-scope representation: Also called "unbundled services" or "discrete task representation," this allows you to hire a lawyer for specific tasks rather than full representation. For example, a lawyer might review documents you drafted, coach you on strategy, or represent you at a single hearing, while you handle the rest of the case yourself. This can significantly reduce costs while still giving you professional guidance on the most critical parts of your case. Not all lawyers offer this, and not all cases are appropriate for it, but it is worth asking about.

Mediation or arbitration: For disputes that do not involve criminal charges or emergency situations, mediation and arbitration can be faster and cheaper alternatives to litigation. In mediation, a neutral third party helps you and the other side negotiate a resolution. In arbitration, a neutral third party makes a binding decision. Both processes are less formal than court, and legal representation may be optional or limited. Many contracts require arbitration, and courts often require mediation before trial.

Legal aid organizations: Legal aid organizations provide free or low-cost legal services to people who meet income eligibility requirements. They typically handle cases involving housing, family law, public benefits, consumer issues, and some other civil matters. They do not handle criminal cases (public defenders do that) or business matters. Legal aid organizations are often overwhelmed with demand, but if you qualify and your case falls within their scope, they can provide high-quality representation at no cost.

Court self-help resources: Many courts offer self-help centers, online resources, form libraries, and instructional materials for people representing themselves. These resources can help you understand court procedures, fill out forms correctly, and prepare for hearings. Some courts also offer free legal advice clinics where volunteer lawyers answer basic questions. While these resources cannot replace a lawyer, they can help you navigate the system more effectively if you cannot afford representation.

Law school clinics: Many law schools operate legal clinics where law students, supervised by experienced attorneys, provide free legal services to low-income clients. The quality of representation is often high, but availability is limited and not all types of cases are handled.

Pro bono services: Some lawyers volunteer a portion of their time to handle cases for free. Bar associations often coordinate pro bono programs. If you cannot afford a lawyer and do not qualify for legal aid, ask the local bar association if pro bono help is available for your type of case.

Understanding fee structures, asking about payment plans, and exploring alternatives helps make legal services more accessible. Many lawyers are willing to work with clients on payment plans, especially for flat-fee services like estate planning or business formation. Do not be afraid to discuss cost openly. A good lawyer would rather work out a payment arrangement than have you go without representation you need.

Why This Chapter Matters

Knowing the law empowers individuals, but knowing the limits of self-help protects them. Google can explain concepts, but it cannot evaluate evidence, negotiate outcomes, or appear in court. Online templates cannot tailor advice to your specific circumstances or warn you about risks you have not considered.

The law is not a DIY project where mistakes are easily fixed. It is a system with rules, procedures, and consequences that can change your life. Representing yourself is sometimes appropriate for simple, low-stakes matters like small claims court, uncontested proceedings, or routine administrative tasks. But for serious matters involving freedom, family, immigration status, significant money, or your future, professional help is not a luxury. It is a necessity.

Recognizing when to seek professional help, and how to do so wisely, can be the difference between resolving a problem and making it worse. The cost of hiring a lawyer is finite and predictable. The cost of not hiring a lawyer when you need one can be catastrophic and permanent.

This book has focused on understanding the law as it affects everyday life. The final step is knowing when understanding alone is not enough. Being informed means knowing what you know, knowing what you do not know, and knowing when to ask for help. The smartest legal decision you can make is recognizing when you need a lawyer and acting on it before it is too late.

Concluding Thoughts

The law touches nearly every part of modern life. It shapes where we live, how we work, who we can marry, how we raise children, how we run businesses, and how we protect ourselves when something goes wrong. It determines what contracts are enforceable, what conduct is criminal, who inherits property, and who can remain in the country. It sets the rules for resolving disputes, punishing wrongdoing, and protecting rights.

Yet for many people, the law feels distant, technical, or deliberately inaccessible. Legal language is dense and confusing. Court procedures seem designed to intimidate. The system feels like it was built for lawyers, not for ordinary people trying to navigate everyday problems. That gap between the law and the people it governs creates fear, confusion, and avoidable harm.

People make decisions every day that have legal consequences, often without realizing it. They sign leases without reading them. They talk to police without understanding their rights. They start businesses without proper structure. They miss court deadlines because they did not realize the deadlines existed. They assume that because something seems unfair, it must be illegal, or that because they did not intend harm, they cannot be held responsible.

These misunderstandings lead to preventable problems. Contracts become traps. Minor issues escalate into major crises. Rights are forfeited through inaction. People lose cases not because they were wrong, but because they did not understand the process or act in time.

This book was written to narrow that gap. It was written for people who want to understand the legal system well enough to protect themselves, make informed decisions, and recognize when they need help. It was written in plain language, without legal jargon, because the law should be accessible to everyone it affects.

Legal Literacy as a Form of Empowerment

Legal literacy does not mean memorizing statutes or arguing cases in court. It does not require years of education or specialized training. It means understanding the basic rules that affect everyday decisions and recognizing when those rules matter.

A legally literate person knows the difference between being charged and being convicted, and understands that an arrest is not the same as guilt. They understand that contracts create obligations that survive changes of heart, and that signing something binds you even if you did not read it. They recognize that deadlines exist in the legal system, and that missing a deadline can forfeit your rights entirely. They know that rights must often be asserted to be protected, and that silence can be interpreted as consent or waiver.

Legal literacy means understanding that the legal system operates on rules, not fairness. It means knowing that what seems obviously unfair to you may be perfectly legal, and that good intentions do not protect you from consequences. It means recognizing that the burden is often on you to act, to preserve evidence, to meet deadlines, and to assert your rights, because the system will not do it for you.

Knowledge reduces panic. When you understand what is happening and why, you can respond strategically instead of emotionally. You can focus on what matters instead of wasting time on what does not. You can make decisions based on likely outcomes instead of guessing.

Legal literacy replaces guesswork with structure. Instead of wondering what might happen, you understand the process. Instead of hoping for the best, you prepare for realistic possibilities. Instead of being paralyzed by uncertainty, you take informed action.

When people understand the legal landscape, they are less likely to be manipulated, rushed into bad decisions, or intimidated into silence. They are less vulnerable to scams, coercion, and exploitation. They can recognize when someone is lying to them about their legal rights or obligations. They can push back when authority is being misused.

Legal literacy turns uncertainty into informed choice. It does not guarantee outcomes, but it gives you agency over how you respond to legal challenges. It allows you to weigh options, understand trade-offs, and make decisions that align with your priorities and values.

How Informed Citizens Protect Themselves

People who understand the law protect themselves in quiet, practical ways. They do not necessarily avoid all legal problems, because some problems are unavoidable, but they minimize harm and preserve their options.

They document important interactions. When they have a disagreement with a landlord, employer, contractor, or business partner, they follow up with written confirmation of what was discussed and agreed to. When they are stopped by police, they make note of the officer's name, badge number, and what was said. When they lend money to a friend, they get a written agreement. They understand that memories fade, stories change, and disputes escalate, but written records endure.

They read what they sign. Before committing to a lease, employment contract, loan agreement, or terms of service, they read the entire document. They pay special attention to sections about obligations, deadlines, termination, fees, and dispute resolution. If they do not understand something, they ask questions or get legal advice. They do not sign under pressure or rush, because they know that once signed, the contract is binding.

They ask questions before problems escalate. When they receive a concerning letter, notice, or legal document, they do not ignore it or assume it will go away. They read it carefully, note any deadlines, and seek clarification or advice before the deadline passes. When something seems wrong in a business transaction, employment situation, or personal relationship, they address it early rather than hoping it will resolve itself.

They recognize red flags early and act before options disappear. They know that criminal charges, court papers, immigration notices, and eviction warnings require immediate attention. They understand that many legal problems have time limits and that waiting can eliminate remedies. They take action while they still have choices, not after those choices are foreclosed.

Informed citizens also understand the limits of self-help. They know when a situation is manageable and when professional guidance is necessary. They do not confuse confidence with competence, and they do not mistake internet information for legal strategy. They are willing to invest in professional help when the stakes are high, the issues are complex, or the consequences are serious. They recognize that the cost of good advice upfront is almost always less than the cost of fixing mistakes later.

Most importantly, informed citizens participate more fully in civic life. They vote with an understanding of how laws are made and changed. They serve on juries with knowledge of the legal system they are part of. They advocate for themselves and others because they understand their rights and responsibilities not as abstract ideas, but as tools that shape real outcomes. They hold institutions accountable because they know what the rules are supposed to be.

Legal literacy makes people more difficult to exploit and easier to help. It makes the system work better for everyone because informed participants make better decisions, resolve disputes more efficiently, and demand accountability from those in power.

A Final Checklist for Navigating Legal Problems

Legal problems can feel overwhelming, especially when they are new and unfamiliar. When you find yourself facing a legal issue, whether it is minor or serious, return to these basic questions. They provide a framework for understanding what you are dealing with and what you need to do next.

When legal issues arise, ask yourself:

What type of legal issue is this? Is it criminal, civil, family, employment, immigration, contract-related, property-related, or something else? Understanding the category helps you identify which rules apply, what procedures to expect, and what type of lawyer or resource you need. Different types of legal problems follow different rules and have different consequences.

Is this governed by state law, federal law, or both? Many legal issues are primarily state matters (like most crimes, family law, contracts, property), while others are federal (immigration, bankruptcy, federal crimes, intellectual property). Some issues involve both state and federal law (like marijuana, employment discrimination, or environmental regulations). Knowing which level of government controls the issue helps you understand where to look for information and which courts have jurisdiction.

Are there deadlines I must meet? Deadlines are everywhere in the legal system: deadlines to respond to lawsuits, file appeals, submit applications, pay fines, appear in court, or assert claims. Missing a deadline can result in automatic loss, forfeiture of rights, or denial of relief. Identify all deadlines immediately and mark them on your calendar with reminders well in advance. If you are not sure whether a deadline applies, assume it does and verify.

What documents, evidence, or records should I preserve? Legal disputes are won and lost on evidence. Identify what documents, photos, videos, emails, texts, receipts, contracts, or other records support your position or might be relevant to your case. Preserve them carefully. Make copies. Store them securely. Do not delete, alter, or destroy anything that might be relevant, even if it seems harmful to your case. Destroying evidence can result in sanctions, criminal charges, or automatic adverse rulings.

What are the short-term and long-term consequences of my choices? Legal decisions often involve trade-offs. Pleading guilty to a minor charge might resolve a criminal case quickly but could affect your immigration status, employment prospects, or professional licenses for years. Settling a lawsuit might save litigation costs but might not fully compensate you for your losses. Breaching a contract might give you immediate relief but could lead to larger damages later. Think beyond the immediate problem to how your choices will affect your future.

Do I need professional legal help? This is often the most important question. If the issue involves potential jail time, significant money, your immigration status, your children, your home, or any other high-stakes consequences, the answer is almost certainly yes. If you are unsure about the law, confused about procedures, facing an opponent with a lawyer, or uncertain about how to protect your rights, the answer is probably yes. If you can afford a consultation (many are free or low-cost), get one. A lawyer can help you understand your situation, evaluate your options, and make informed decisions, even if you ultimately decide to handle some or all of the matter yourself.

You do not need all the answers immediately. Legal problems unfold over time, and information becomes clearer as the process moves forward. But asking the right questions early can prevent small problems from becoming irreversible ones. It can help you prioritize what matters, avoid common mistakes, and preserve your options for as long as possible.

These questions are not just for emergencies. They are useful for everyday decisions too. Before signing a lease, starting a business, creating a will, or making any significant legal commitment, run through this checklist. It takes only a few minutes and can save you months or years of problems.

A Closing Thought

The law is not just a system for resolving disputes after something goes wrong. It is a framework for making informed decisions before problems arise. It is a set of rules that, when understood, can be used to protect yourself, pursue opportunities, and shape outcomes.

Understanding the law, even at a basic level, is an act of self-protection. It allows you to navigate the world with more confidence and less vulnerability. It helps you spot problems early, respond effectively when they arise, and avoid mistakes that create unnecessary hardship.

Legal knowledge belongs to everyone. The rules that govern your life should not be a mystery. You do not need to be a lawyer to understand your rights, your obligations, and the processes that affect you. You have the right to know how the system works, what your options are, and when you need help.

The more people understand the rules that govern their lives, the more fair, predictable, and accessible the system becomes. When people know their rights, they assert them. When they understand procedures, they follow them. When they recognize injustice, they challenge it. An informed public makes the legal system work better for everyone.

Legal literacy is not a luxury or a specialized skill reserved for professionals. It is a basic life competency, as important as financial literacy or health literacy. Just as you need to understand how money works to manage your finances, and how your body works to maintain your health, you need to understand how the law works to protect your rights, fulfill your obligations, and make informed decisions.

That understanding begins here, with the decision to learn, to ask questions, and to take the law seriously as something that affects you personally. It continues every time you read before you sign, document what matters, meet a deadline, seek help when you need it, or stand up for your rights when they are threatened.

The legal system is not perfect. It is often slow, expensive, complicated, and frustrating. It does not always produce fair outcomes. But it is the system we have, and understanding it gives you power within it. Knowledge does not guarantee victory, but ignorance almost guarantees vulnerability.

You now have a foundation. You understand the basics of criminal law, civil law, family law, employment law, housing law, consumer protection, immigration law, business law, and estate planning. You know when to act, when to wait, when to ask for help, and when to insist on your rights. You know that the law is not magic or mystery but a system of rules that can be learned, understood, and used.

That understanding begins here and continues every time you choose clarity over confusion, preparation over panic, and knowledge over assumption. Take what you have learned, apply it to your life, share it with others, and never stop asking questions. The law is yours to understand, and understanding it is your best protection.

Appendices

The chapters in this book focus on understanding how the law works and how it affects everyday life. They explain concepts, principles, and processes that apply broadly across situations and jurisdictions. These appendices are designed to help readers take the next step: finding reliable resources, accessing help when money is tight, and understanding common legal documents they may encounter.

Legal problems rarely announce themselves clearly. They develop gradually, emerge from misunderstandings, or arrive suddenly in the form of court papers or official notices. When they do, most people need more than general understanding. They need specific answers to specific questions: What does this form mean? Where do I file this? Who can help me? What are my options in my state?

These appendices provide starting points for those practical questions. They are not comprehensive, because legal resources vary by location and change over time, but they point you in the right direction. They help you identify trustworthy sources, avoid common mistakes, and find assistance when you need it most.

Use these appendices as a reference guide. Return to them when you face a specific legal issue, need to locate resources in your area, or encounter a document you do not understand. Combined with the knowledge you have gained from the previous chapters, these tools will help you navigate legal challenges with greater confidence and clarity.

Using These Appendices

These appendices are not substitutes for legal advice. They are tools for orientation, helping readers identify where to look, who to ask, and what to expect. They cannot account for every situation, jurisdiction, or individual circumstance. Legal problems are fact-specific, and the information here is necessarily general.

Use these appendices as starting points. When you face a legal issue, turn to the appropriate appendix to find resources that can provide more specific guidance. Follow the links, make the calls, visit the offices. Ask questions, gather information, and make informed decisions.

Combined with the chapters in this book, these appendices provide a foundation for navigating legal issues thoughtfully, responsibly, and with greater confidence. You now understand the legal concepts that govern everyday life, and you know where to turn when you need help applying those concepts to your situation.

The law may be complex, but access to understanding does not have to be. Knowledge is power, and you now have the knowledge to protect yourself, assert your rights, and make informed decisions. Use it wisely.

Appendix A: State-by-State Legal Resources

Because most everyday legal issues are governed by state law, accurate information depends on location. Family law, landlord-tenant law, criminal procedure, probate, business formation, and many other areas vary significantly from state to state. What is true in California may not be true in Texas. A form that works in New York may be invalid in Florida. Deadlines, procedures, and even the names of courts differ across jurisdictions.

This means that generic legal advice, while sometimes useful for understanding concepts, is often insufficient for taking action. You need information that is specific to your state, current, and authoritative. Fortunately, each state maintains official resources that explain laws, procedures, and rights in plain language, often designed specifically for people who are not lawyers.

Starting Points: Where to Look for State-Specific Information

When looking for state-specific legal information, start with these trusted sources. They are reliable, current, and designed to serve the public.

State Court Websites

State court systems maintain official websites that are often the single best resource for understanding court procedures, filing requirements, and your rights in legal proceedings. These websites are usually organized by court type (trial courts, appellate courts, supreme court) and often include dedicated sections for the public.

State court websites often include:

Self-help sections: Many states have developed extensive self-help resources for common legal issues like divorce, custody, eviction, small claims, name changes, guardianship, and restraining orders. These sections explain the process step-by-step, often with videos, flowcharts, and plain-language guides. The quality of these resources has improved dramatically in recent years as courts recognize that most people cannot afford lawyers for every legal problem.

Some states offer self-help centers within courthouses where you can receive in-person assistance. Staff members (often paralegals or volunteer lawyers) can help you understand procedures, fill out forms, and prepare for hearings. They cannot provide legal advice about what decisions you should make, but they can explain how the system works and what your options are.

Court forms: Official, fillable forms for initiating cases, responding to lawsuits, requesting orders, and other court filings. Using the correct, current form is critical. Forms from other states, outdated forms, or forms purchased from commercial sources may not be accepted by the court. Courts increasingly provide forms that can be filled out electronically, saved, and either printed for filing or submitted online if electronic filing is available.

Many court websites now offer "interview-style" form completion tools. These are interactive programs that ask you questions in plain language, then automatically fill out the correct legal forms based on your answers. This technology reduces errors and makes form completion much easier for people without legal training.

Filing instructions: Detailed instructions on how to complete forms, where to file them, what fees are required, and what happens next. These instructions often include checklists to ensure you have not missed required documents or steps. Pay careful attention to filing deadlines. Missing a deadline can result in losing your case by default, even if you have a strong legal position.

Instructions typically explain whether you must file in person, by mail, or electronically. They also explain how many copies to file, whether documents must be served on other parties, and what proof of service is required. Following these instructions precisely prevents delays and rejected filings.

Explanations of common legal processes: Descriptions of how cases proceed, what to expect at hearings, how to present evidence, and what judges will consider when making decisions. Some courts offer video tutorials or in-person workshops that walk you through common procedures like small claims trials, restraining order hearings, or divorce proceedings.

Understanding the process reduces anxiety and improves outcomes. Knowing what to expect helps you prepare properly, organize your evidence, and present your case effectively. Courts want you to succeed in navigating the system, even without a lawyer, so they invest in these educational resources.

Fee waivers and payment plans: Information on how to request a waiver of filing fees if you cannot afford them, or how to arrange payment plans for court costs. Filing fees can range from $50 for small claims cases to $500 or more for complex civil cases. For people with limited income, these fees create a barrier to justice. Fee waiver applications ask about your income, expenses, assets, and household size. If approved, you can proceed without paying fees.

Some courts also waive fees for service of process (delivering legal papers to other parties), court reporters, and other costs. Fee waivers do not eliminate the obligation to follow court rules and deadlines, but they do make the system accessible to people who otherwise could not afford to participate.

Local court rules: In addition to statewide rules, individual courts may have local rules about formatting, scheduling, electronic filing, and courtroom conduct. Failing to follow local rules can result in rejected filings or sanctions. Local rules might specify margin sizes for documents, font requirements, page limits for motions, or procedures for requesting hearing dates.

Local rules also govern courtroom behavior: when to stand, how to address the judge, whether you may bring electronic devices into the courtroom, and how to present evidence. While judges are generally patient with self-represented parties, you are still expected to conduct yourself professionally and follow basic courtroom procedures.

Electronic filing systems: Many courts now require or offer electronic filing (e-filing) for certain types of cases. Court websites provide instructions for registering for e-filing accounts, uploading documents, paying fees online, and receiving electronic notice of court actions. E-filing can be more convenient than filing in person, but it requires careful attention to technical requirements like file formats, size limits, and submission deadlines.

To find your state's court website, search for "[your state] courts" or "[your state] judicial branch." Look for the official government site (usually ending in .gov). Once there, look for links labeled "Self-Help," "Public Resources," "Representing Yourself," or "Forms and Instructions."

State Bar Associations

Every state has a bar association, which is the organization that licenses and regulates lawyers. Bar associations serve both lawyers and the public, and they maintain extensive resources for people seeking legal information or representation.

Bar associations often provide:

Lawyer referral services: These services match you with lawyers in your area who practice in the relevant field. Referral services typically screen lawyers for licensing and good standing, and many offer initial consultations at reduced rates (often $25 to $50 for 30 minutes). This is an excellent way to get professional advice at low cost, even if you cannot afford full representation.

During an initial consultation, you can explain your situation, ask questions, get preliminary advice, and decide whether to hire the lawyer for further representation. Even if you ultimately represent yourself, a brief consultation can help you understand your options, identify potential problems, and develop a strategy.

Lawyer referral services usually ask about your legal issue, your location, and sometimes your budget. They then provide contact information for two or three lawyers who handle that type of case. You call the lawyers directly to schedule your consultation. The reduced-fee consultation is a benefit of using the referral service; the lawyer has agreed to this arrangement in exchange for client referrals.

Public education materials: Brochures, videos, articles, and guides on common legal topics like wills, small claims court, landlord-tenant law, divorce, and consumer rights. These materials are usually written in plain language and reviewed by lawyers for accuracy. They explain legal concepts, outline procedures, describe common pitfalls, and suggest resources for further assistance.

Many bar associations produce video series on legal topics, offer webinars, and maintain libraries of written guides that can be downloaded for free. These materials are updated regularly to reflect changes in law and are tailored to your state's specific rules and procedures.

Consumer guides: Information on how to hire a lawyer, what to expect from the attorney-client relationship, how to file complaints about lawyers, and how to avoid legal scams. These guides help you become an informed consumer of legal services.

Topics covered include how lawyers charge for their services (hourly rates, flat fees, contingency fees), what questions to ask before hiring a lawyer, how to read and understand fee agreements, what to do if you disagree with your lawyer's advice or bills, and how the disciplinary process works if a lawyer behaves unethically.

Pro bono and legal aid directories: Lists of organizations and programs that provide free or low-cost legal services, including eligibility requirements and contact information. Bar associations maintain these directories as a public service, helping connect people who need legal help with organizations that can provide it.

These directories are organized by practice area (family law, housing, immigration, etc.) and by location. They include information about income limits, types of cases handled, application processes, and contact details. Checking the directory is often the fastest way to find appropriate free or low-cost assistance.

Know Your Rights resources: Many bar associations publish guides explaining your rights in specific situations, like traffic stops, arrest, eviction, or employment termination. These guides are practical, focusing on what you can and cannot do, what officials can and cannot do, and what consequences may follow from different choices.

For example, a guide on traffic stops might explain that you must provide your license and registration when asked, that you have the right to refuse a search of your vehicle in most circumstances, and that you have the right to remain silent. A guide on eviction might explain how much notice your landlord must give, what reasons justify eviction, and how to respond to an eviction lawsuit.

Ethics hotlines: Some bar associations operate hotlines where you can ask questions about lawyer ethics and professional conduct. If you are concerned about how a lawyer has treated you, or if you want to know whether certain behavior is appropriate, you can call for guidance before deciding whether to file a formal complaint.

Fee arbitration programs: If you have a dispute with a lawyer about fees or billing, many bar associations offer fee arbitration programs. These programs provide a neutral third party who reviews the bill, listens to both sides, and issues a decision about what fee is reasonable. This process is faster and cheaper than filing a lawsuit.

To find your state bar association, search for "[your state] bar association" or "[your state] state bar." Again, use the official .gov or .org site. Most state bars have prominent "For the Public" or "Find a Lawyer" sections on their websites.

Attorney General Offices

Each state has an attorney general (AG) who serves as the state's chief legal officer. The AG's office enforces consumer protection laws, investigates fraud, handles civil litigation on behalf of the state, and provides legal guidance on state law.

State attorney general offices publish:

Consumer protection information: Guides on avoiding scams, understanding your rights when buying goods or services, how to file complaints about businesses, and how to report fraud. AG offices often maintain hotlines or online complaint forms where you can report problems with businesses, contractors, telemarketers, or online sellers.

Consumer protection divisions investigate complaints and can take enforcement action against businesses that violate consumer protection laws. While they cannot resolve individual disputes or get your money back, they can identify patterns of misconduct and pursue legal action that benefits all consumers. They also publish alerts about common scams and fraudulent schemes.

Topics covered in consumer protection materials include:

Auto sales and repairs: Your rights when buying new or used cars, lemon laws, dealer obligations, and how to resolve disputes with mechanics.

Home improvement and contractors: How to choose a contractor, what should be in written contracts, how to verify licenses and insurance, and what to do if work is substandard or incomplete.

Debt collection: What debt collectors can and cannot do, how to dispute debts, how to stop harassment, and your rights under federal and state debt collection laws.

Credit reports and identity theft: How to get free credit reports, how to dispute errors, steps to take if your identity is stolen, and how to place fraud alerts or credit freezes.

Telemarketing and robocalls: How to stop unwanted calls, how to register for the Do Not Call list, and how to report illegal telemarketing.

Online shopping and e-commerce: Your rights when buying online, how to avoid fake websites, what to do if products are not delivered or are defective, and how to dispute charges with your credit card company.

Charitable giving: How to verify that charities are legitimate, how donations are used, and how to report fundraising fraud.

Landlord-tenant issues: Summaries of key landlord-tenant laws, security deposit rules, eviction procedures, and tenant rights regarding repairs and habitability.

Employment rights materials: Explanations of state labor laws, wage and hour protections, discrimination prohibitions, and how to file complaints with state labor agencies. State labor departments (sometimes separate from the AG's office but often linked) enforce laws regarding minimum wage, overtime, meal and rest breaks, wage theft, workplace safety, and unemployment insurance.

Materials explain what to do if your employer fails to pay you, refuses to provide required breaks, misclassifies you as an independent contractor to avoid paying benefits, or retaliates against you for asserting your rights. They describe how to file wage claims, request unemployment benefits, and report safety violations.

State AG offices also enforce employment discrimination laws (often in coordination with federal agencies) and publish guides explaining protections against discrimination based on race, gender, age, disability, religion, national origin, sexual orientation, and other protected characteristics. These guides explain how to recognize discrimination, how to file complaints, and what remedies are available.

Housing issues guidance: Information on tenant rights, landlord obligations, fair housing laws, and how to report housing discrimination or predatory lending. Fair housing laws prohibit discrimination in renting, buying, and financing housing based on protected characteristics. AG offices investigate complaints and can bring enforcement actions against landlords, real estate agents, and lenders who violate these laws.

Materials also cover predatory lending practices, including high-interest payday loans, car title loans, mortgage fraud, and foreclosure rescue scams. If you are facing foreclosure, AG resources explain your options, including loan modifications, payment plans, and legal protections against wrongful foreclosure.

Alerts about scams and enforcement actions: Regular updates on current scams targeting residents (like IRS impersonation, lottery fraud, tech support scams, romance scams, or cryptocurrency fraud) and announcements about enforcement actions against companies or individuals who violated the law. These alerts help you recognize and avoid fraud.

Scam alerts describe how the scam works, what warning signs to look for, and what steps to take if you have been targeted. They often include real examples of scam messages or calls so you can recognize them. Staying informed about current scams significantly reduces your risk of becoming a victim.

Legal opinions: Formal opinions interpreting state law, usually written for government agencies but sometimes relevant to public questions about what the law requires. These opinions address novel or unclear legal questions and provide authoritative guidance on how state law should be interpreted. While they are technical and written for lawyers, they can be useful for understanding how the AG's office views particular legal issues.

Data breach notifications: Many state AG offices maintain lists of data breaches affecting state residents. If a company experiences a data breach that exposes personal information, they are required to notify affected individuals and, in many states, the attorney general. These notifications help you take protective steps like changing passwords, monitoring credit reports, and watching for signs of identity theft.

Health care and insurance resources: Information about patient rights, how to file complaints about health care providers or insurers, understanding health insurance coverage, and resolving billing disputes. Some AG offices have dedicated health care divisions that handle complaints and enforce health care fraud laws.

To find your state attorney general, search for "[your state] attorney general" and use the official government website. Look for sections labeled "Consumer Protection," "Consumer Resources," or "File a Complaint."

Local Government Websites

Cities and counties have their own legal rules and resources, particularly for issues related to property, business operations, and local services. Local law often goes beyond state law, creating additional rights and obligations.

Local government websites often provide:

Housing codes and landlord-tenant ordinances: Many cities have rental housing regulations that go beyond state law, covering issues like security deposits, habitability standards, rent control, eviction procedures, and tenant protections. Some cities require landlords to register rental properties, obtain rental licenses, and comply with inspection requirements.

Local housing codes specify minimum standards for heating, plumbing, electricity, pest control, and structural safety. If your rental unit does not meet these standards, you may have grounds to demand repairs, withhold rent (in some jurisdictions), or terminate your lease. Local code enforcement departments inspect properties and can order landlords to make repairs or face fines.

Rent control and rent stabilization ordinances, where they exist, limit how much and how often landlords can increase rent. These ordinances also often provide additional protections against eviction, requiring landlords to have "just cause" to terminate tenancies. Understanding local rent control rules is essential for both landlords and tenants.

Business licenses and permits: Information on how to obtain business licenses, permits for specific activities (like food service, construction, or selling alcohol), and zoning regulations that determine where businesses can operate. Starting a business requires compliance with local licensing requirements, which vary by business type and location.

Local governments regulate businesses to protect public health and safety. Restaurants must obtain health permits and pass inspections. Contractors must be licensed and bonded. Home-based businesses may need special permits. Selling goods on the street requires vendor licenses. Local websites explain what permits you need, how to apply, what fees apply, and what inspections or approvals are required.

Zoning information: Zoning maps and rules that control land use, whether you can operate a business from home, and what types of development are allowed in different areas. Zoning divides cities and counties into districts (residential, commercial, industrial, agricultural) and specifies what activities are permitted in each district.

Before buying property or starting a business, check zoning rules to ensure your intended use is allowed. Zoning regulations affect whether you can build additions, rent out rooms, park commercial vehicles, keep certain animals, or operate businesses from your home. Violating zoning rules can result in fines, orders to cease operations, or even demolition orders for illegal construction.

Many local governments now provide online zoning maps and lookup tools where you can enter an address and see what zoning district applies, what uses are permitted, and what restrictions exist. You can also apply for variances (exceptions to zoning rules) or conditional use permits if you want to use property in ways not automatically allowed.

Local ordinances: City and county laws on topics like noise, parking, nuisance violations, animal control, building codes, tree removal, and property maintenance. Violating local ordinances can result in fines, corrective orders, or even criminal charges in some cases.

Common local ordinances include:

Noise ordinances: Limits on loud music, construction noise, barking dogs, and other disturbances. These ordinances typically specify quiet hours (often 10 p.m. to 7 a.m.) and acceptable noise levels.

Parking regulations: Where you can and cannot park, how long you can park in one spot, permit requirements for residential parking, and penalties for violations.

Property maintenance: Requirements to maintain yards, remove trash, repair fences, control weeds, and keep properties in good condition. Failure to maintain property can result in fines and even city-ordered cleanup at the owner's expense.

Animal control: Leash laws, limits on the number of pets, requirements for licensing and vaccinations, and rules for controlling dangerous or nuisance animals.

Smoking regulations: Where smoking and vaping are prohibited, including parks, beaches, restaurants, bars, and near building entrances.

Short-term rental regulations: Rules governing Airbnb and similar rentals, including licensing requirements, occupancy limits, and restrictions on where short-term rentals are allowed.

Complaint and inspection departments: Contact information for reporting housing code violations, unsafe conditions, illegal activity, or seeking inspections of rental properties. Local governments have code enforcement officers who investigate complaints, inspect properties, and issue citations for violations.

If you are a tenant living in substandard conditions, you can request an inspection. If violations are found, the landlord is ordered to make repairs within a specific timeframe. Landlords who fail to comply face escalating fines and potential legal action. Some jurisdictions allow tenants to withhold rent or use rent money to make repairs themselves if landlords fail to address serious habitability problems.

Public records access: Information on how to request public records under state open records laws. Local governments maintain records on property ownership, building permits, business licenses, government contracts, meeting minutes, budgets, employee salaries, and much more. You have the right to inspect and copy most public records, though some exceptions apply for privacy and security reasons.

Public records requests are useful for researching properties before buying, investigating businesses, verifying contractors' licenses and permits, monitoring government spending, and holding officials accountable. Most local governments have designated public records officers and specific procedures for submitting requests.

Local court information: For cities and counties with their own courts (like municipal courts or county courts), information about filing cases, small claims procedures, traffic ticket contests, and court schedules. Municipal courts typically handle traffic violations, city ordinance violations, and small civil cases. County courts may handle evictions, small claims, misdemeanors, and preliminary hearings for serious crimes.

To find your local government resources, search for "[your city or county] government" or "[your city or county] official website." City and county websites are usually organized by department, so look for "Housing,"

"Planning," "Building and Safety," "Consumer Affairs," "Code Enforcement," or similar sections.

State Legislature Websites

Each state maintains a legislative website where you can read current laws (statutes), track bills under consideration, and learn about your elected representatives. Understanding what the law actually says is critical for asserting your rights and making informed decisions.

State legislature websites typically include:

State codes and statutes: Searchable databases of all state laws, organized by subject area. You can search by keyword, browse by topic, or look up specific code sections. State codes are the permanent laws passed by the legislature, covering everything from criminal law to family law to business regulations.

Reading statutes requires care. Legal language is precise and sometimes difficult to understand. Look for definitions sections at the beginning of each chapter, which explain key terms. Pay attention to exceptions, conditions, and cross-references to other statutes. If a statute is unclear, look for court cases or attorney general opinions that interpret it.

Bill tracking: Information about proposed legislation currently under consideration. You can search for bills by number, subject, or sponsor. Each bill's page shows its current status (in committee, passed one house, awaiting governor's signature, etc.), the text of the bill, amendments, voting records, and scheduled hearings.

Tracking bills helps you stay informed about potential changes to laws that affect you. If you have strong views on proposed legislation, you can contact your representatives, submit written comments, or testify at public hearings.

Committee information: Details about legislative committees, including membership, schedules, agendas, and how to participate in hearings. Committees review bills before they go to the full legislature for a vote. Most committees hold public hearings where citizens can provide input.

Legislative reports and studies: Research reports, fiscal analyses, and policy studies produced by legislative staff or commissioned by the legislature. These documents provide background information on policy issues, analyze the potential impacts of proposed laws, and summarize public testimony.

Contact information for legislators: Names, districts, party affiliations, contact information, and office hours for your state representatives and senators. You have the right to communicate with your elected officials about laws and policies that affect you. Most legislators maintain district offices where constituents can meet with them or their staff.

To find your state legislature website, search for "[your state] legislature" or "[your state] general assembly" (some states use different names). Look for sections labeled "Laws," "Statutes," "Bills," or "Legislative Information."

State Administrative Agencies

Beyond courts, legislatures, and attorney general offices, states have numerous administrative agencies that regulate specific areas and provide public resources:

State labor departments: Enforce wage and hour laws, investigate workplace safety violations, process unemployment claims, and provide information about workers' rights. If you have problems with unpaid wages, workplace discrimination, or denied unemployment benefits, the labor department is your first stop.

State revenue departments: Handle tax issues, including income tax, sales tax, property tax, and business taxes. If you have questions about tax obligations, need to resolve tax disputes, or want to set up payment plans for tax debt, contact the revenue department.

Licensing boards: Regulate professions like medicine, nursing, law, real estate, contracting, cosmetology, and many others. These boards issue licenses, investigate complaints against professionals, and can discipline or revoke licenses for misconduct. If you have problems with a licensed professional, filing a complaint with the licensing board can result in investigation and sanctions.

Insurance departments: Regulate insurance companies, investigate complaints about unfair practices, and provide consumer information about insurance coverage. If your insurance company denies a claim you believe should be covered, or if you have problems with policy cancellations or rate increases, the insurance department can help.

Public utility commissions: Regulate utilities like electricity, gas, water, and telecommunications. They approve rate increases, investigate service complaints, and ensure that utilities provide adequate service. If you have billing disputes or service problems with utilities, the public utility commission may be able to assist.

Health departments: Enforce public health laws, inspect restaurants and food facilities, investigate disease outbreaks, and provide information about health services. Local health departments often handle environmental health issues like sewage problems, contaminated water, and pest infestations.

Environmental agencies: Enforce environmental laws, regulate pollution, manage natural resources, and provide information about environmental hazards. If you are concerned about pollution, hazardous waste, water quality, or other environmental problems, contact your state environmental agency.

Departments of motor vehicles: Handle driver licensing, vehicle registration, title transfers, and traffic safety programs. DMV websites provide information about licensing requirements, how to register vehicles, what to do if you buy or sell a car, and how to contest license suspensions.

Social services agencies: Administer public benefits programs like Medicaid, food assistance (SNAP), cash assistance (TANF), child welfare services, and adult protective services. If you need public benefits or have problems with benefit applications or terminations, these agencies provide assistance and handle appeals.

To find state agencies, search for the agency name plus your state, or visit your state government's main website and look for an agency directory.

Best Practices for Online Legal Research

When researching online, always confirm that information applies to your state and is current. Laws change frequently through legislation, court decisions, and regulatory updates. A guide written five years ago may no longer reflect current law. An article about California law does not help you if you live in Michigan.

Verify the source: Use official government websites (.gov) or trusted legal organizations (.org). Be cautious of commercial sites (.com) that may be trying to sell products or services, or that may contain inaccurate or outdated information. Some commercial sites offer forms or services that appear official but are actually private businesses charging for information or forms that are available for free from courts.

Government websites are recognizable by the .gov domain. Nonprofit organizations use .org domains. Law schools, bar associations, legal aid organizations, and court systems are trustworthy sources. Be especially skeptical of sites that require payment for forms or information before showing you what you are buying.

Check the date: Look for when the information was published or last updated. If the date is not visible, the information may be outdated. Legal guides should be updated at least annually, and ideally more frequently for areas where law changes rapidly.

Courts and government agencies typically date their forms and publications. If you cannot find a date, contact the organization to ask whether the information is current. Using outdated forms or following outdated procedures can result in rejected filings, missed deadlines, and lost cases.

Confirm jurisdiction: Make sure the information applies to your state and, if relevant, your county or city. Federal law applies everywhere, but most everyday legal issues are governed by state or local law. An excellent guide to landlord-tenant law in Oregon is useless if you live in Florida.

When reading legal information online, look for clear statements about which jurisdiction the information covers. National websites sometimes provide state-specific pages or dropdown menus to select your state. Always verify that you are reading information for your location.

Cross-reference: If possible, verify information by checking multiple trusted sources. If one source says something different from others, investigate further or consult a professional. Discrepancies might indicate that the law is unclear, that one source is outdated, or that different jurisdictions have different rules.

For important matters, do not rely on a single source. Compare information from the court website, the state bar, and legal aid organizations. If they all say the same thing, you can be confident the information is accurate.

Read carefully and completely: Legal documents and guides are written precisely. Words matter. Pay attention to conditions, exceptions, and qualifications. A statement that "you must file within 30 days" means exactly that, not 31 days or "about a month." A requirement that you "serve copies on all parties" means everyone involved, not just the person on the other side.

Many legal mistakes happen because people skim information, miss important details, or assume they understand when they do not. Slow down. Read carefully. Take notes. Make sure you understand before taking action.

Understand the difference between legal information and legal advice: Legal information explains what the law says and how it generally applies. Legal advice tells you what you specifically should do in your particular situation. Websites, books, and self-help materials provide information. Lawyers provide advice.

You can use legal information to understand your situation and make informed decisions, but you should not assume that general information applies perfectly to your specific facts. If your situation is complicated, if there are significant consequences to getting it wrong, or if you are uncertain about what to do, consult a lawyer for advice tailored to your circumstances.

Be cautious of forums and social media: Online forums, Facebook groups, and social media posts can provide emotional support and general information, but they are not reliable sources of legal advice. What worked for someone else may not apply to your situation, and advice from non-lawyers can be dangerously wrong.

People who post on forums are usually not lawyers, and even if they claim to be, you cannot verify their credentials or rely on their information. Laws vary by state and change over time. Someone's experience in Ohio three years ago may be completely irrelevant to your situation in Georgia today. Forum posts can be helpful for understanding others' experiences and learning what questions to ask, but never rely on them as your only source of information.

Document what you find: Save copies of forms, guides, and other materials you find online. Print them or save them as PDFs. Legal websites change, information is updated, and pages are sometimes removed. Having your own copies ensures you can refer back to the information you relied on.

Keep notes about where you found information, including the website address, the date you accessed it, and what it said. This documentation can be useful if you need to prove you relied on official information, or if you need to find updated versions later.

Know when to stop researching and get help: Legal research can be overwhelming. Issues that seem simple often turn out to be complex. If you find yourself confused, reading contradictory information, or uncertain about how to proceed, it is time to consult a professional. Many people waste weeks researching when a 30-minute consultation with a lawyer would provide clarity and direction.

Understanding Jurisdictional Differences

Jurisdiction refers to the geographic area and the type of legal authority that governs a particular issue. Understanding jurisdiction is critical because the wrong information for the wrong jurisdiction can lead you astray.

Federal vs. state jurisdiction: Some legal issues are governed by federal law (the same everywhere in the United States) and some by state law (different in each state). Federal law covers issues like immigration, bankruptcy, Social Security, federal taxes, patents, copyrights, and violations of federal criminal law. State law covers issues like divorce, child custody, most criminal prosecutions, landlord-tenant disputes, wills and estates, personal injury, contracts, and most business regulation.

Some issues involve both federal and state law. Employment discrimination, for example, is prohibited by both federal law (Title VII, ADA, ADEA) and state laws, which may provide additional protections. When researching, determine whether your issue is governed by federal law, state law, or both.

State variations: Even when the general legal principle is the same across states, details vary. Consider divorce law: all states allow no-fault divorce, but residency requirements differ (some states require six months' residency, others require one year), grounds for divorce vary, property division rules are different (community property vs. equitable distribution), and procedures for filing and serving divorce papers are not uniform.

Similarly, landlord-tenant law varies widely. Some states require 30 days' notice to terminate a month-to-month tenancy; others require 60 days. Some states allow landlords to enter rental units with 24 hours' notice; others require more. Security deposit limits and return deadlines differ. Eviction procedures and timelines vary. Always research your specific state's law.

Local variations: Within states, cities and counties may have their own rules. As discussed above, local governments enact ordinances on housing, business licensing, zoning, and other local matters. A tenant in San Francisco has different rights than a tenant in rural California because San Francisco has extensive local tenant protection laws. Always check whether your city or county has local rules that go beyond state law.

Court jurisdiction: Different courts handle different types of cases. Small claims courts handle civil cases involving modest amounts of money (limits vary by state, typically $5,000 to $10,000). Family courts handle divorce, custody, and domestic relations matters. Probate courts handle estates and guardianships. Criminal courts handle criminal prosecutions. Knowing which court handles your type of case is essential for filing correctly.

Additionally, courts have geographic jurisdiction. You must file in the correct county, usually where the defendant lives, where the incident occurred, or where property is located (rules vary by case type). Filing in the wrong court results in your case being dismissed or transferred, wasting time and money.

Keeping Information Current

Laws change constantly. Legislatures pass new statutes. Courts issue new decisions that change how laws are interpreted. Agencies adopt new regulations. What was true last year may not be true today.

Track legal changes: Subscribe to updates from state courts, bar associations, and legal aid organizations. Many provide email newsletters or RSS feeds alerting subscribers to changes in law, new court decisions, or updated procedures. Following these updates keeps you informed.

Verify before relying: Before taking action based on legal information, especially if that information is more than a year old, verify that it is still current. Check the court website for updated forms. Confirm that statutes have not been amended. Ask whether procedures have changed.

Watch for effective dates: When laws change, they do not always take effect immediately. New legislation may have an effective date months or even a year after it is passed. Court rules changes are often announced weeks in advance to give people time to prepare. Pay attention to effective dates to ensure you are following the current rules.

Understand the difference between settled and unsettled law: Some areas of law are well-established and stable. Other areas are in flux, with ongoing litigation, pending legislation, or recent changes that have not yet been fully interpreted. If you are dealing with an area where law is changing rapidly, be especially cautious and consider seeking professional advice.

When to Move Beyond Self-Help Resources

Self-help resources are valuable, but they have limits. Some situations require professional legal assistance:

Complex legal issues: If your legal problem involves multiple areas of law, complicated facts, significant amounts of money, or difficult legal questions, self-help may not be sufficient. Examples include business disputes involving multiple parties, contested estates with complicated assets, or civil rights cases raising novel legal theories.

High stakes: The more serious the potential consequences, the more important it is to have professional help. Criminal charges that could result in jail time, cases that could result in losing your home or custody of your children, or disputes involving large sums of money warrant hiring a lawyer if at all possible.

Opposing party has a lawyer: If the other side is represented by a lawyer and you are not, you are at a significant disadvantage. Lawyers know the rules, understand strategy, can anticipate problems, and present cases persuasively. While you can represent yourself against a lawyer, doing so is difficult and risky.

Procedural complications: If you do not understand court procedures, keep making mistakes with filings, or feel overwhelmed by the process, get help. Missing deadlines, filing incorrect documents, or failing to properly serve papers can result in losing your case regardless of the merits.

Negotiations and settlements: Lawyers are skilled negotiators who understand the value of cases and can often achieve better settlements than self-represented parties. If you are considering settling a case, consulting a lawyer about whether the settlement is fair can prevent you from accepting too little or giving up important rights.

Appeals: Appealing a court decision is a specialized and complex process with strict deadlines and procedural requirements. If you lost at trial and want to appeal, you need a lawyer. Appellate courts have extremely technical rules, and mistakes are almost never excusable.

Do not let pride or stubbornness prevent you from seeking help when you need it. Representing yourself in appropriate situations (like simple small claims cases or uncontested matters) is perfectly reasonable. But attempting to handle complex, high-stakes cases without professional help often leads to poor outcomes that could have been avoided.

Final Thoughts on State Resources

The legal resources available to you depend on where you live. Some states have invested heavily in self-help resources, offer extensive pro bono programs, and maintain user-friendly court websites. Other states lag behind, with fewer resources and less assistance available to self-represented parties.

Regardless of where you live, start with official government sources. They are more reliable, more current, and more relevant than commercial websites or general information. Take advantage of free resources like court self-help centers, lawyer referral services, and legal aid organizations.

Approach legal research methodically. Identify your specific legal issue. Determine which area of law applies. Find state-specific resources. Read carefully and thoroughly. Verify that information is current. Take notes and save documents. Ask questions when you do not understand. And recognize when a problem exceeds your ability to handle it alone.

Laws change, and outdated guidance can be as harmful as no guidance at all. Using a form from 2015 may result in your filing being rejected. Following advice based on a law that was repealed could lead to losing your case. Always verify that information is current before relying on it.

You are now equipped with knowledge of where to look, what to look for, and how to evaluate what you find. Use this knowledge wisely. Legal problems are stressful, but access to good information reduces that stress and improves your chances of achieving a fair outcome. The resources are available. Now you know how to find them.

Appendix B: Free and Low-Cost Legal Help

Legal assistance is not limited to those who can afford private attorneys. Many organizations exist to provide help at reduced or no cost, funded by government grants, charitable donations, or volunteer lawyer time. While these resources are often overwhelmed with demand and cannot help everyone, they are critical safety nets for people facing serious legal problems without the means to pay for representation.

Understanding what resources are available and how to access them can make the difference between losing your rights and protecting them. This appendix provides a comprehensive guide to finding and using free and low-cost legal services.

Legal Aid Organizations

Legal aid organizations are nonprofit entities that provide free legal services to people who meet income and asset eligibility requirements. These organizations are funded by a combination of federal and state grants, private donations, and court filing fees. They employ staff attorneys and paralegals who handle cases for clients at no charge.

Legal aid is the primary source of free legal representation for low-income Americans. These organizations handle hundreds of thousands of cases each year, from preventing wrongful evictions to protecting victims of domestic violence to securing disability benefits for people unable to work.

What Legal Aid Organizations Handle

Legal aid organizations typically focus on civil legal matters (not criminal defense) affecting basic human needs:

Housing: Eviction defense, habitability complaints, subsidized housing issues, foreclosure prevention, housing discrimination, landlord-tenant disputes, security deposit recovery, repairs and maintenance issues, lease violations, public housing terminations.

Family law: Divorce, custody, child support, domestic violence protective orders, guardianship, adoption, paternity, visitation rights, modification of custody or support orders, termination of parental rights, grandparent visitation.

Employment: Wage theft, unemployment benefits, workplace discrimination, wrongful termination, unpaid overtime, independent contractor misclassification, workplace safety violations, retaliation for whistleblowing, denial of family or medical leave.

Public benefits: Assistance with Social Security, Medicaid, food stamps (SNAP), disability benefits, veterans' benefits, SSI (Supplemental Security Income), denial or termination of benefits, appeals of agency decisions, nursing home coverage.

Immigration: Asylum, deportation defense, family-based immigration, naturalization, VAWA (Violence Against Women Act) petitions, U visas for crime victims, T visas for trafficking victims, DACA (Deferred Action for Childhood Arrivals), adjustment of status.

Consumer issues: Debt collection defense, credit reporting errors, predatory lending, utility shutoffs, repossession, bankruptcy, unfair business practices, scams targeting seniors or vulnerable populations, identity theft.

Elder law: Issues affecting seniors, including elder abuse, guardianship, nursing home rights, Medicare and Medicaid, powers of attorney, advance directives, age discrimination, financial exploitation.

Education: Special education rights for children with disabilities, school discipline issues, discrimination, denial of services, IEP (Individualized Education Program) disputes.

Health: Access to medical care, health insurance denials, patient rights, medical debt, disability accommodations, mental health treatment access.

What Legal Aid Organizations Do Not Handle

Legal aid organizations do not handle certain types of cases, including most criminal matters (except some post-conviction issues like expungements or record sealing), fee-generating cases (like personal injury or medical malpractice where a lawyer could be paid from a settlement), and cases on behalf of businesses or for-profit entities. They generally cannot help with simple wills or estate planning unless the client is elderly or has special circumstances.

Income Eligibility Requirements

Legal aid organizations have strict income and asset limits. Generally, you must earn below 125% to 200% of the federal poverty level to qualify, though some programs have higher limits for specific case types. As of 2025, this means:

For a single person: annual income below approximately $15,000 to $30,000 depending on the program

For a family of four: annual income below approximately $31,000 to $62,000 depending on the program

These limits vary by state and by the specific legal aid program. Some programs serving victims of domestic violence or seniors may have more flexible eligibility criteria. Most programs also consider your assets, though they typically exclude your primary residence and one vehicle.

When you apply to legal aid, you will need to provide proof of income such as pay stubs, tax returns, benefit statements, or a letter from your employer. If you have no income, you may need to provide a sworn statement explaining your situation.

How to Find Legal Aid in Your Area

Online searches: Search for "[your state or county] legal aid" or "[your city] legal services." Most legal aid organizations have websites with information about their services, eligibility requirements, and application processes.

LawHelp.org: Visit LawHelp.org, a national directory of legal aid programs and resources. You can search by state and by legal issue to find organizations that can help with your specific problem.

State bar associations: Call your state bar association's referral service and ask for legal aid contact information. Bar associations maintain lists of legal aid providers throughout the state.

Court self-help centers: Contact your local court's self-help center for referrals. Court staff can direct you to legal aid organizations serving your area.

211 hotline: Dial 211 from any phone to reach a community resource hotline that can provide referrals to legal aid and other social services in your area.

Libraries: Ask librarians at your public library for help finding legal aid resources. Many libraries maintain information about local legal services.

What to Expect When You Contact Legal Aid

When you first contact a legal aid organization, you will likely go through an intake process. This usually involves:

Initial screening: You will be asked basic questions about your legal problem, your income, and your household size to determine if you meet eligibility requirements.

Detailed intake: If you appear eligible, you will be asked to provide more detailed information about your legal issue. Be prepared to explain your situation clearly and provide any relevant documents.

Document gathering: You may be asked to provide proof of income, identification, and documents related to your legal problem (such as court papers, eviction notices, or letters from government agencies).

Wait time: Many legal aid programs have waiting lists. You may not receive help immediately. Ask how long the wait typically is and what you should do in the meantime.

Case acceptance decision: Not all cases can be accepted. Legal aid organizations must prioritize based on the severity of the problem, the likelihood of success, the resources required, and other factors.

Be prepared for the possibility that legal aid programs are full and cannot take your case. They receive far more requests than they can handle. Nationwide, legal aid organizations can help only about 20% of people who seek their services due to limited funding and overwhelming demand.

If you are turned away, ask if they can refer you to other resources or provide limited assistance like document review, advice, or self-help materials. Some legal aid organizations offer "brief services" where they cannot represent you fully but can help you understand your options or review documents you have prepared yourself.

Tips for Working with Legal Aid

Apply as early as possible: Do not wait until the last minute. Legal problems are easier to solve when addressed early, and legal aid organizations need time to review your case.

Be honest and complete: Provide all relevant information, even if you think it might hurt your case. Your lawyer needs the full picture to help you effectively.

Keep all documents organized: Maintain a file with all papers related to your legal problem. Bring copies (not originals) to your appointments.

Respond promptly: If legal aid asks you for additional information or documents, provide them as quickly as possible. Delays on your part can result in your case being closed.

Attend all appointments: Missing appointments can result in your case being closed. If you cannot make an appointment, call as soon as possible to reschedule.

Follow your lawyer's advice: Your legal aid attorney is working to help you. Follow their instructions and recommendations.

Pro Bono Programs

"Pro bono" is Latin for "for the public good," and it refers to legal services provided by lawyers for free. Many lawyers volunteer a portion of their time to handle cases for people who cannot afford representation. Pro bono programs are typically coordinated by bar associations, nonprofit organizations, or law firms.

Pro bono services are similar to legal aid but are provided by volunteer private attorneys rather than staff attorneys at nonprofit organizations. Pro bono lawyers may handle a wider range of cases, including some types that legal aid does not cover. A corporate attorney who normally works on business transactions might volunteer to handle a consumer protection case, or a family law specialist might take on custody matters for low-income parents.

How Pro Bono Programs Work

Pro bono programs match volunteer lawyers with people who need legal help. The process typically involves:

- **Intake and screening:** You contact the pro bono program and provide information about your legal issue and financial situation.
- **Case review:** Program staff or volunteer attorneys review your case to determine if it is appropriate for pro bono representation.
- **Matching:** If your case is accepted, the program matches you with a volunteer attorney who has expertise in the relevant area of law.
- **Representation:** The volunteer attorney represents you at no charge, just as they would a paying client.

Types of Pro Bono Programs

Bar association programs: State and local bar associations often coordinate pro bono projects. These may include legal advice clinics, volunteer panels, or specific initiatives targeting particular legal needs.

Law firm programs: Large and mid-sized law firms typically have pro bono coordinators who manage volunteer opportunities for their attorneys. Some firms dedicate significant resources to pro bono work.

Nonprofit coordination: Organizations like the Volunteer Lawyers Project or Pro Bono Net coordinate volunteers and match them with clients.

Court-based programs: Some courts operate pro bono programs where volunteer lawyers provide representation to people appearing without attorneys.

Issue-specific programs: Some pro bono programs focus on particular issues such as veterans' legal needs, immigrants' rights, or small business formation.

How to Access Pro Bono Services

State or local bar associations: Contact your state or local bar association and ask about pro bono programs. Many bar associations have dedicated pro bono coordinators who can explain available services.

Online searches: Search for "pro bono" + [your state or city]. Many pro bono programs have websites with application information.

Legal aid referrals: Inquire with legal aid organizations, which sometimes coordinate pro bono referrals. If they cannot take your case, they may be able to refer you to a pro bono volunteer.

Law firm websites: Visit websites of large law firms in your area and look for information about pro bono programs or community service. Some firms have online forms for pro bono requests.

Specialty bar associations: Contact specialty bar associations (such as women lawyers' associations, Hispanic bar associations, or LGBT bar associations) that may coordinate pro bono services for their communities.

Pro bono programs often have intake processes and case selection criteria. Not all requests will be accepted, as volunteer lawyers have limited time and typically prioritize serious cases with clear merit. Cases involving straightforward legal issues, significant impact on the client's life, and reasonable likelihood of success are more likely to be accepted.

What to Expect from Pro Bono Representation

Pro bono representation is professional legal representation provided without charge. Your pro bono attorney owes you the same duties of competence, diligence, and loyalty as they owe to paying clients. You should expect:

- **Competent representation:** The attorney will apply their knowledge and skill to your case.
- **Communication:** The attorney will keep you informed about your case and respond to your questions.
- **Confidentiality:** Everything you tell your attorney is protected by attorney-client privilege.
- **Professional conduct:** The attorney will represent your interests zealously within the bounds of the law.

However, understand that pro bono attorneys are volunteering their time in addition to their regular work responsibilities. This may mean:

- Communication might be less frequent than with a full-time legal aid attorney

- Court dates and deadlines will be prioritized, but non-urgent matters may take longer
- The attorney may have limited time for extensive research or investigation compared to a paid engagement

These limitations do not mean pro bono representation is inferior. Many pro bono volunteers are highly skilled attorneys who take their volunteer work very seriously. But it helps to understand the practical realities of volunteer representation.

Law School Clinics

Many law schools operate legal clinics where law students, supervised by experienced attorney-professors, provide free legal services to low-income clients. These clinics serve a dual purpose: they give law students practical experience while providing much-needed legal help to the community.

Law school clinics are often hidden gems in the world of free legal services. The quality of representation is typically excellent because students work under close faculty supervision, conduct thorough research, and bring energy and dedication to their cases.

Areas of Practice

Law school clinics typically specialize in specific areas such as:

- **Immigration:** Asylum applications, deportation defense, family-based petitions, naturalization, DACA, removal proceedings, immigration court representation.
- **Housing and eviction defense:** Eviction defense, habitability issues, subsidized housing, security deposits, landlord-tenant disputes, fair housing violations.
- **Small business formation and advice:** Entity formation, contract review, trademark registration, business planning, nonprofit formation.
- **Tax law:** Tax preparation, disputes with the IRS, innocent spouse relief, offers in compromise, tax debt resolution.
- **Veterans' rights:** Veterans' benefits, discharge upgrades, disability claims, appeals to the Board of Veterans' Appeals.

- **Criminal appeals or post-conviction relief:** Appeals of criminal convictions, sentence reductions, expungements, record sealing, clemency petitions.
- **Civil rights:** Police misconduct, discrimination, prisoners' rights, disability rights, First Amendment issues.
- **Environmental law:** Environmental justice, clean air and water, public health, community advocacy.
- **Consumer protection:** Predatory lending, debt collection, credit reporting, consumer fraud, bankruptcy.
- **Innocence projects:** Investigating and litigating claims of actual innocence for wrongfully convicted individuals.
- **Intellectual property:** Patent and trademark issues, copyright, licensing agreements.
- **Workers' rights:** Wage theft, unemployment benefits, workplace discrimination, labor organizing.
- **Health law:** Health insurance denials, access to medical care, public health advocacy.

Not every law school offers every type of clinic. The clinics available depend on the school's size, location, and faculty expertise.

Quality of Representation

The quality of representation from law school clinics is often very high. Students are closely supervised by experienced attorneys who are usually professors specializing in that area of law. Students conduct thorough research, have access to faculty expertise, and often spend more time on cases than busy practicing attorneys can afford to spend.

Law students in clinics are highly motivated. They want to learn, they want to do well, and they want to help their clients. They approach cases with fresh perspectives and thoroughness.

Cases tend to move more slowly than with private attorneys, as students are learning while working, but the level of attention and care can be excellent. If your case has an urgent deadline, make sure to mention this during intake so the clinic can assess whether they can handle it.

How to Find Law School Clinics

Law school websites: Search for law schools in your state and visit their websites. Look for sections labeled "Clinics," "Community Services," "Legal Services," "Centers," or "Clinical Programs."

Direct contact: Contact the law school directly and ask which clinics are accepting clients. Call the main number and ask to be connected to the clinical programs office.

Legal aid referrals: Check with legal aid or bar associations for referrals to local clinics. They often maintain lists of law school clinics and their areas of practice.

Online directories: Some states maintain directories of law school clinics and their practice areas.

University websites: If you are near a university with a law school, check the university's community engagement or service pages for information about legal clinics.

Application Process

Law school clinics have intake processes and case selection criteria. They often prioritize cases that provide good learning opportunities for students, which usually means cases with interesting legal issues rather than purely routine matters. A straightforward uncontested divorce might not be accepted, while an eviction case raising novel questions about landlord obligations might be ideal.

When you apply to a law school clinic:

- **Complete the intake process:** Fill out application forms thoroughly and provide all requested information about your legal issue and financial situation.
- **Provide documentation:** Gather and provide relevant documents such as court papers, contracts, letters, or notices related to your legal problem.
- **Be patient:** Law school clinics often operate on academic calendars. Cases are typically accepted at the beginning of semesters, and there may be breaks during exam periods or summer. Ask about timing when you apply.
- **Explain why your case is interesting:** If your case involves unusual facts or novel legal questions, mention this. Clinics look for cases that

will challenge students and teach them important skills.

- **Follow up:** If you do not hear back within a reasonable time, follow up with the clinic to check on the status of your application.

Working with a Law School Clinic

When you work with a law school clinic:

- **You will work primarily with students:** One or more law students will handle your case under faculty supervision. The supervising attorney (usually a professor) reviews all work and makes final decisions.

- **Expect thorough preparation:** Students typically prepare extensively for hearings, meetings, and negotiations. They may ask you many questions as they learn about your case.

- **Communication may involve multiple people:** You might communicate with both students and the supervising attorney. Make sure everyone stays informed about important developments.

- **Be available for meetings:** Clinics often need to meet with you multiple times to prepare your case. Be flexible and responsive to scheduling requests.

- **Academic calendar affects timing:** Law school clinics follow academic calendars, which means there may be busy periods (near exams) when communication slows and break periods when students are not available.

- **Trust the process:** Even though students are still learning, they are working hard on your case and have expert supervision. Give them the benefit of the doubt and follow their advice.

Court Self-Help Centers

Many courts, especially in larger jurisdictions, operate self-help centers that provide assistance to people representing themselves in legal matters. These centers are staffed by court employees, paralegals, or volunteer lawyers who can provide information, guidance on procedures, and help with forms, but usually cannot provide legal advice or represent you in court.

Self-help centers recognize that many people cannot afford attorneys and need help navigating the court system. They exist to make the legal process more accessible and to help people avoid mistakes that could harm their cases.

What Court Self-Help Centers Can Help With

Understanding court procedures: Self-help center staff can explain how the court process works, what steps you need to take, what documents you need to file, and what will happen at hearings or trials.

Choosing the correct forms: Courts use many different forms for different purposes. Self-help centers can help you identify which forms you need for your specific situation.

Filling out forms correctly and completely: Staff can review your forms to make sure you have filled them out properly, included all necessary information, and signed in the right places.

Filing procedures, fees, and deadlines: Self-help centers can explain how to file documents with the court, how much the filing fees are, whether you qualify for a fee waiver, and what deadlines apply to your case.

Preparing for hearings or trials: Staff can explain what to expect at court appearances, what documents to bring, how to present evidence, and general courtroom procedures and etiquette.

Accessing legal aid or lawyer referral services: Self-help centers maintain information about legal aid, pro bono programs, and lawyer referral services. They can help you find representation if possible.

Understanding court orders and judgments: If you have received a court order or judgment and do not understand it, self-help center staff can explain what it means and what you need to do to comply.

Language assistance: Many self-help centers provide services in multiple languages or can arrange for interpreters.

What Self-Help Centers Cannot Do

Provide legal advice: Self-help center staff cannot tell you what decision to make in your case, what legal strategy to pursue, or whether you should accept a settlement offer. They can explain your options but cannot recommend one option over another. This limitation exists because staff are not your attorneys and do not have a duty to advocate for your interests.

Represent you in court: Self-help center staff cannot appear in court with you, speak on your behalf, or act as your attorney.

Predict outcomes: Staff cannot tell you whether your case will succeed or what the judge is likely to decide. Every case depends on specific facts and the judge's discretion.

Help with cases against the government: In some circumstances, such as when you are suing a government agency, self-help centers operated by that same government may not be able to assist you due to conflicts of interest.

Draft documents for you: While staff can help you fill out standard forms, they cannot write custom legal documents like motions, briefs, or contracts.

Contact the other party: Self-help centers cannot negotiate with the other side in your case or communicate with them on your behalf.

Guarantee your forms are correct: While staff can review forms for completeness, the ultimate responsibility for accuracy rests with you.

How to Find a Court Self-Help Center

Court websites: Visit your local court's website and look for "Self-Help," "Family Law Facilitator," "Public Services," "Self-Represented Litigants," or similar sections.

Call the court clerk: Call the court clerk's office and ask if they have a self-help center, where it is located, and what hours it is open.

Visit the court: Visit the court in person and ask for the self-help center location. Look for signs directing you to the self-help center or ask security guards or information desk staff.

State court websites: Many state court systems have websites with information about self-help centers throughout the state.

Legal aid referrals: Legal aid organizations can tell you whether your local court has a self-help center.

Additional Resources from Self-Help Centers

Many self-help centers also offer:

- **Workshops:** Group sessions on common legal processes such as filing for divorce, responding to an eviction, or requesting a restraining order.

- **Instructional videos:** Many courts create videos explaining procedures and how to fill out forms. These may be available online or at the courthouse.

- **Written guides:** Detailed guides on common legal processes, often available in multiple languages.

- **Form packets:** Pre-assembled packets of all the forms you need for common cases, with instructions for completing them.

- **Free legal advice clinics:** Some self-help centers host regular clinics where volunteer lawyers provide brief legal advice on specific days. You may be able to speak with a lawyer for 15-30 minutes about your case.

- **Computers and printers:** Many self-help centers have computers with internet access and printers available for public use, allowing you to access online forms and information.

- **Notary services:** Some self-help centers offer free notary services for court documents.

Tips for Using Self-Help Centers Effectively

- **Arrive early:** Self-help centers can be busy, especially early in the morning and on Mondays. Arrive early to avoid long waits.

- **Bring all relevant documents:** Bring everything related to your case, including court papers, letters, contracts, photos, and any other evidence. Bring copies, not originals.

- **Write down your questions:** Before visiting, write down specific questions you need answered. This helps you remember everything and use your time efficiently.

- **Be prepared to wait:** Depending on how busy the center is, you may wait an hour or more. Bring something to occupy your time.

- **Take notes:** Write down the information and advice you receive. It is easy to forget details when you are stressed.

- **Ask for clarification:** If you do not understand something, ask the staff to explain it again or in different terms. Do not leave confused.

- **Get names:** Note the name of the person who helped you in case you need to follow up later.

- **Be respectful:** Self-help center staff are trying to help many people with limited resources. Be patient and courteous even if you are frustrated with your legal situation.

- **Return if needed:** Do not hesitate to return to the self-help center if you have additional questions as your case progresses.

Other Sources of Assistance

Beyond legal aid, pro bono programs, law school clinics, and self-help centers, several other resources can provide legal help or support:

Law Libraries

County law libraries are open to the public and contain legal research materials, including statutes, case law, practice guides, form books, and legal treatises. Law librarians can help you find resources but cannot provide legal advice.

What you can find at law libraries:

- Statutes and codes (the written laws passed by legislatures)
- Case law (court decisions interpreting and applying the law)
- Practice guides and handbooks for specific areas of law
- Form books with sample legal documents
- Legal encyclopedias explaining legal concepts
- Self-help books on common legal issues
- Computers with access to legal databases

How law librarians can help:

- Show you how to use legal research tools
- Help you locate relevant statutes or cases
- Explain how legal materials are organized
- Suggest resources for your type of legal issue
- Teach you basic legal research skills

What librarians cannot do:

- Interpret the law for your specific situation
- Tell you how to apply the law to your case
- Recommend what you should do
- Fill out legal forms for you

To find your county law library, search for "[your county] law library" or check your county's website. Many law libraries offer free public access, though some may charge a small fee for non-attorneys.

Mediation Services

Community mediation centers offer low-cost or free mediation for disputes involving neighbors, landlords and tenants, small businesses, and family matters. Mediation can resolve conflicts without going to court.

What is mediation?

Mediation is a process where a neutral third party (the mediator) helps people in a dispute communicate and reach their own agreement. The mediator does not decide who is right or wrong but facilitates a conversation that allows both sides to understand each other and find common ground.

Types of disputes suitable for mediation:

- Neighbor disputes (noise, boundaries, property damage)
- Landlord-tenant issues (deposits, repairs, lease violations)
- Family conflicts (custody, visitation, elder care)
- Small business disputes (partnerships, contracts, customer complaints)
- Workplace conflicts
- Consumer complaints
- Community issues

Benefits of mediation:

- Costs much less than going to court

- Resolves disputes faster than litigation
- Allows you to maintain relationships with the other party
- Gives you control over the outcome rather than having a judge decide
- Keeps matters private rather than public
- Can result in more creative solutions than court could order
- Less stressful and formal than court proceedings

How to find mediation services:

- Search for "community mediation center" + [your city or county]
- Contact your local court and ask about mediation programs
- Check with legal aid organizations for mediation referrals
- Visit the website of the National Association for Community Mediation at www.nafcm.org

Many community mediation centers charge fees on a sliding scale based on income, and some offer completely free mediation for low-income individuals.

Nonprofit Advocacy Organizations

Groups focused on specific issues sometimes provide legal help, advice, or referrals in their areas of focus. These organizations advocate for particular communities or causes and may have staff attorneys or partnerships with volunteer lawyers.

Types of nonprofit advocacy organizations:

- **Housing rights organizations:** Help with evictions, housing discrimination, habitability issues, and foreclosure prevention. Examples include tenant unions, fair housing councils, and housing advocacy nonprofits.
- **Workers' rights organizations:** Assist with wage theft, workplace discrimination, wrongful termination, and labor organizing. Examples include worker centers, labor unions, and employment justice projects.

- **Immigrant rights organizations:** Provide immigration legal services, know-your-rights training, and defense against deportation. Many serve specific immigrant communities.
- **Disability rights organizations:** Advocate for people with disabilities in areas like accessibility, discrimination, special education, and government benefits.
- **Civil liberties organizations:** Groups like the ACLU (American Civil Liberties Union) take on cases involving constitutional rights, free speech, privacy, and discrimination.
- **LGBTQ+ advocacy organizations:** Provide legal support on issues like discrimination, family law, name changes, and transgender rights.
- **Veterans' service organizations:** Help veterans access benefits, appeal denials, and address legal issues related to military service.
- **Elder rights organizations:** Focus on issues affecting seniors, including elder abuse, guardianship, nursing home rights, and age discrimination.
- **Consumer advocacy groups:** Help with predatory lending, debt collection, consumer fraud, and unfair business practices.
- **Environmental justice organizations:** Work on issues affecting community health and environment, including pollution, toxic exposure, and environmental regulation.

To find advocacy organizations in your area, search online for "[your issue] advocacy" + [your state or city], or ask legal aid organizations and self-help centers for referrals.

Union or Membership Organizations

If you belong to a union, professional association, or membership organization, check whether they offer legal assistance as a benefit.

Unions: Many labor unions provide free legal representation to members for workplace issues such as grievances, discipline, discrimination, wage disputes, and workers' compensation. Some unions also offer legal services for personal matters like wills, real estate, or traffic tickets.

Professional associations: Associations for teachers, nurses, engineers, and other professionals sometimes offer legal advice hotlines, document review, or representation for professional licensing issues and workplace disputes.

Member benefit organizations: Groups like credit unions, automobile associations (AAA), and identity theft protection services sometimes include legal assistance as a membership benefit, such as a toll-free legal advice hotline or discounts on legal services.

Alumni associations: Some college and university alumni associations offer legal referral services or discounted legal services to graduates.

Check your membership materials or contact your organization's member services department to learn what legal benefits are available.

Lawyer Referral Services

Bar associations operate lawyer referral services that connect people with attorneys in their area. While these services usually provide referrals to attorneys who charge fees, many offer:

- Initial consultations at reduced rates (often $25-$50 for a 30-minute consultation)
- Screening to ensure the attorney has experience in the relevant area of law
- Information about attorneys who offer payment plans or reduced fees
- Referrals to legal aid or pro bono services if you qualify

To find a lawyer referral service, contact your state or local bar association or visit the American Bar Association's website at www.findlegalhelp.org.

Online Legal Resources

Numerous websites provide legal information, self-help guides, and forms:

- **LawHelp.org:** Comprehensive directory of legal aid programs and resources by state, with self-help articles on common legal issues.
- **Justia:** Free legal information, case law, and explanations of legal topics.

- **Nolo:** Self-help legal books, articles, and forms (some free, some paid).
- **Court websites:** Most courts provide forms, instructions, and informational guides on their websites.
- **Legal aid websites:** Many legal aid organizations publish self-help materials on their websites available to everyone, not just their clients.
- **State bar associations:** Often publish consumer guides on common legal issues.

Be cautious with online information. Laws vary significantly by state, and online information may not be current or applicable to your situation. Use online resources as a starting point, but verify information with local legal aid, court self-help centers, or attorneys when possible.

Law School Legal Advice Clinics

In addition to the full-service clinics described earlier, many law schools operate legal advice clinics (sometimes called "student practice" clinics) where you can receive brief consultations with law students supervised by attorneys. These clinics typically do not provide representation but offer:

- Answers to legal questions
- Review of documents or forms
- Explanation of your legal options
- Referrals to other resources

These clinics are usually free and may be available on a walk-in basis or by appointment.

Religious and Community Organizations

Churches, mosques, temples, synagogues, and other faith-based organizations sometimes offer legal clinics or have partnerships with volunteer attorneys who provide free advice to community members. Community centers, nonprofit social service agencies, and neighborhood organizations may also host periodic legal advice clinics.

Ask community organizations in your area whether they offer legal assistance or can connect you with volunteer attorneys.

Private Attorneys with Reduced Fees or Payment Plans

Some private attorneys offer reduced fees for low-income clients, sliding scale fees based on income, or payment plans that allow you to pay over time. While not free, these arrangements can make private representation more affordable.

When contacting private attorneys:

- Explain your financial situation upfront
- Ask if they offer reduced fees for low-income clients
- Inquire about payment plans or flat fees rather than hourly billing
- Ask if they offer "unbundled" or "limited scope" services where they help with only part of your case (such as reviewing documents or providing advice) rather than full representation

Some attorneys will reduce their fees for clients who do some of the work themselves, such as gathering documents, conducting factual research, or filling out forms.

The Value of Limited Assistance

Even when full representation is unavailable, limited advice or document review can prevent serious mistakes. A 30-minute consultation with a lawyer, even if you pay a modest fee, can clarify your options, identify mistakes you were about to make, and point you in the right direction.

What limited assistance can accomplish:

- Help you understand the strength of your legal position
- Identify legal issues you had not recognized
- Explain the likely outcomes of different courses of action
- Catch errors in documents you have prepared
- Point you to relevant laws or court rules
- Help you prioritize the most important aspects of your case

- Prevent you from waiving rights or missing deadlines

Types of limited assistance:

- **Advice-only consultations:** A lawyer reviews your situation, explains your options, and advises you on how to proceed, but does not represent you in court or negotiate on your behalf.
- **Document review:** A lawyer reviews documents you have prepared (such as court forms, contracts, or settlement agreements) and suggests corrections or improvements.
- **Coaching:** A lawyer provides ongoing advice and coaching as you represent yourself, helping you prepare for hearings and make strategic decisions, but does not appear in court with you.
- **Ghostwriting:** A lawyer helps you draft pleadings or motions that you file yourself. (Note: Court rules in some jurisdictions require disclosure that an attorney assisted with drafting.)
- **Unbundled services:** A lawyer handles specific tasks in your case (such as a hearing or negotiation) while you handle other parts yourself.

Limited assistance is particularly valuable in the early stages of a legal matter. Getting advice before you take action can prevent problems that would be difficult or impossible to fix later. For example:

- Advice before signing a settlement can ensure you are not giving up valuable rights
- Document review before filing can prevent procedural mistakes that delay your case
- A consultation before responding to a lawsuit can help you raise all available defenses

When to Seek Help

Asking for help early increases the chances of finding affordable options and preserving your legal rights. Many legal problems become much worse when ignored or handled incorrectly. Seek legal assistance as soon as possible when:

- You receive a court summons or notice of a lawsuit

- You are facing eviction or foreclosure
- You receive a notice of termination of government benefits
- You are arrested or charged with a crime
- You are a victim of domestic violence
- You receive a notice of deportation proceedings
- You face workplace discrimination or wrongful termination
- You are injured due to someone else's negligence
- You need to establish custody or child support
- You face garnishment of your wages or bank account
- You receive notice of a tax audit or IRS collection action
- Your child is being denied necessary special education services

Do not assume you cannot afford help without investigating your options. Many people who think they do not qualify for free services are actually eligible. Even if you do not qualify for free representation, limited assistance or reduced-fee services may be available.

Preparing for Your First Contact with Legal Services

To make the most of your initial contact with any legal service provider, prepare by:

- **Gathering relevant documents:** Collect all papers related to your legal issue, including court documents, contracts, letters, notices, bills, photographs, and any other relevant evidence.
- **Writing a timeline:** Create a written timeline of important events in chronological order with dates if possible.
- **Listing key people:** Make a list of important people involved in your situation with their contact information.
- **Identifying your goals:** Think about what outcome you hope to achieve and what would be acceptable alternatives.
- **Noting deadlines:** Identify any deadlines you are aware of, such as response dates for court papers or expiration of time limits.

- **Preparing questions:** Write down specific questions you need answered.
- **Gathering financial information:** Have proof of income and information about your assets and debts ready, as most free services require financial eligibility.

Being organized and prepared helps legal service providers assess your case quickly and increases the likelihood they can help you.

Conclusion

Free and low-cost legal help is available, though finding it requires persistence. Do not give up if the first organization you contact cannot help. Try multiple resources, ask for referrals, and keep looking until you find assistance or at least advice that helps you understand your options.

Remember that the legal system is complex, and mistakes can have serious consequences. Professional legal help, even if limited, is almost always better than trying to navigate the system entirely alone. Take advantage of every resource available to you, and do not hesitate to ask for help.

Glossary of Legal Terms From Law in Real Life

A

Affidavit / Declaration

A written statement made under oath, affirming that the information provided is true. Used as evidence in court proceedings. A written statement of facts that someone swears or affirms to be true before an authorized official (such as a notary public, court clerk, or other officer). The person making the statement (the affiant) signs it under penalty of perjury, making it a legally binding document that can be used as evidence in court proceedings. A **declaration** is a written statement of facts that someone signs under penalty of perjury, but without requiring a notary or other official to witness it. The person declares the contents to be true to the best of their knowledge. In many jurisdictions, declarations have the same legal weight as affidavits but with less formality in their execution. The main distinction is that affidavits require witnessing and formal oath-taking before an authorized official, while declarations simply require the signer's signature under penalty of perjury. Both carry legal consequences if the statements are knowingly false.

Alimony

Also called spousal support or maintenance, is a court-ordered payment that one spouse makes to the other during or after a divorce. Its purpose is to provide financial support to the lower-earning or financially dependent spouse, helping them maintain a reasonable standard of living. Alimony is not automatic and is intended to address economic imbalances resulting from the marriage. Courts consider factors like marriage length, each spouse's income and earning capacity, age, health, and contributions to the household when deciding whether to award alimony and how much.

Answer
A formal written response to a complaint or petition in a lawsuit, in which the defendant addresses the claims made against them.

Appeals Court
A court that reviews decisions made by lower courts to determine if the law was applied correctly. Does not re-examine facts or hear new evidence.

Arbitration
A form of alternative dispute resolution where a neutral third party (arbitrator) hears both sides and makes a binding decision. Often required by consumer contracts and employment agreements.

Arrest
Being taken into police custody based on probable cause that a crime has been committed. Can occur with or without handcuffs.

Assault
Intentionally causing another person to fear imminent harmful or offensive contact. Does not require actual physical touching.

At-Will Employment
Employment arrangement where either the employer or employee can end the relationship at any time, for any legal reason or no reason at all, without advance notice.

Attorney-Client Privilege
Legal protection that keeps communications between a lawyer and client confidential. Allows clients to speak freely without fear their statements will be used against them.

B

Background Check
Investigation into a person's criminal, financial, employment, or personal history. Commonly used by employers, landlords, and financial institutions.

Bail
Money or conditions set by a court to ensure a defendant returns for trial while released from custody. Not a punishment, but a guarantee of appearance.

Bankruptcy
Legal process allowing individuals or businesses unable to pay debts to get relief or reorganize their finances under court supervision. Can result in discharge of certain debts.

Battery
Intentional and unlawful physical contact with another person without their consent. Differs from assault, which only requires fear of contact.

Beneficiary
Person or entity designated to receive assets from a will, trust, life insurance policy, or retirement account.

Beyond a Reasonable Doubt
The highest standard of proof in the legal system, required in criminal cases. Means the evidence leaves no reasonable doubt in a rational person's mind about guilt.

Bond
A financial guarantee (often through a bail bondsman) that a defendant will appear in court. Typically costs a percentage of the total bail amount.

Breach of Contract
Failure to perform obligations promised in a legally binding agreement. Can be minor or material depending on the significance of the failure.

Burden of Proof
Obligation to prove one's claims in a legal proceeding. In criminal cases, the prosecution bears this burden. In civil cases, typically the plaintiff does.

C

Capacity
Legal ability to enter into a contract or make legal decisions. May be limited by age, mental state, or other factors.

Chapter 7 Bankruptcy
Type of bankruptcy where most debts are discharged after non-exempt assets are sold to pay creditors. Also called liquidation bankruptcy.

Chapter 13 Bankruptcy
Type of bankruptcy where debts are reorganized into a repayment plan over three to five years. Allows people to keep property while catching up on payments.

Child Support
Court-ordered financial payments from one parent to another to help cover costs of raising a child. Belongs to the child, not the receiving parent.

Civil Law
Area of law governing disputes between private parties (individuals, businesses, organizations). Results in money damages or court orders, not jail time.

Civil Liability
Legal responsibility for causing harm to another person or entity in a non-criminal context. Usually results in financial compensation.

Class Action
Lawsuit filed by one or more people on behalf of a larger group who suffered similar harm. Common in consumer protection and product liability cases.

Closing
The final step in a real estate transaction where documents are signed, money is exchanged, and ownership officially transfers.

Closing Costs
Fees and expenses paid at the end of a real estate transaction, including title insurance, appraisal fees, attorney fees, and recording charges.

Codicil
Legal document that modifies or adds to an existing will without replacing it entirely.

Collateral
Property pledged as security for a loan. If the borrower fails to repay, the lender can take possession of the collateral.

Community Property
Legal system used in some states where most assets and debts acquired during marriage are owned equally by both spouses.

Complaint
A legal document that starts a lawsuit by explaining what happened and what the plaintiff wants the court to do.

Conservatorship
Legal arrangement where a court appoints someone to manage the financial affairs or personal care of an adult unable to do so themselves.

Consideration
Something of value exchanged between parties in a contract. Required for most contracts to be legally binding.

Consumer Protection Laws
Federal and state laws designed to protect buyers from unfair business practices, defective products, and deceptive advertising.

Contested (Divorce/Case)
A legal proceeding where parties disagree on major issues and require court intervention to resolve disputes.

Contingency Fee
Payment arrangement where a lawyer receives a percentage of money recovered only if the case is won. Common in personal injury cases.

Contract
A legally enforceable agreement between two or more parties involving an offer, acceptance, and exchange of something valuable.

Conviction
Official finding of guilt in a criminal case, established either through guilty plea or jury/judge verdict at trial.

Copyright
Legal protection for original creative works like books, music, art, and software. Arises automatically when a work is created.

Cosigner
Person who agrees to be legally responsible for a loan or debt if the primary borrower fails to pay. Equally liable for the full amount.

Counterclaim
Claim made by a defendant against a plaintiff in response to the plaintiff's lawsuit. Filed as part of the same legal proceeding.

Court Order
Official instruction from a judge requiring someone to do or not do something. Violating a court order can result in contempt charges.

Credit Report
Detailed record of a person's credit history, including loans, payment history, and outstanding debts. Used to determine creditworthiness.

Creditor
Person, business, or institution to whom money is owed.

Criminal Law
Area of law dealing with behavior the government has decided is harmful to society. Cases brought by the government can result in jail, fines, or criminal records.

Criminal Record
Official documentation of arrests, charges, and convictions accessible to employers, landlords, and background check companies.

Custody
Legal authority and responsibility regarding a child's care and upbringing. Includes both legal custody (decision-making) and physical custody (where the child lives).

D

Damages
Money awarded in a lawsuit to compensate for losses, injuries, or harm caused by another party.

Debtor
Person or entity who owes money to another.

Declaration
A written statement of facts that someone signs under penalty of perjury, but without requiring a notary or other official to witness it. The person declares the contents to be true to the best of their knowledge. In many jurisdictions, declarations have the same legal weight as affidavits but with less formality in their execution.

Decree
Final court order or judgment, often used in divorce and family law cases.

Deed
Legal document transferring ownership of real property from one party to another.

Default
Failure to fulfill a legal obligation, such as missing loan payments or failing to respond to a lawsuit.

Default Judgment
Court ruling in favor of one party because the other party failed to respond or appear. Can occur when a defendant ignores a lawsuit.

Defendant
The person or entity being sued in a civil case or charged with a crime in a criminal case.

Defamation
False statement that harms someone's reputation. Includes both libel (written) and slander (spoken).

Delinquent
Overdue or unpaid, typically referring to debts or required payments.

Deportation
Formal legal process (officially called removal) by which the government orders a non-citizen to leave the United States.

Deposition
Formal questioning of a witness under oath before trial, with answers recorded for later use.

Detention
Temporary stop by police based on reasonable suspicion that a crime may be occurring. Person is not free to leave but has not been arrested.

Discovery
Pre-trial phase where both sides exchange information, documents, and testimony to build their cases.

Discrimination
Unfair treatment based on protected characteristics such as race, sex, religion, national origin, disability, or age.

Dismissal
Court order ending a case without a full trial. Can be with or without prejudice (ability to refile).

Divorce
Legal dissolution of a marriage by court order.

Domestic Violence
Abuse or threats of abuse between family or household members or intimate partners. Can be physical, emotional, sexual, or financial.

Down Payment
Initial upfront payment made when purchasing a large item like a house or car. Usually a percentage of the total purchase price.

Due Process
Constitutional guarantee that the government must follow fair procedures before depriving someone of life, liberty, or property.

Durable Power of Attorney
Legal document allowing someone to make decisions on your behalf even if you become incapacitated.

DUI/DWI
Driving Under the Influence or Driving While Intoxicated. Criminal offense of operating a vehicle while impaired by alcohol or drugs.

E

Easement
Legal right to use someone else's property for a specific purpose, such as a shared driveway or utility access.

Emancipation
Legal process freeing a minor from parental control and granting them adult legal status before reaching age 18.

Embezzlement
Crime of stealing money or property entrusted to your care, often committed by employees against employers.

Eminent Domain
Government power to take private property for public use with fair compensation to the owner.

Encumbrance
Claim, lien, or liability attached to property that may decrease its value or restrict its use.

Equitable Distribution
Legal system used in most states where marital property is divided fairly (but not necessarily equally) in divorce.

Escrow
Arrangement where a neutral third party holds money or documents until certain conditions are met. Common in real estate transactions.

Estate
All property, assets, and debts left behind when someone dies.

Estate Planning
Process of arranging how your assets will be managed and distributed after death or if you become incapacitated.

Eviction
Legal process by which a landlord removes a tenant from rental property. Must follow specific procedures and cannot be done without court involvement.

Evidence
Information presented in court to prove or disprove facts, including documents, testimony, and physical objects.

Executor
Person named in a will to carry out the deceased's wishes and manage the estate through probate.

Exempt Employee
Worker who meets specific salary and job duty criteria and is therefore not entitled to overtime pay under federal law.

Expungement
Legal process that erases or destroys a criminal record, making it unavailable to most background checks.

F

Fair Credit Reporting Act (FCRA)
Federal law regulating how consumer credit information is collected, shared, and used. Gives consumers rights to dispute inaccurate information.

Fair Debt Collection Practices Act (FDCPA)
Federal law protecting consumers from abusive debt collection practices, including harassment and false statements.

Fair Housing Act
Federal law prohibiting discrimination in housing based on race, color, religion, sex, national origin, disability, or family status.

Fair Labor Standards Act (FLSA)
Federal law establishing minimum wage, overtime pay, and child labor standards.

False Arrest
Unlawful restraint of a person's freedom of movement by another claiming legal authority.

Family and Medical Leave Act (FMLA)
Federal law allowing eligible employees to take unpaid, job-protected leave for family and medical reasons.

Federal Law
Laws created by the national government that apply across all states. Covers areas like immigration, interstate commerce, and civil rights.

Felony
Serious criminal offense that can result in prison sentences over one year, substantial fines, and loss of certain civil rights.

Fiduciary
Person or entity with legal duty to act in another's best interest, such as trustees, guardians, and executors.

Foreclosure
Legal process where a lender takes possession of property due to the borrower's failure to make mortgage payments.

Fraud
Intentional deception for personal gain or to cause harm to another. Can be criminal or civil.

G

Garnishment
Court-ordered process where money is withheld from wages or bank accounts to pay a debt or judgment.

Good Faith
Honest intention and fair dealing in transactions. Required in many contractual relationships.

Grand Jury
Group of citizens who review evidence presented by prosecutors to decide whether there is enough reason to formally charge someone with a crime.

Green Card
Document granting lawful permanent residence in the United States. Holders may live and work indefinitely but are not citizens.

Gross Negligence
Extreme carelessness or reckless disregard for the safety or lives of others. More serious than ordinary negligence.

Guardian
Person appointed by a court to make decisions for a minor or incapacitated adult.

Guardian ad Litem
Person appointed by a court to represent the best interests of a child or incapacitated person in legal proceedings.

H

Habeas Corpus
Legal action requiring authorities to bring a detained person before a court to determine if their imprisonment is lawful.

Habitable
Condition of rental property that meets basic standards for safe, healthy living, including working utilities, heat, and freedom from serious hazards.

Harassment
Unwelcome conduct based on protected characteristics that is severe or

pervasive enough to create a hostile environment or involves quid pro quo demands.

Hearsay
Out-of-court statement offered to prove the truth of the matter asserted. Generally not admissible as evidence with many exceptions.

Heir
Person entitled to inherit property from someone who dies without a will, determined by state intestacy laws.

Homestead Exemption
Legal provision protecting a portion of home equity from creditors in bankruptcy or debt collection. Amount varies by state.

Hostile Work Environment
Workplace where harassment based on protected characteristics is severe or pervasive enough to create an abusive atmosphere.

I

Identity Theft
Crime of using someone else's personal information without permission, typically for financial gain.

Implied Warranty
Unwritten guarantee that a product is fit for its intended purpose and of merchantable quality. Automatically applies to most sales.

Indictment
Formal accusation from a grand jury that a person has committed a crime. Not a declaration of guilt, just an allegation allowing the case to proceed.

Independent Contractor
Worker who operates independently rather than as an employee. Generally not entitled to minimum wage, overtime, or employee benefits.

Informed Consent
Agreement to something after receiving full information about risks, benefits, and alternatives. Required in medical procedures and research.

Inheritance
Property or assets received from someone who has died, either through a will or intestate succession laws.

Injunction
Court order requiring someone to do something or stop doing something.

Insolvency
Financial state where debts exceed assets or inability to pay debts as they come due.

Intellectual Property
Legal rights protecting creations of the mind, including trademarks, copyrights, and patents.

Interrogation
Formal questioning by law enforcement designed to obtain information or a confession.

Intestate
Dying without a valid will. State law determines how property is distributed.

Irrevocable Trust
Trust that cannot be changed or cancelled once created. Often used for estate planning and asset protection.

J

Joint and Several Liability
Legal principle where multiple defendants can each be held responsible for the entire amount of damages, allowing the plaintiff to collect from any or all of them.

Joint Custody
Custody arrangement where both parents share legal decision-making authority and/or physical care of a child.

Joint Tenancy
Property ownership by two or more people with right of survivorship, meaning surviving owners automatically inherit deceased owner's share.

Judgment
Official court decision determining the rights and obligations of parties in a case.

Judgment Lien
Legal claim against property based on a court judgment for unpaid debt.

Jurisdiction
Authority of a court to hear a case and make decisions. Can be limited by geography, subject matter, or amount in dispute.

Jury
Group of citizens selected to evaluate evidence and decide factual questions in certain legal cases.

Jury Duty
Civic obligation to serve as a juror when summoned by a court. Employers generally cannot fire employees for jury service.

L

Landlord
Property owner who rents or leases property to another person (tenant).

Larceny
Crime of unlawfully taking someone else's property with intent to permanently deprive them of it. Another term for theft.

Lease Agreement
Contract between landlord and tenant outlining rental terms, payment amounts, duration, and responsibilities.

Legal Aid
Nonprofit organizations providing free legal services to qualifying low-income individuals.

Legal Custody
Authority to make major decisions about a child's life, including education, healthcare, and religious upbringing.

Legal Separation
Court-recognized arrangement where spouses live apart and divide assets but remain legally married.

Lemon Law
Consumer protection law providing remedies when a new vehicle has substantial defects that cannot be repaired after reasonable attempts.

Liability
Legal responsibility for harm, loss, or debt.

Liability Insurance
Coverage that protects against claims for injuries or damage caused to others.

Libel
Written or published false statement that damages someone's reputation. Form of defamation.

Lien
Legal claim against property used as security for a debt or obligation.

Limited Liability Company (LLC)
Business structure that creates a legal entity separate from owners, providing liability protection while allowing flexible management.

Liquidation
Converting assets into cash, often in bankruptcy or business closure.

Living Trust
Trust created during a person's lifetime to manage assets and avoid probate. Can be revocable or irrevocable.

Living Will
Document stating your wishes for end-of-life medical care if you cannot communicate. Different from a standard will.

M

Malpractice
Professional negligence by a doctor, lawyer, or other licensed professional that causes harm to a client or patient.

Marital Property
Assets and debts acquired during marriage. Treatment varies by state (community property vs. equitable distribution).

Mediation
Alternative dispute resolution process where a neutral third party helps disputing parties reach voluntary agreement.

Medical Power of Attorney
Legal document authorizing someone to make healthcare decisions on your behalf if you cannot.

Minimum Wage
Lowest hourly pay rate an employer may legally offer. Can be set by federal, state, or local law (highest applies).

Minor
Person under the legal age of adulthood, typically 18. Has limited legal capacity to enter contracts or make certain decisions.

Miranda Rights
Constitutional protections that must be explained when someone is in custody and being interrogated, including the right to remain silent and right to an attorney.

Misdemeanor
Less serious criminal offense typically punishable by fines, probation, community service, or jail sentences up to one year.

Mistrial
Trial that ends without a verdict due to procedural error, jury deadlock, or other fundamental problem.

Modification
Court-ordered change to an existing order, such as adjusting child support or custody arrangements based on changed circumstances.

Mortgage
Loan secured by real property. Borrower pledges property as collateral, and lender can foreclose if payments are not made.

Motion
Formal request asking a court to make a specific ruling or take particular action in a case.

N

Naturalization
Legal process by which a foreign citizen becomes a U.S. citizen after meeting residency and other requirements.

Negligence
Failure to exercise reasonable care, resulting in harm to another person.

No-Fault Divorce
Divorce that does not require proving wrongdoing by either spouse. Common grounds include irreconcilable differences.

No-Fault Insurance
Auto insurance system where drivers file claims with their own insurance regardless of who caused the accident.

Non-Compete Agreement
Contract restricting an employee from working for competitors or starting a competing business for a specified time and area after leaving employment.

Non-Disclosure Agreement (NDA)
Contract requiring parties to keep certain information confidential.

Non-Exempt Employee
Worker entitled to minimum wage and overtime pay protections under federal and state law.

Notary Public
Official authorized to witness signatures, administer oaths, and verify identities on legal documents.

Notice
Formal communication informing someone of legal proceedings, rights, or obligations. Must be given properly to be legally effective.

Notice to Quit
Written notice from landlord to tenant requiring them to vacate the property or correct a lease violation within a specified time.

O

Offer
Proposal to enter into a contract with specific terms. First step in contract formation.

Ordinance
Law passed by a local government such as a city or county.

Overtime
Additional pay (typically 1.5 times regular rate) required for non-exempt employees who work beyond a set threshold, usually 40 hours per week.

Overstay
Remaining in the United States beyond the authorized period of a visa or admission. Can trigger bars on future reentry.

P

Paralegal
Trained legal assistant who works under attorney supervision but cannot give legal advice or represent clients in court.

Parole
Supervised early release from prison before completing full sentence. Conditions must be followed to avoid returning to prison.

Partnership
Business structure where two or more people share ownership, profits, and liabilities.

Patent
Legal protection for inventions and technological processes, granting exclusive rights to make, use, or sell the invention for a limited time.

Perjury
Crime of lying under oath in a legal proceeding or on a sworn document.

Permanent Residence
Immigration status allowing someone to live and work in the U.S. indefinitely. See Green Card.

Personal Injury
Harm to body, mind, or emotions caused by another's negligence or intentional conduct. Basis for lawsuits seeking compensation.

Personal Property
Movable items that can be owned, as opposed to real property (land and buildings).

Petition
Formal written request to a court asking for specific legal action or relief.

Physical Custody
Refers to where a child lives and who provides day-to-day care.

Plaintiff
Person or entity bringing a lawsuit against another party in a civil case.

Plea Agreement (Plea Deal)
Negotiated agreement where a defendant pleads guilty, often to reduced charges or for lighter sentencing, in exchange for avoiding trial.

Power of Attorney
Legal document authorizing someone to act on another person's behalf in legal or financial matters.

Precedent
Prior court decision that serves as an example or rule for deciding similar cases in the future.

Preliminary Hearing
Court proceeding where a judge determines if there is enough evidence to proceed with criminal charges.

Premises Liability
Legal responsibility of property owners for injuries occurring on their property due to unsafe conditions.

Prenuptial Agreement (Prenup)
Contract entered before marriage defining how certain matters (property, debts, support) will be handled if the marriage ends.

Preponderance of the Evidence
Standard of proof in most civil cases, meaning more likely than not (essentially 51% certainty).

Probable Cause
Reasonable basis to believe a crime has been committed and that a particular person is involved. Lower standard than proof beyond a reasonable doubt.

Probate
Court-supervised process of settling a deceased person's estate, including validating wills, paying debts, and distributing assets.

Probation
Supervised sentence served in the community instead of jail, with specific conditions that must be followed.

Pro Bono
Legal services provided for free, typically by lawyers volunteering their time.

Product Liability
Legal responsibility of manufacturers and sellers for injuries caused by defective or dangerous products.

Promissory Note
Written promise to pay a specific amount of money at a particular time or on demand.

Prosecutor
Government attorney who brings criminal charges and represents the state in criminal cases.

Protective Order
Court order designed to protect someone from harassment, abuse, or threats. Also called restraining order.

Proximate Cause
Legal concept that an injury must be a reasonably foreseeable result of the defendant's action to establish liability.

Public Defender
Attorney provided by the government to represent defendants who cannot afford a lawyer in criminal cases.

Punitive Damages
Money awarded to punish a defendant for particularly harmful or malicious conduct, beyond compensating the plaintiff for losses.

Q

Qualified Domestic Relations Order (QDRO)
Court order dividing retirement plan assets between spouses in divorce.

Quiet Title
Legal action to establish clear ownership of property when title is disputed or clouded.

Quitclaim Deed
Document transferring whatever ownership interest someone has in property without guaranteeing they actually own it or that title is clear.

R

Real Property
Land and anything permanently attached to it, including buildings and structures.

Reasonable Accommodation
Changes or adjustments to a job, workplace, or housing to enable a person with a disability to have equal opportunities.

Reasonable Doubt
See Beyond a Reasonable Doubt.

Rebuttal
Evidence or argument presented to contradict or disprove the other party's claims.

Referee
Court-appointed official who conducts hearings and makes recommendations or decisions in certain legal matters.

Refinance
Replacing an existing loan with a new one, typically to get better terms or interest rates.

Registered Agent
Person or business designated to receive legal documents on behalf of a company.

Release
Agreement giving up a legal claim or right, often in exchange for payment or settlement.

Remand
Sending a case back to a lower court for further proceedings.

Removal
See Deportation.

Rent Control
Laws limiting how much and how often landlords can increase rent.

Repossession
Taking back property that was used as collateral for a loan when the borrower fails to make payments.

Rescission
Cancelling a contract and returning parties to their positions before the agreement was made.

Res Judicata
Legal principle preventing the same dispute between the same parties from being relitigated after a final judgment.

Restitution
Court-ordered payment from a defendant to a victim to compensate for losses caused by a crime.

Restraining Order
Court order prohibiting someone from contacting or coming near another person. See Protective Order.

Retainer
Upfront fee paid to hire an attorney, often held in a special account and used as work is performed.

Retaliation
Adverse action taken against someone for engaging in legally protected activity, such as reporting harassment or filing a complaint.

Revocable Trust
Trust that can be changed or cancelled by the person who created it during their lifetime.

Right of Survivorship
Automatic transfer of property ownership to surviving joint owner(s) when one owner dies.

Right of Way
Legal right to pass through property owned by another, often for access to landlocked property.

Right to Remain Silent
Constitutional protection against self-incrimination. You cannot be forced to testify or answer questions that might incriminate you.

S

Sealed (Records)
Criminal records hidden from public view but not destroyed. Access is restricted to certain government agencies.

Search Warrant
Court order authorizing law enforcement to search a specific location for specific evidence.

Security Deposit
Money paid at the start of a tenancy to cover potential damage or unpaid rent. Must be returned (minus lawful deductions) after tenancy ends.

Self-Defense
Legal justification for using reasonable force to protect yourself from imminent harm.

Sentencing
Process where a court imposes punishment after a criminal conviction, which may include jail, fines, probation, or other penalties.

Separate Property
Assets owned before marriage or received as gifts or inheritances during marriage. Generally not divided in divorce.

Service of Process
Formal delivery of legal documents to notify someone of court proceedings. Must follow specific legal requirements.

Settlement
Agreement between parties to resolve a dispute without going to trial or completing litigation.

Severance Pay
Compensation sometimes provided to employees upon termination of employment. Not legally required in most cases.

Sexual Harassment
Unwelcome sexual advances, requests for sexual favors, or other verbal or physical conduct of a sexual nature in the workplace or other settings.

Sheriff's Sale
Public auction of property ordered by a court to satisfy a judgment or debt.

Slander
Spoken false statement that damages someone's reputation. Form of defamation.

Small Claims Court
Informal court designed for disputes involving relatively small amounts of money, often without lawyers.

Sole Custody
Custody arrangement where one parent has exclusive legal decision-making authority and/or physical care of a child.

Sole Proprietorship
Simplest business structure where the business and owner are legally the same. Offers no personal liability protection.

Spousal Support
Financial assistance one spouse may be required to pay the other after separation or divorce. Also called alimony.

Stalking
Repeated unwanted contact, following, or harassment that causes fear for safety.

Standing
Legal right to bring a lawsuit based on having suffered actual or threatened injury.

State Law
Laws created by individual states that govern most everyday matters like marriage, property, criminal offenses, and employment.

Statute
Written law passed by a legislative body.

Statute of Frauds
Legal requirement that certain contracts must be in writing to be enforceable, such as real estate sales and contracts lasting over one year.

Statute of Limitations
Legal deadline setting the maximum time someone has to file a lawsuit or bring criminal charges after an event occurs.

Stay
Court order temporarily stopping legal proceedings or enforcement of a judgment.

Stipulation
Agreement between parties in a lawsuit about certain facts or procedures, reducing issues the court must decide.

Strict Liability
Legal responsibility for harm regardless of fault or negligence. Often applies to defective products or inherently dangerous activities.

Subpoena
Court order requiring someone to testify or produce documents.

Subrogation
Legal right of an insurer who has paid a claim to recover that amount from the party responsible for the loss.

Summons
Official notice informing someone they are being sued and must respond by a specific deadline.

Surety
Person or company that guarantees payment of another's debt or performance of another's obligation.

T

Tenant
Person who rents or leases property from a landlord.

Tenancy at Will
Rental arrangement with no fixed term that either party can terminate with proper notice.

Tenancy in Common
Property ownership by two or more people where each owns a share that can be sold or inherited independently. No right of survivorship.

Testamentary Trust
Trust created through a will that takes effect after the person's death.

Testator
Person who creates a will.

Testimony
Statements made by witnesses under oath in court or during depositions.

Third Party
Person or entity not directly involved in a legal agreement or transaction but who may have related rights or interests.

Title
Legal ownership of property. In real estate, proof of ownership transferred through documented chain of ownership.

Title Insurance
Insurance protecting property buyers and lenders against defects in title or ownership claims.

Title Search
Examination of public records to verify legal ownership and check for liens or claims against property.

Tort
Wrongful act or injury for which a civil lawsuit can be brought, excluding breach of contract.

Trademark
Legal protection for words, names, symbols, logos, and slogans that identify the source of goods or services and distinguish them from others.

Trial Court
Court where cases are initially heard, evidence is presented, and factual determinations are made.

Trust
Legal arrangement where one person (trustee) holds and manages property for the benefit of another (beneficiary).

Trustee
Person or institution responsible for managing assets in a trust according to the trust terms.

U

Unconscionable
Contract or clause so unfair or one-sided that a court may refuse to enforce it.

Uncontested (Divorce/Case)
Legal proceeding where parties agree on all major issues and do not require court intervention to resolve disputes.

Unemployment Benefits
Temporary financial assistance for workers who lose jobs through no fault of their own.

V

Verdict
Formal decision by a jury or judge determining the outcome of a trial.

Visa
Permission to enter or remain in the United States for a specific purpose and time period. Does not guarantee permanent residence.

W

Warrant
Court order authorizing law enforcement to take specific action, such as conducting a search or making an arrest.

Will
Legal document stating how a person's property should be distributed after death and who should be responsible for carrying out those wishes.

Workers' Compensation
Insurance system providing benefits to employees injured on the job, typically covering medical costs and lost wages.

Work Authorization
Legal permission allowing a non-citizen to work in the United States under specific conditions.

Wrongful Termination
Firing an employee for a reason prohibited by law or in violation of a contract, such as retaliation or discrimination.

Z

Zoning
Local government regulations controlling how land and property can be used in specific areas (residential, commercial, industrial, etc.).

This glossary is for educational purposes and does not constitute legal advice. Laws vary by jurisdiction and change over time. Consult a qualified attorney for guidance on specific legal matters.

About the Author

Ngozi E. Bolin, Esq. brings more than three decades of extensive legal and litigation experience to this comprehensive guide on consumer rights and protection. With a distinguished career spanning multiple jurisdictions and legal disciplines, Ms. Bolin offers readers the benefit of deep legal knowledge, strategic insight, and practical courtroom wisdom grounded in real-world practice.

Educated under the British Commonwealth legal system and having studied at the Harvard Extension School, Ms. Bolin brings a uniquely global perspective to the law. Her international legal career began with her admission as a Barrister and Solicitor of the Supreme Court of Nigeria in 1989. She later relocated to the United States, where she was admitted to the New York State Bar in 1991, the United States Court of Appeals for the Second Circuit, and the California State Bar in 2013.

Throughout her career as a seasoned trial attorney, Ms. Bolin has been committed to making legal knowledge more accessible and affordable. She has been a strong advocate of unbundled legal services, empowering consumers to better understand the legal system and assert their rights with confidence. Her practice has encompassed a broad range of areas, including consumer protection, personal injury, contract, employment law, unfair business practices, real estate, bankruptcy, probate, and insurance disputes.

Ms. Bolin has successfully negotiated and litigated numerous cases, consistently emphasizing fair settlements and practical outcomes for her clients. Her professional record includes participation in significant cases such as Louis Capital Markets, LP v. Refco Group Ltd., LLC, et al. (9

Misc.3d 283, 801 N.Y.S.2d 490, N.Y. Co. 2005), addressing issues of corporate misconduct and fiduciary duties; Giordano v. Thomson, et al. (438 F. Supp. 2d 35, E.D.N.Y. 2005); and Davis v. Commercial Bank of New York (275 F. Supp. 2d 418, S.D.N.Y. 2003), involving employee benefits and unjust enrichment.

Through her writing and legal work, Ms. Bolin continues to bridge the gap between complex legal principles and the everyday concerns of consumers, offering guidance that is both authoritative and practical.

Made in United States
Orlando, FL
04 November 2026

90201363R00208